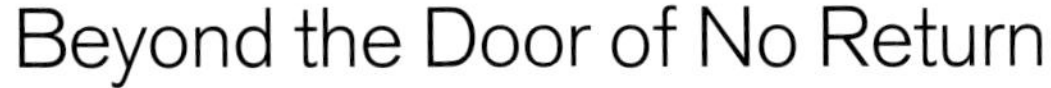

Beyond the Door of No Return

Selene Wendt

Beyond the Door of No Return

Confronting Hidden Colonial Histories
through Contemporary Art

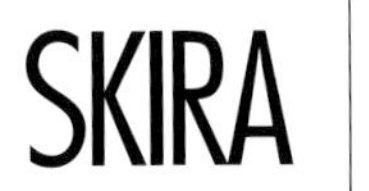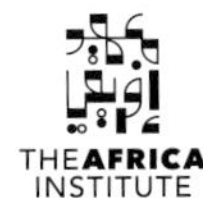

Selene Wendt's *Beyond the Door of No Return* represents the first in a series of co-publications between The Africa Institute, Sharjah, and Skira, one of the oldest and leading publishers in the field of art and visual culture.

We are proud to inaugurate this collaboration with Wendt's book, which features a group of African and African diaspora artists who are all at the forefront of a conceptualism that is intertwined with cutting-edge decolonial thinking. Drawing on extensive research that brings together cultural studies and postcolonial theory, with particular emphasis on stories of resistance and rebellion against colonial rule, the volume shifts the focus away from the deeply entrenched Eurocentric perspectives of contemporary art.

The featured artworks convey narratives of empowerment that also help expose some of the lesser-known and, in some cases, consciously hidden details of colonial history, such as Norwegian involvement in the transatlantic slave trade. Seen through the lens of contemporary art, the book provides valuable insight into the entanglements and overlaps that connect the colonial histories of Scandinavia and Europe to Africa, the Caribbean, and the Americas. In turn, these narratives shed light on the many factors that have contributed to the perpetuation of colonial power structures today, seen most evidently in social injustices and related inequalities such as poverty, forced migration, and racism.

The Africa Institute is an interdisciplinary academic research institute dedicated to the study, research, and documentation of Africa and the African diaspora and their manifold connections with the wider world. It is conceived as a research-based think-tank and a postgraduate studies institution, offering both Master's and PhD programs, which aims to train a new generation of critical thinkers. Hence, collaborations with publishers such as Skira are essential to The Africa Institute's mission of enhancing knowledge production and, by extension, public awareness of all aspects of African and African diaspora arts and culture.

Hoor Al-Qasimi
Salah M. Hassan

Cover
John Akomfrah
Vertigo Sea, 2015
Detail

Art Director
Marcello Francone

Design
Luigi Fiore

Editorial Coordination
Sataan Al-Hassan
Emma Cavazzini

Copy Editor
Carlotta Santuccio

Layout
Paola Ranzini Pallavicini

First published in Italy in 2021 by
Skira editore S.p.A.
Palazzo Casati Stampa
via Torino 61
20123 Milano, Italy
In association with
The Africa Institute, Sharjah

www.skira.net

Printed and bound in Italy. First edition

ISBN: 978-88-572-4560-7

Distributed in USA, Canada, Central
& South America by ARTBOOK |
D.A.P. 75, Broad Street Suite 630,
New York, NY 10004, USA.
Distributed elsewhere in the world
by Thames and Hudson Ltd.,
181A High Holborn, London
WC1V 7QX, United Kingdom.

*The author has received
a writer's grant from the
Norwegian Non-Fiction Writers
and Translators Association,
Fritt Ord, and Arts Council
Norway. This publication
was supported by Fritt Ord.*

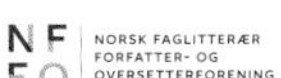
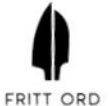
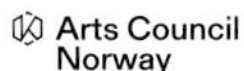
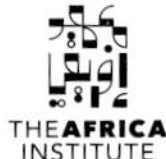
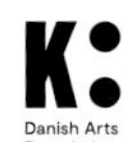

Contents

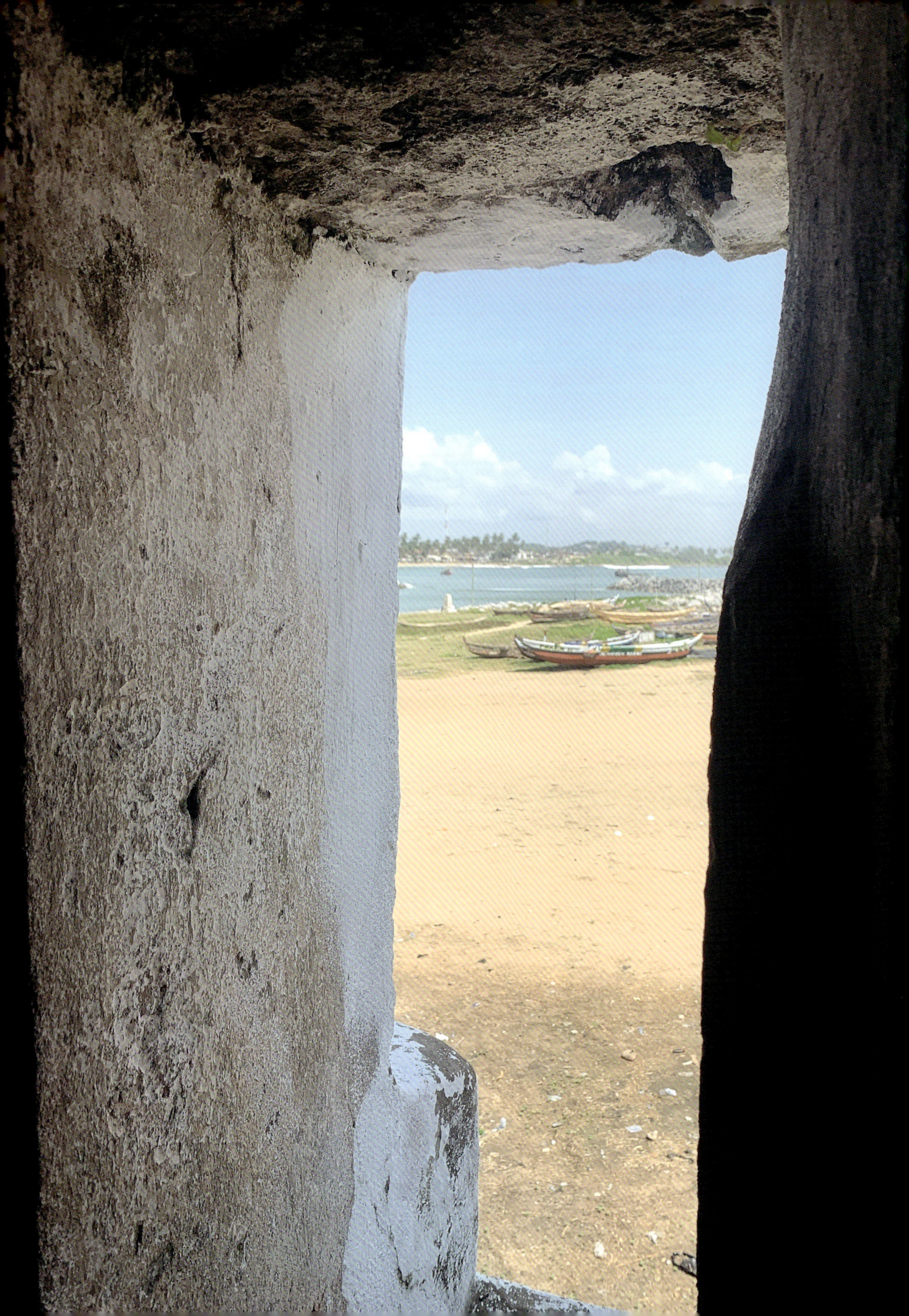

Introduction

Nothing could have prepared me for the experience of visiting Osu Castle in Accra, Ghana, where countless Africans were held captive and tortured over extended periods of time. After weeks and even months of confinement in total darkness, they were led through the Door of No Return into the blindingly bright sun and shuffled onto the beach where slave ships awaited offshore. The enslaved Africans were then packed onto the ships and transported across the Atlantic to the West Indies where they were sold to work on plantations. As a Norwegian, it felt even worse knowing that this particular site, also known as Christiansborg Fort, was mostly under Danish-Norwegian rule between 1661 and 1814 (when Norway became independent of Denmark). Relatively few people are aware of this part of Danish-Norwegian history, with the exception of a fairly small group of academics dedicated to postcolonial research, the descendants of Danish-Norwegian colonial rule in Ghana and the West Indies, and a growing number of contemporary artists who are dedicated to confronting the colonial past.

Seen through the lens of contemporary art, my interest lies in exposing the lesser-known details of colonial history, with particular emphasis on stories of resistance and rebellion against colonial rule. The contemporary artists featured in this book are all at the forefront of decolonial thinking. Through their artworks, they convey compelling narratives of resistance that shed light on the entangled colonial histories that connect Europe, Africa, the Caribbean, and the Americas. Collectively, these artists provide crucial

Elmina Castle, Ghana,
The Door of No Return
Photo: Selene Wendt

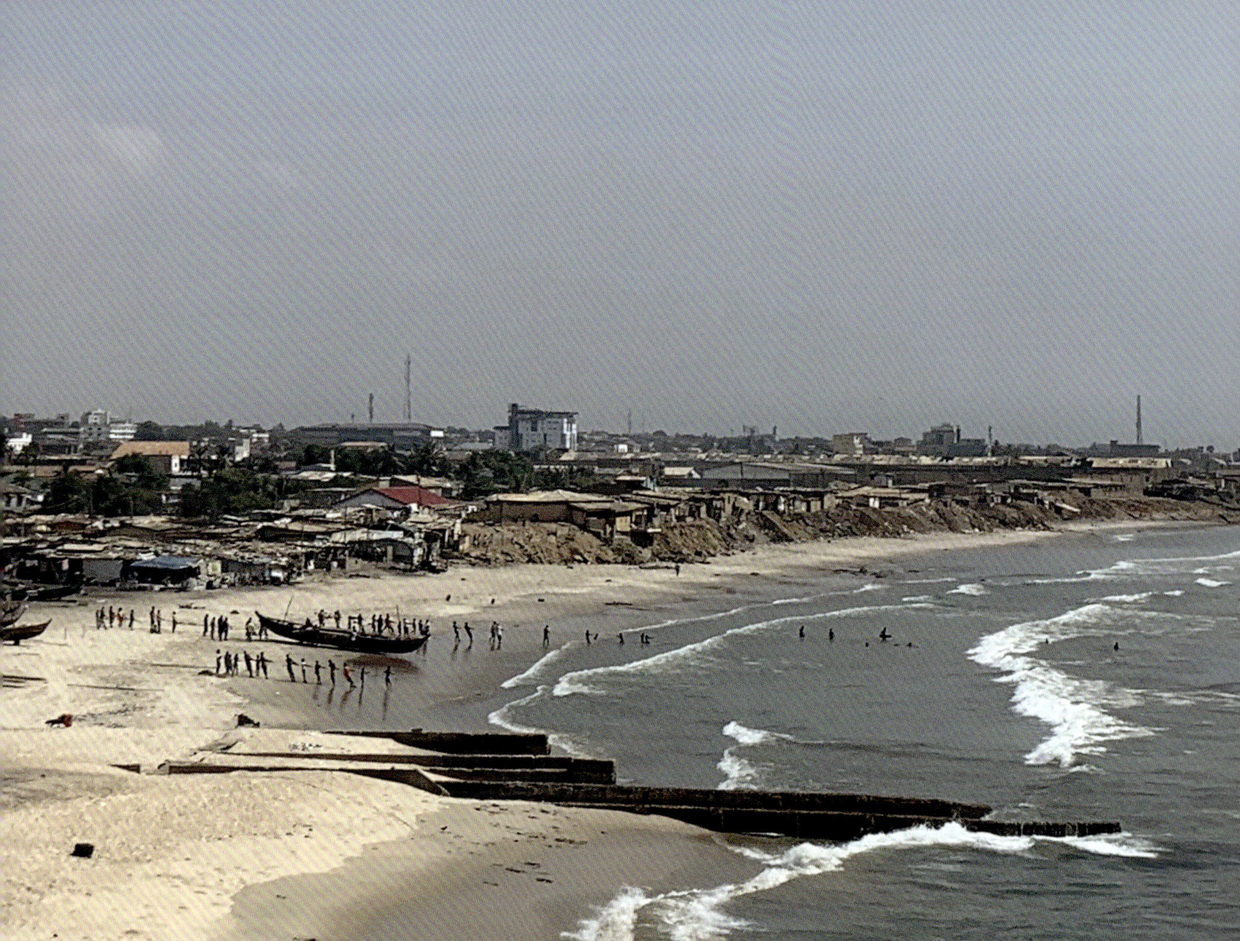

View from Osu Castle, Ghana
Photo: Selene Wendt

insight into aspects of colonial history that have been overlooked, such as Norwegian involvement in the transatlantic slave trade.

Up until fairly recently, the widely accepted narrative has been that Norway has no colonial history in relation to Africa and the Caribbean. It wasn't until 2017—on the occasion of the one-hundred-year anniversary of Denmark selling the Virgin Islands to the United States for 25 million dollars in gold—that Denmark really began to acknowledge its own colonial past. This was marked by cultural initiatives on both sides of the Atlantic that reexamined, questioned, and confronted Denmark's colonial history through scholarship, conferences, exhibitions, and the extensive digitalization of historical archives.[1] The fact that Norwegian shipping and trade profited from the transatlantic slave trade has typically been dismissed under the excuse that Norway was under Danish rule during the colonial era.[2] In fact, quite a few Norwegian merchants, investors, and ship-owners were directly involved in the shipment of enslaved Africans to the Caribbean as

12

part of the triangular trade between Denmark-Norway, the Gold Coast (Ghana), and the West Indies (St. Croix, St. Thomas, and St. John). Even after 1803, when the shipment of enslaved people from Africa to the Caribbean was abolished under the Danish flag, Danes and Norwegians continued to profit from slave ownership and the plantation economy along the Gold Coast and in the Danish West Indies.

Paraphrasing Stuart Hall, the works featured in this book address the circumstances in which we now find ourselves, how they arose, and question what forces are sustaining them and what forces are available to change them.[3] This means confronting histories that have been swept aside as inconsequential and, even worse, consciously hidden. Despite a recent increase in the number of Norwegians who are engaged in decolonial thinking, Norway's colonial past in relation to Africa and the Caribbean is far from common knowledge.

The urgency to decolonize the mind, which also means decolonizing the power structures and institutions that contribute to the perpetuation of coloniality today, is among the most important topics of our time. As conveyed by the artists featured in this book, this involves recognizing and addressing the consequences of colonial history. In the continued aftermath of colonialism, it's our shared responsibility to question the grand narratives of history that have been written by the West. We must work collectively towards an inclusive understanding of world history, one that involves multiple, diverse perspectives.

As the title suggests,
Pensée archipélique *emphasizes*
the importance of archipelagic thinking,
conveyed through a rich visual narrative
that also speaks of creolization,
the philosophy and poetics of relation,
world mentality, and opacity.

The Sea is History

As set forth in my exhibition and book *The Sea is History*, Stuart Hall's and Édouard Glissant's contributions to cultural theory provide valuable insight into processes of migration, which in turn helps to reveal the diverse, overlapping narratives that typically define diaspora aesthetics. The artworks featured in *The Sea is History* convey the intricate cultural tapestry that migration creates, both historically and within a contemporary context. It's about understanding history to better understand the present.

The numerous parallels between Stuart Hall's scholarship and Édouard Glissant's philosophy of the entanglements of worldwide relation, and how their interests and research intersected, are part of a distinct trajectory that mirrors what Hall described as "the syncretic character of Caribbean culture and . . . the violent fractures and brutal ruptures of its history."[4] It's important to keep in mind that the violent fractures within Caribbean culture were, and still are, a direct result of colonial history.

Due greatly to the direct influence of Stuart Hall's own diaspora experience on the development of his thinking, his writing provides crucial insight into the link between history and personal experience as an integral aspect of the shared diaspora experience. This is eloquently described in Hall's posthumously published biography *Familiar Stranger*:

> At the core of the diasporic experience is a variant of what W. E. B. DuBois called 'double consciousness': that of belonging to more than one world, of being both 'here' and 'there', of thinking about 'there' from 'here' and vice versa; of being 'at home' – but never wholly – in both places; neither fundamentally the same, nor totally different. It thus entails a very different conception of identity's

relations to cultural traditions from that of conventional notions, which tend to emphasize remaining true to one's primordial origins and imply continuity, fixity and an unchanging rootedness. Here, 'routes' (change, movement, transformations, adaptation, being always 'in process') are just as important as 'roots', if not more so: an example of what Paul Gilroy calls culture as 'the changing same'.[5]

The distinction between *roots* versus *routes* is a topic that Stuart Hall frequently returned to during his lifetime. He was among those, including Édouard Glissant, Paul Gilroy, and Kobena Mercer, who have suggested that we should think of culture not necessarily in terms of roots, but rather in terms of routes—a concept that embraces an expansive and inclusive notion of culture. This encompasses the routes by which people migrate as well as how culture migrates, develops, and changes through time. As a direct result of migration, a rich canvas of different cultures is woven along these routes, an idea which Glissant elaborated on throughout his writing.

As a respected scholar and longtime friend of Édouard Glissant during his lifetime, we can look to the filmmaker, writer, and cultural theorist Manthia Diawara for insight into Glissant's *Philosophie de la Relation* (Philosophy of Relation). He sums up the essence of Glissant's thinking succinctly:

> Glissant recognizes and enables a relation between different people and places, animate and inanimate objects, visible and invisible forces, the air, the water, the fire, the vegetation, animals and humans. Glissant the poet became a philosopher to reveal the fluidity of relation beyond the closed doors of systems of discrimination, segregation, and rejection, and to insist that difference is more constructive when viewed as a by-product of solidarity and conciliation between two or more elements of the *Tout-Monde* (One-World).[6]

Diawara's films capture Glissant's interest in a shift from the idea of globalization to *mondialité*, or world mentality. He emphasizes the relevance of Glissant's worldview:

Glissant suggested that we needed to enter into a site of world and mind that was less prone to discovery and conquest, and to espouse a philosophy of relation that looked at our differences not as that which divides us, but which links us individually and collectively in the *Tout-Monde*, where the communication between our intuitions knew no frontiers of language, territory, or power.[7]

Glissant's concept of *mondialité* and the idea of *échos-monde*, understood as the world of things resonating with one another, is more relevant than ever. Nowhere is this more powerfully conveyed through visual means than in Manthia Diawara's films. In 2009, Diawara accompanied Édouard Glissant on a transatlantic journey from Hampton to Brooklyn on the *Queen Mary II*. The results are seen in *Édouard Glissant: One World in Relation*, a film that successfully captures the essence of Glissant's poetics and philosophy of relation and his concept of *tout-monde*, or the world in its entirety. Along with *An Opera of the World* (2017) and *Pensée archipélique* (Archipelagic Thinking) (2019), Diawara's approach to Glissantian theory has had a tremendous impact on raising awareness and interest in Glissant worldwide. The similarities and overlaps between these three films unite them into a comprehensive trilogy. *Pensée archipélique* was adapted from the full film into a three-screen video installation made specifically for *The Sea is History*. Both versions offer a visual and aural emersion into Glissant's *Poèmes complets* (Complete Poems) and illuminate fundamental aspects of his worldview. As the title suggests, *Pensée archipélique* emphasizes the importance of archipelagic thinking, conveyed through a rich visual narrative that also speaks of creolization, the philosophy and poetics of relation, world mentality, and opacity.

Reflecting on the importance of thinking consciously, inclusively, and generously about relationships between all human beings, these films emphasize the need for a shared commitment to human rights, empathy, and human dignity. In a world where these values are constantly being challenged, Diawara pinpoints the implications of the current situation: "As Glissant would put it, we are in danger of losing our capacity to tremble within the trembling of others, the migrants."[8]

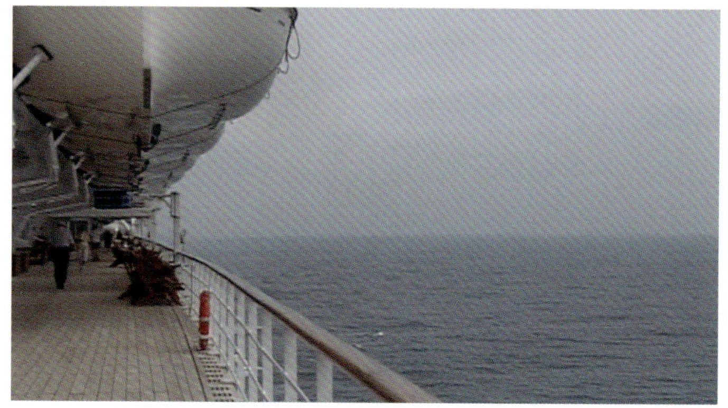

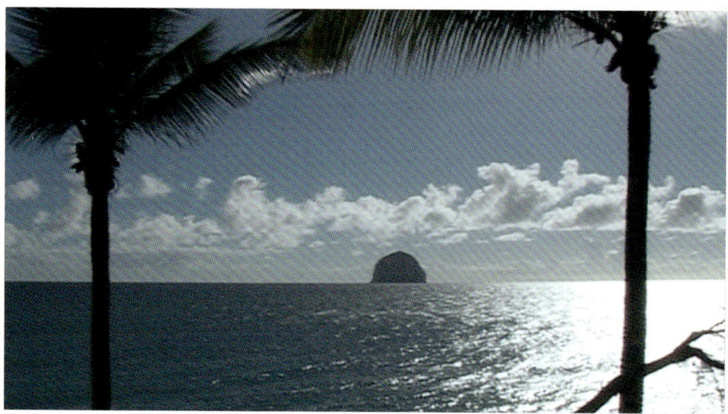

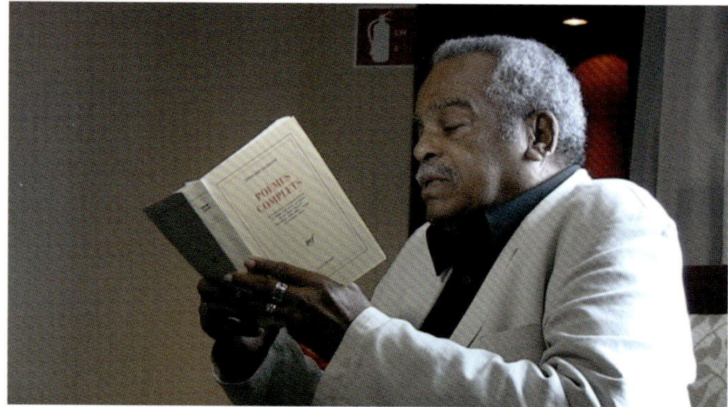

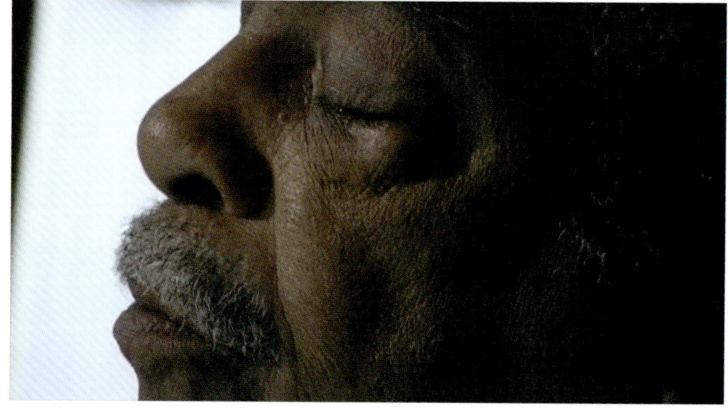

Manthia Diawara
*Édouard Glissant: One
World in Relation*, 2009
K'a Yéléma Productions
Film stills
48 minutes

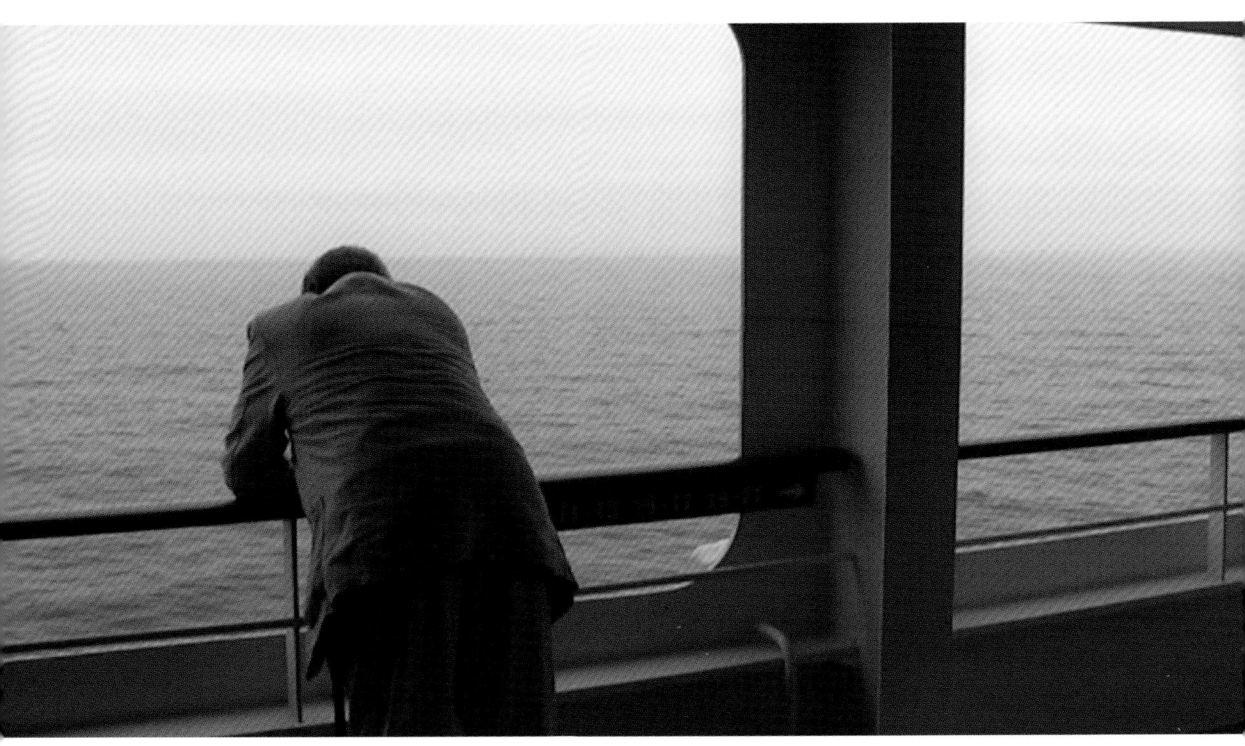

By bringing together the experiences of artists who have transcultural roots, this book explores and questions the multiple, overlapping routes that connect Europe, Africa, the Americas, and the Caribbean. As Stuart Hall pointed out, "in this post-colonial moment, the sensibilities of colonialism are still potent. We—all of us—are still its inheritors, still living in its terrifying aftermath."[9]

Hopefully, a careful consideration of these topics will help to untangle some of the knots that come in the way of breaking free from the continued effects of colonialism and the many forms of oppression that have been inherited from it. Clearly, only through a true understanding of the past can we even begin to negotiate a nuanced discussion about the present, which also involves talking about topics such as forced migration and racism. Because, as Hall so eloquently stated, "A past which is forgotten, or rendered inconsequential, will take its historic revenge."[10]

If we think about music within the context of Glissant's relational thinking, the historical weight of the call and response that unites musicians through time and across geographies, the overlaps and crossovers of music, and the constant back and forth between musical genres, particularly within the South Atlantic, are all abundantly clear.

Listening to the Echoes of the South Atlantic

Interestingly, the most powerful decolonial artistic strategies are often interdisciplinary. In fact, the deep interconnectivity between music and history and the idea that music can function as a response to history are key to understanding the wider framework of diaspora aesthetics. Building on its role within the context of what Paul Gilroy refers to as "the Atlantic as a system of cultural exchanges,"[11] we can recognize the importance of music as a collective language of resistance and solidarity. This was the focus of my exhibition *Listening to the Echoes of the South Atlantic*, which conveyed the significance of music as an expression of cultural experience and history. Emphasis was placed on sonic politics and the historical, cultural, and social implications of specific types of music, understood in relation to the entangled histories of the South Atlantic.

Listening to the Echoes of the South Atlantic highlighted interdisciplinary approaches that reflect a deep understanding of music and its migrating histories. As the works in the exhibition conveyed, music and sound are particularly effective means of bringing historical narratives into contemporary space. As a highly interdisciplinary exhibition, the sonic heartbeat was found in socially engaged and historically conscious art practices that extend beyond the strict parameters of visual art, music, or performance.

Ever since W. E. B. Du Bois penned his seminal work, *The Souls of Black Folk* (1903), the deep interconnectivity between Black musical traditions has been abundantly clear. More than a century later, the book is still a key resource for inspiration, analysis, and reflection for anyone interested in the interconnected histories of Black Atlantic music. The sociopolitical implications of music within the Atlantic triangle have also been extensively researched by contemporary scholars and writers, such as Paul Gilroy,

Greg Tate, and Fred Moten, to name only a few. Paul Gilroy in particular has played a pivotal role in conveying the extent to which music moves back and forth between continents, countries, and cultures within the Black Atlantic.

In this regard, Édouard Glissant's observations about "the cry of the Plantation" are quite illuminating. In *Poétique de la Relation* (Poetics of Relation), he describes the vital connection between orality (speech) and music:

> It is not just literature. When we examine how speech functions in this Plantation realm, we observe that there are several almost codified types of expression. Direct, elementary speech, articulating the rudimentary language necessary to get work done; stifled speech, corresponding to the silence of this world in which knowing how to read and write is forbidden; deferred or disguised speech, in which men and women who are gagged keep their words close. The Creole language integrated these three modes and made them jazz.

> It is understandable that in this universe every cry was an event. Night in the cabins gave birth to this other enormous silence from which music, inescapable, a murmur at first, finally burst out into this long shout—a music of reserved spirituality through which the body suddenly expresses itself. Monotonous changes, syncopated, broken by prohibitions, set free by the entire thrust of bodies, produced their language from one end of this world to the other. These musical expressions born of silence: Negro spirituals and blues, persisting in towns and growing cities; jazz, *biguines*, and calypsos, bursting into barrios and shantytowns; salsas and reggaes, assembled everything blunt and direct, painfully stifled, and patiently differed into this varied speech. This was the cry of the Plantation, transfigured into the speech of the world.[12]

These observations extend directly from Glissant's poetics and philosophy of relation and are perfectly in tune with his concept of *échos-monde*. If we think about music within the context of Glissant's relational thinking, the historical weight of the call and response that unites musicians through time and across geographies, the overlaps and crossovers of music, and the constant back and forth between musical genres, particularly within the South Atlantic, are all abundantly clear. Glissant's concept of universal interconnectivity is perhaps nowhere more evident than in relation to music. He returns to these ideas in a subsequent passage about *échos-monde*, which emphasizes the multiple, meaningful connections between music, art, literature, and architecture. Here, he describes *échos-monde* as an interactive, interdependent totality and posits that thought creates music:

> William Faulkner's work, Bob Marley's singing, Benoît Mandelbrot's theories are *échos-monde*. Wilfredo Lam's painting (flowing together) or that of Roberto Matta (flowing apart); the architecture of Chicago, as well as the disorder of the shantytowns of Rio or Caracas; Ezra Pound's *Cantos*, and also the marching of schoolchildren in Soweto, are all examples of *échos-monde*.[13]

Glissant's observations about poetry also apply to music. He states: "The world's poetic force (its energy), kept alive within us, fastens itself by fleeting, delicate shivers, onto the rambling prescience of poetry in the depths of our being."[14]

It's here, at the intersection between art, music, poetry, and literature, that we can access a deeper understanding of the overlapping and entangled histories that connect Norway not only to Denmark and Europe, but also to Africa and the Caribbean.

By highlighting the stories of those who have been historically silenced, we gain access to a more nuanced understanding of colonial history and the factors which have contributed to the continued effects of colonialism today.

From Africa to the West Indies on Danish-Norwegian Slave Ships

In order to achieve a clear understanding of the ways in which Norway profited from colonial trade, it's worth mentioning briefly that Denmark-Norway's first colony was located in Tranquebar, India (1620-1845).[15] Tranquebar was established nearly forty years before Denmark-Norway invested in trading forts along the coast of Guinea (West Africa) and before becoming involved in the slave trade between Guinea and the West Indies. The first person in charge of the Danish-Norwegian colony Tranquebar, known today as Tharangambadi, was the Danish Admiral Ove Gjedde, who went on to enjoy a profitable existence in Norway. Gjedde invested in the Kongsberg Silver Mines in 1628 and was subsequently appointed director of the silver mines in 1630.[16] He later invested in Fossum Ironworks in Skien, before establishing Ulefoss Ironworks in 1657.[17] He is mentioned here as a classic example of the many Danes and Norwegians who not only profited from positions of colonial governance, they were also handsomely rewarded when they returned to Denmark-Norway.

At the height of Danish-Norwegian colonial presence in Guinea there were numerous trading stations, forts, and castles situated along what was commonly referred to as the Gold Coast, with Christiansborg Fort as the headquarters for the slave trade.[18] As the site where thousands upon thousands of enslaved Africans were imprisoned and tortured, and as the primary point of departure for Danish-Norwegian transatlantic trade, Christiansborg Fort is irreparably tainted by the atrocities of its colonial history. In 1652, Swedish Africa Company first built an earthen trading lodge at the site, located in Osu, Accra. The Danes took over the property in 1661 and subsequently built a stone fort and named it Christiansborg Fort after Christian IV. Over time, the fort was enlarged and converted to a castle with the eventual plan to turn it into a museum.[19] Christiansborg Fort was so vital to the Danish-Norwegian economy that between 1688 and 1747 an image of the castle was depicted on Danish-Norwegian coinage, including the ducat coin made from West African gold.[20] In 1850, Denmark sold Christiansborg to the British for £10,000 along with the forts Augustaborg, Fredensborg, Kongensten, Prinsensten and Prøvesten, as well as the plantations of the Akuapem Mountains.[21] Additionally, Cape Coast Castle (also known as Carlsborg or Carulsborg), which was first built by Swedish Africa Company in 1652, was also briefly occupied by Danish West India Company in 1658. Several more transfers of power occurred between the Danes, the Dutch, and the Swedes until 1664, when the British took over the castle and maintained control until 1957.[22]

Similarly, the history of Danish-Norwegian colonization of the West Indies extends over centuries, beginning with the unsuccessful occupation of St. Thomas in 1666. Denmark regained control in 1672 after having established Danish West India Company in 1671 to handle shipping, colonization, and trade on St. Thomas. In 1674, Danish West India Company took over Danish holdings on the Gold Coast of Africa and the name was changed to Danish West India and Guinea Company.[23] St. John was annexed in 1718, and St. Croix was eventually purchased by Christian VI from France in 1733. In 1754, the Danish crown purchased Danish West India and Guinea Company[24] and thereby took over direct colonial rule of the West Indies until 1917 when Denmark sold the Danish West Indies to the United States and they became the U.S. Virgin Islands.

Although the exact numbers vary, most estimates indicate that approximately one hundred and twenty thousand enslaved Africans were shipped under the Danish flag from Guinea to the West Indies. It's no secret that the conditions on board were horrific, and many died of disease, hunger, thirst, or suicide during the transatlantic crossing. The shipment of enslaved Africans under the Danish flag started on a fairly small scale, but gradually more and more individuals were transported from the Gold Coast to the West Indies. Although King Frederik VI ruled in 1792 that the transatlantic shipment of slaves would be abolished in 1803, paradoxically, the greatest number of enslaved people were transported between 1793 and 1802. During those years alone, two thousand five hundred enslaved Africans were transported to the former Danish West Indies every year. This was because plantation owners in the former Danish West Indies wanted to acquire as many enslaved laborers as possible prior to abolition.[25] Even after 1803, slavery still continued in West Africa and in the West Indies, and Danes and Norwegians went on to profit from the plantation economy well beyond that date.

Ships generally sailed a triangular route between Denmark, Guinea, and the West Indies. Leaving from Denmark, the ships were stocked with weapons, gunpowder, and alcohol. In Guinea the ships picked up enslaved Africans, ivory, and gold before sailing on to the West Indies, where the enslaved were sold to plantation owners. Finally, the ships were loaded with sugar, tobacco, coffee, rum, and other goods before sailing back to Denmark. The entire voyage typically took up to eighteen months—often with a layover of up to six months in Guinea to collect enslaved laborers. During the first few decades of trade, about half of the ships sailed the triangular route, but from the 1730s the triangular trade ebbed away.[26]

The first slave ship to sail under the Danish flag was owned by a trader from Bergen. *Cornelia*, which arrived in St. Croix in 1674 with one hundred and three enslaved individuals, was owned by Jørgen Thormøhlen (also known as Jørgen Thor Møhlen). Not only was he responsible for the first shipment of enslaved Africans to the West Indies under the Danish flag, he was also contracted in 1690 to lease St. Thomas and its surrounding islands from Danish West India and Guinea Company. Having leased the right to trade, he profited greatly from the plantation economy, and had full control over the plantations, forts, and enslaved laborers.[27]

Among the individuals who were directly involved in or profited from the triangular trade and the transatlantic slave trade are some of the most prominent names in Norwegian history. A comprehensive list would include anyone who invested in the triangular trade, the traders, the ship-owners, the men who built the ships, the captains who sailed the ships, the governors and tradesmen who were placed in charge of colonial interests, the priests who kept quiet, the doctors who let people die, and the wealthy Danes and Norwegians who kept African and West Indian slaves as servants in their homes. The list should also include those who profited from other aspects of European colonization of Africa, such as those who stole Nkisi artifacts and treasures from the Kingdom of Kongo and subsequently sold them to ethnographic museums throughout Scandinavia.

Among the most well-known slave ships to sail under the Danish flag was *Fredensborg*. As one of very few excavated slave ships in the world today, it has been a vital source of information regarding Denmark-Norway's involvement in the transatlantic slave trade. The history of *Fredensborg* is most thoroughly documented in Leif Svalesen's book *The Slave Ship Fredensborg*. There is a lot to be learned from the details of the ship's final voyage. *Fredensborg* sailed from Copenhagen in June 1767, arriving at Christiansborg Fort on the Gold Coast in October. It remained anchored there until April 1768, when the ship departed for St. Croix loaded with goods and two hundred and fifty-one enslaved Africans, including women and children. Also, since several members of the ship's crew had fallen ill, an additional nine enslaved Africans were brought on board to man the deck. Prior to boarding the ship, the enslaved were branded with Danish West India and Guinea Company's mark of ownership, the letter "S" inside the shape of a heart. The enslaved were chained together and were each designated a space measuring only $180 \times 40 \times 70$ centimeters. At least twenty-four enslaved Africans died during the transatlantic journey, and the rest were sold to plantation owners upon arrival in St. Croix.[28] During the return trip to Denmark, in 1768, *Fredensborg* sank off the coast of Norway and the shipwreck was eventually discovered by local divers in 1974.[29]

Despite the facts, and even the most well-documented evidence, there continues to be surprisingly little interest in exposing the details of Norway's colonial history. While the transatlantic slave trade is undoubtedly the most horrific aspect of the triangular trade, Denmark-Norway was also involved in direct trade to and from the West Indies and profited greatly from all aspects of the plantation economy, even after slavery was abolished.

As an art historian and curator of contemporary art, I will leave the task of conveying the lengthy details about Norway's colonial history, including the list of all the individuals involved, to the historians. My interest lies in shedding light on narratives of rebellion against colonial rule, told primarily from the perspective of the descendants of the enslaved and seen through the lens of contemporary art. There is empowerment in the stories of individuals such as Venus Johannes, Mary Thomas, Anna Heegaard, and Olaudah Equiano, who fought fearlessly against slavery and colonial rule. These are stories of resistance that help, at least partially, to set the historical records straight. By highlighting the stories of those who have been historically silenced, we gain access to a more nuanced understanding of colonial history and the factors which have contributed to the continued effects of colonialism today, most evidently witnessed in the prevalence of racism, poverty, and forced migration.

Positioned directly in front of the eighteenth-century warehouse that was built for Danish West India Company, the monument stands as a strong visual reminder of Denmark-Norway's colonial history and is a beautiful act of empowerment and resistance.

I Am Queen Mary

Jeannette Ehlers was among the first in Scandinavia to address colonial history through contemporary art. Her artworks confront Denmark's (and Norway's) colonial past directly, asking viewers to question what it means to be an inheritor of colonial history. Recently, she gained international attention for her collaborative monument with La Vaughn Belle, *I Am Queen Mary* (2018). As the first monument in Denmark to address the country's colonization of the Virgin Islands (1672–1917), its relevance within the framework of Scandinavian decolonial discourse is unprecedented. *I Am Queen Mary* memorializes the Crucian freedom fighter Mary Thomas, commonly known as Queen Mary, who was an important leader of the Fireburn labor revolt, which took place in St. Croix.

> The Fireburn began on October 1, 1878 as an uprising against the contractual servitude that continued to bind workers to the plantation system after the 1848 abolition of slavery in the former Danish West Indies. As its name suggests, this insurrection for better working and living conditions involved burning down most of Frederiksted as well as sugar cane fields on a great number of St. Croix's plantations. Along with Mary Thomas, the three women Axeline 'Agnes' Elizabeth Salomon, Matilde McBean and Susanna 'Bottom Belly' Abrahamson led the largest labor revolt in Danish colonial history. They were arrested and sent to Denmark in 1882 to serve prison sentences in Christianshavn's Women's Prison. Their sentences were later commuted and they were returned to St. Croix. They are venerated in U.S. Virgin Islands cultural mythology as the Queens of the Fireburn.[30]

The massive sculpture stands on a plinth composed of 1.5 tons of coral imported from St. Croix, referencing the coral that was once cut by hand

Jeannette Ehlers
Whip it Good, 2013–
ongoing
Interactive performance
Brundyn Gallery, Cape
Town, 2015
Photo: Nikolaj Recke

Whip it Good was first
commissioned in 2013
by Art Labour Archive
and Ballhaus
Naunynstrasse, Berlin

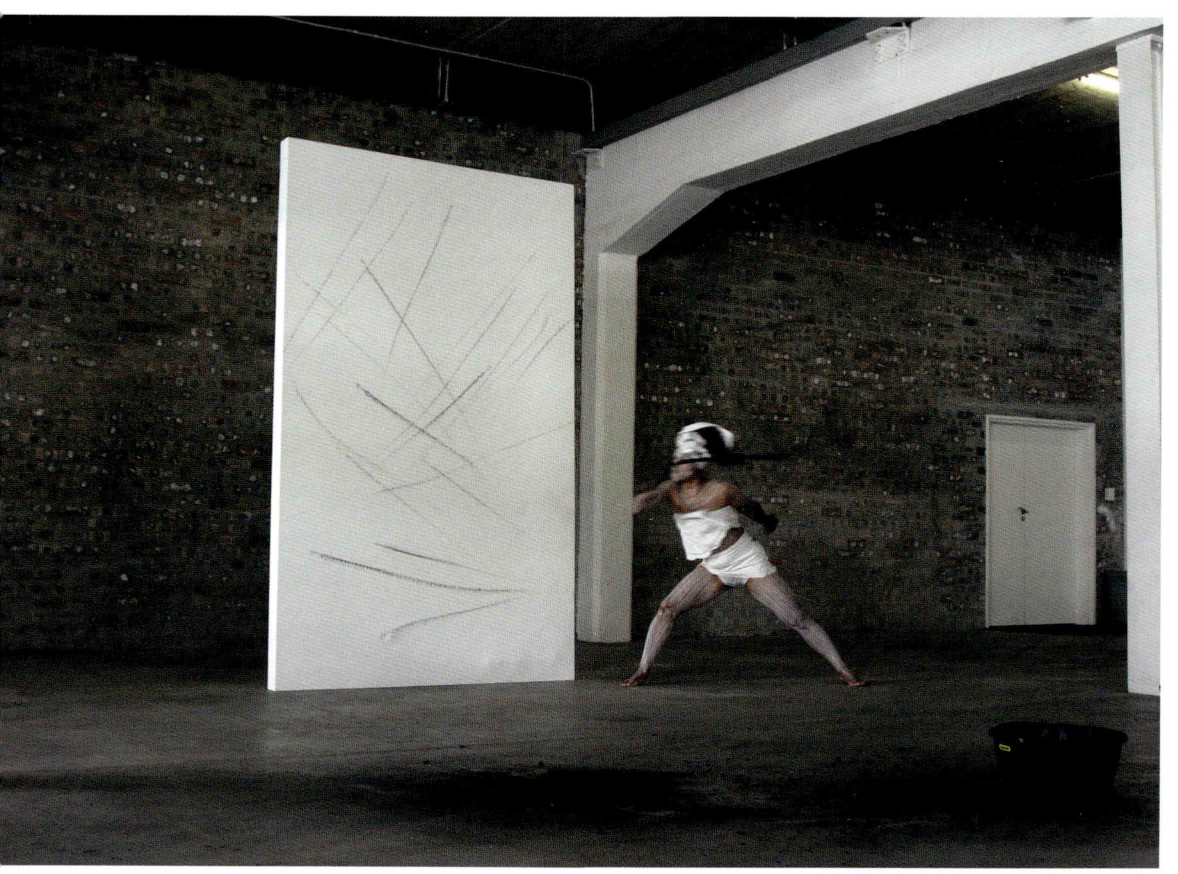

La Vaughn Belle
Trading Post, 2015
Reclaimed coral stones
cut from the ocean
by enslaved Africans,
plexiglass
91.4 × 45.7 × 45.7 cm
Photo: Tamia Williams

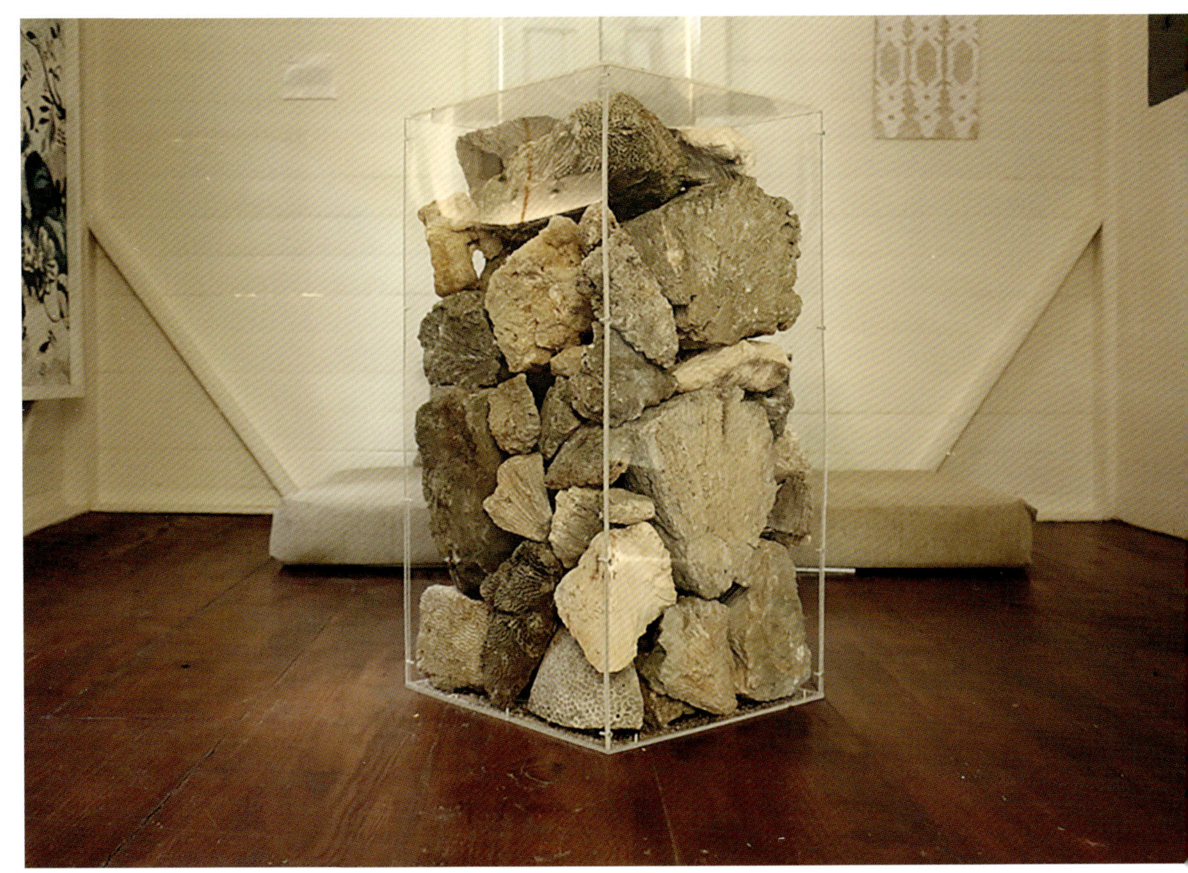

by enslaved Africans and used in the foundations of buildings in the former Danish West Indies. The implementation of coral in Ehlers's and Belle's collaborative monument was inspired by an earlier work by La Vaughn Belle entitled *Trading Post* (2015), comprised of coral encased in plexiglass. Already a strong sociopolitical statement in its own right, the transformation from a freestanding work to the double significance of its purpose as the foundation of a decolonial monument, inserted into a colonial space, imbues it with additional layers of meaning. In the journey from St. Croix to Copenhagen, in the transition from colonial trading post to colonial warehouse, a crucial conceptual shift takes place. Ultimately, the transport of the coral from the Virgin Islands to Denmark is an effective reversal of Danish-Norwegian colonial trade routes. Positioned directly in front of the eighteenth-century warehouse that was built for Danish West India Company, the monument stands as a strong visual reminder of Denmark-Norway's colonial history and is a beautiful act of empowerment and resistance.

Imbuing the work with additional layers of meaning, Ehlers and Belle used 3D body scanning technology to combine their physical likenesses into a hybrid female figure. Their monumental statue commands the space as a fusion of bodies and overlapping historical narratives. Ultimately, *I Am Queen Mary* is more than a monument to the heroines who fought against colonial rule; it functions as a transhistorical intervention into contemporary cultural space. It's highly significant that Ehlers and Belle embody Queen Mary as a powerful symbol of solidarity between the inheritors of Denmark's colonial legacy on both sides of the Atlantic. It's equally important that Queen Mary sits on a peacock chair and holds a cane bill and a torch, echoing the seated pose of Ehlers's performance and video work *Whip it Good*, which in turn references the iconic image of Huey P. Newton, leader of the Black Panther Party, seated on a peacock chair holding a rifle and a spear in his hands.[31] Ehlers and Belle meld multiple overlapping histories into a narrative that emphasizes the direct connection between history and contemporary society. Every detail in the work tells part of an interconnected story, which is a narrative that began with the slave trade and still continues today.

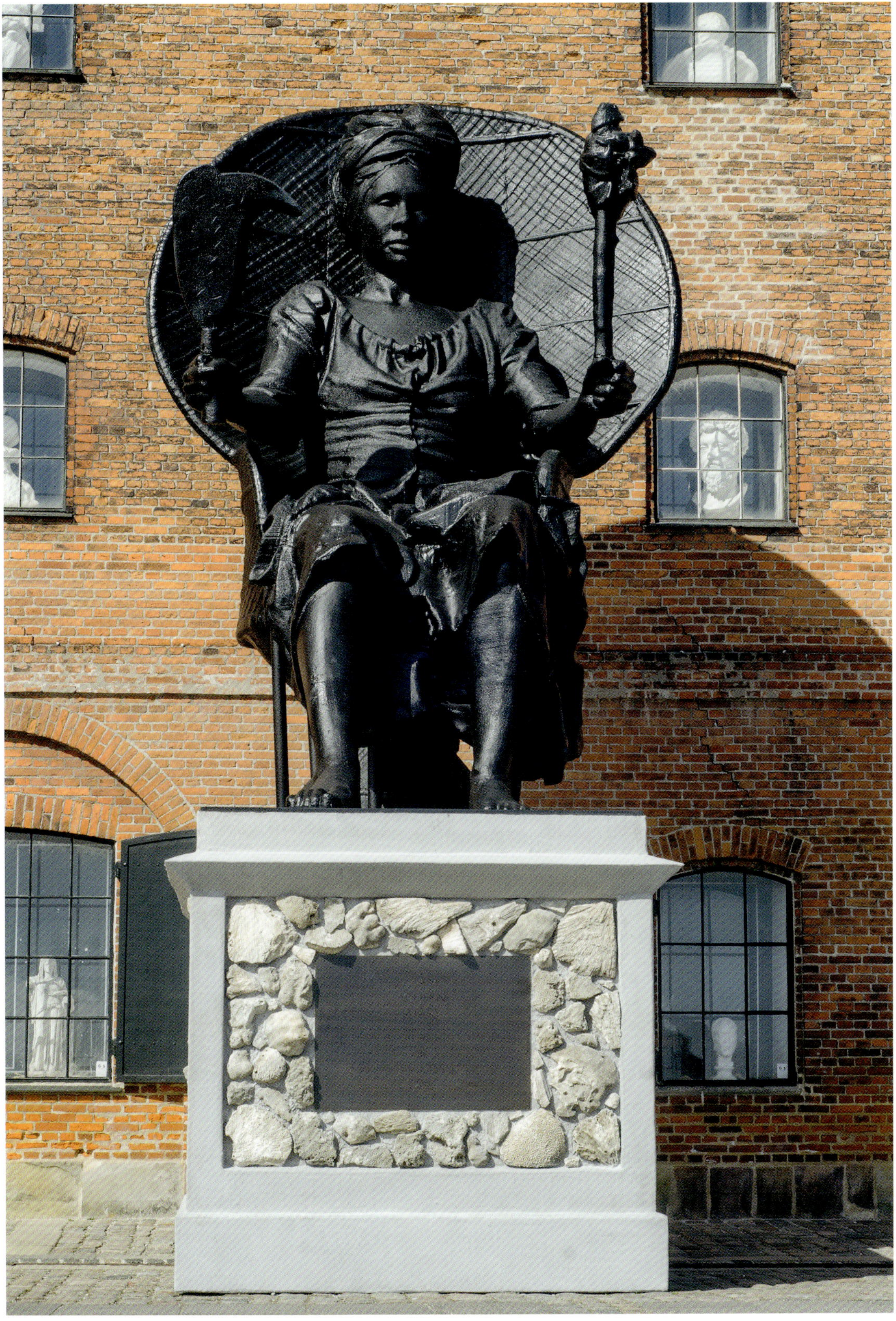

*Occupying colonial space as
Jeannette Ehlers does, positioning her
body in this space, the work functions
as a powerful act of resistance.
Paradoxically, she achieves visibility
through her own invisibility as she exorcises
the colonial demons out of the manor.*

Occupying Colonial Space

Ehlers's video *Black Magic at the White House* (2009), featured in the exhibition *Listening to the Echoes of the South Atlantic*, involves a similar strategy of decolonial intervention. In this video Ehlers performs a Vodou dance at Marienborg, which has a strong connection to the triangular trade. Jeannette Ehlers explains:

> It was built as a summer residence for the Commander Olfert Fischer in 1744, who since sold it to merchant Peter Windt, who also had created a great deal of wealth from the slave and sugar trade, and who even brought slaves with him to his home in Denmark. Several other traders from the colonial era have owned and put their stamp on Marienborg, and today it still plays an important role in Denmark, in terms of its position as the official residence (since 1962) of the country's prime minister.[32]

Since the full impact of *Black Magic at the White House* depends on our awareness of the history of the manor where it was filmed, the video begins with the image of an embroidered cloth featuring a depiction of Marienborg followed by winter scenes that make it fairly clear that the setting is Denmark. It's interesting to consider the implications of the fact that Jeannette Ehlers's performance is essentially an invisible dance. More precisely, we see her dancing, but she is invisible. We see the outline of her body, but we don't actually see her. She is camouflaged right into the antique wallpaper and hardwood floor. In that invisibility, essentially an erasure, she has created a bold sand radical work. The insistent and rhythmical beat of the drum is equally crucial to the impact of the work. Images of a *vévé* being drawn suggest that she is performing a Vodou ritual. Occupying colonial space as she does, positioning her body in this space, the work functions as a powerful act of resistance. Paradoxically, she achieves visibility through her own invisibility as she exorcises the colonial demons out of the manor. Ultimately, the work addresses Denmark-Norway's unspoken histories and relocates these histories at the center of the narrative. As such, paraphrasing Fred Moten, the work is a staging of the piercing insistence of the excluded.[33]

Throughout her work, Jeannette Ehlers explores specific historical events and people, with particular emphasis on those who were at the forefront of the struggle for emancipation, such as Queen Mary. Her works read as captivating history lessons and a critical questioning of the historical details of Danish colonial rule, which have generally been told from a colonizer's perspective. For instance, Peter von Scholten, often credited for having worked to improve the conditions for "free people of color" and enslaved laborers, and also for his efforts to abolish slavery, is referenced in her video *Three Steps of Story* (2009). Here, she conveys a more nuanced account of his role, along the lines of what is cited by the Danish National Archives: "Peter von Scholten was probably encouraged in his fight for the cause of the enslaved laborers by Anna Heegaard, who was a 'free-colored' and with whom he lived on St. Croix even though he had a wife back home in Copenhagen."[34] Anna Heegaard certainly seems to have had a positive influence on von Scholten, and together they fought for improved conditions for the "free-colored" and enslaved laborers. However, regarding von Scholten declaring the emancipation of slaves in 1848, it's hard to believe that his motivation was entirely humanitarian. In retrospect, it seems more likely that his most urgent goal was to avert a slave rebellion.

Much attention is also given to the fact that von Scholten and Heegaard invited both slave owners and "free-colored" to attend the balls that they frequently arranged at his residence. Ehlers's video frames this story within a contemporary context, thereby emphasizing the direct link between past and present. Inserting herself into the narrative, she dances through the mirrored ballroom of Government House in St. Croix, resulting in a critical questioning of white colonial space and the internal power structures of white space which still continue to this day. The fact that this was a colonial space where slave owners could dance and mingle freely with their "free-colored" mistresses is typically mentioned in defense of Peter von Scholten by those who still give him full credit for emancipating the enslaved.

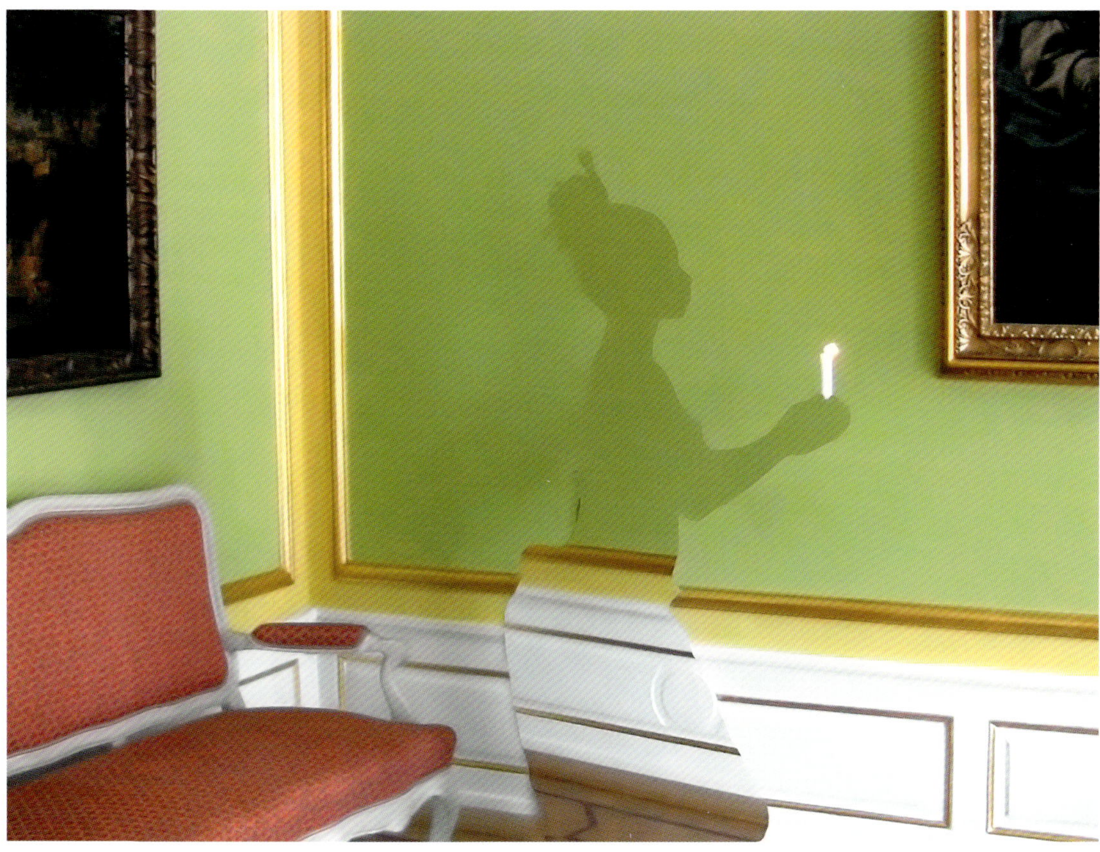

A more balanced account of the individuals and events that led to the emancipation of the enslaved in 1848 gives credit to General Buddhoe, the man who led St. Croix's struggle for liberty:

> In July 1848, a slave rebellion started on St. Croix. Big crowds of enslaved laborers from the town and the plantations took complete control of the small town of Frederiksted. One of the leading men among the rebels was the enslaved laborer John Gottlieb, called General Buddhoe.

> The situation was critical. Von Scholten saw no other recourse than taking matters into his own hands in order to ward off and to avert a devastating rebellion. On July 3, 1848, he drove to Frederiksted, spoke to the rebels and abolished slavery in the Danish possessions in the West Indies effective immediately. It has since been said that von Scholten and John Gottlieb entered into a secret prior agreement, but there is no proof to document this claim.

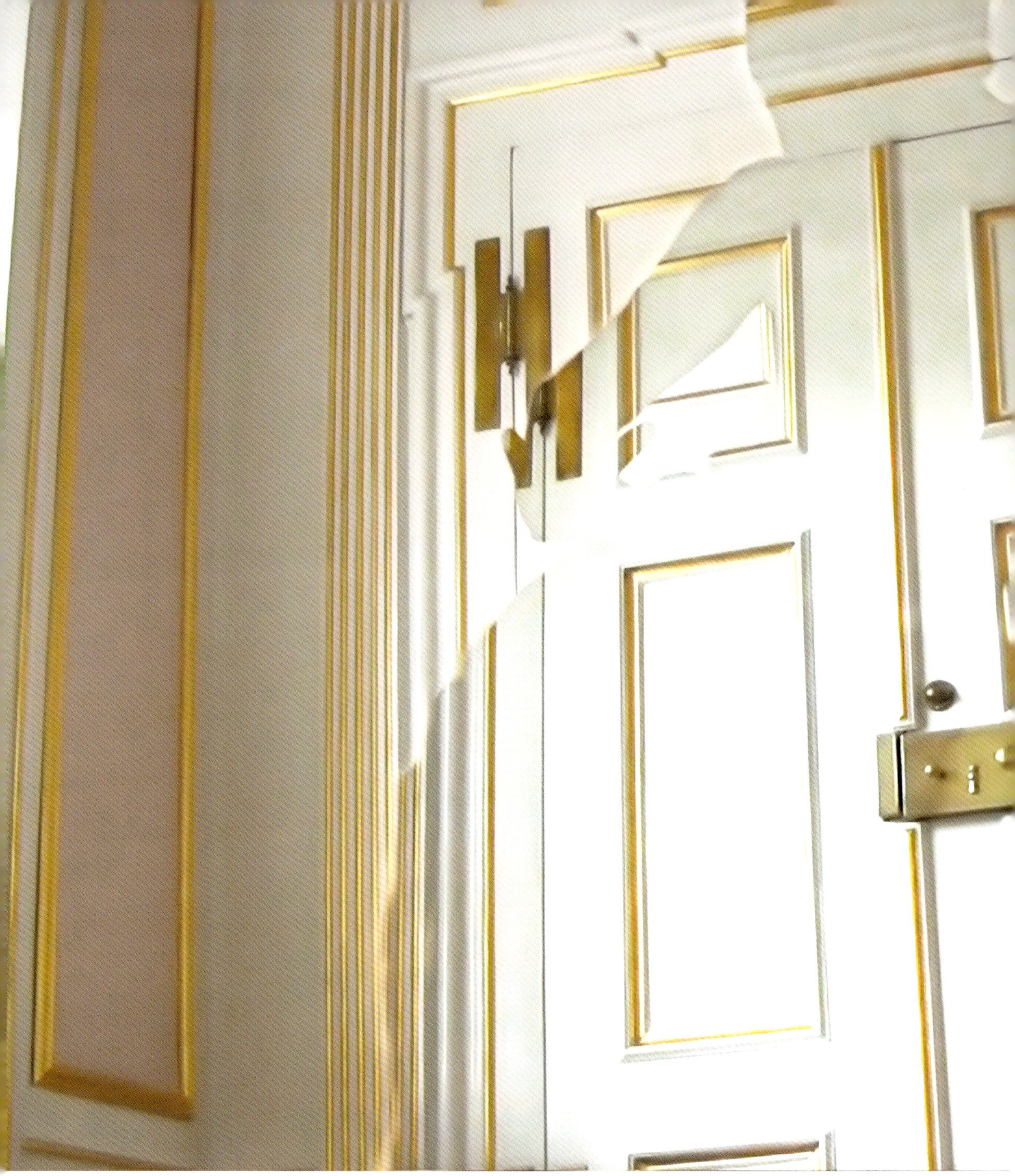

Jeannette Ehlers
Black Magic at the White House, 2009
Video still
3 minutes 46 seconds

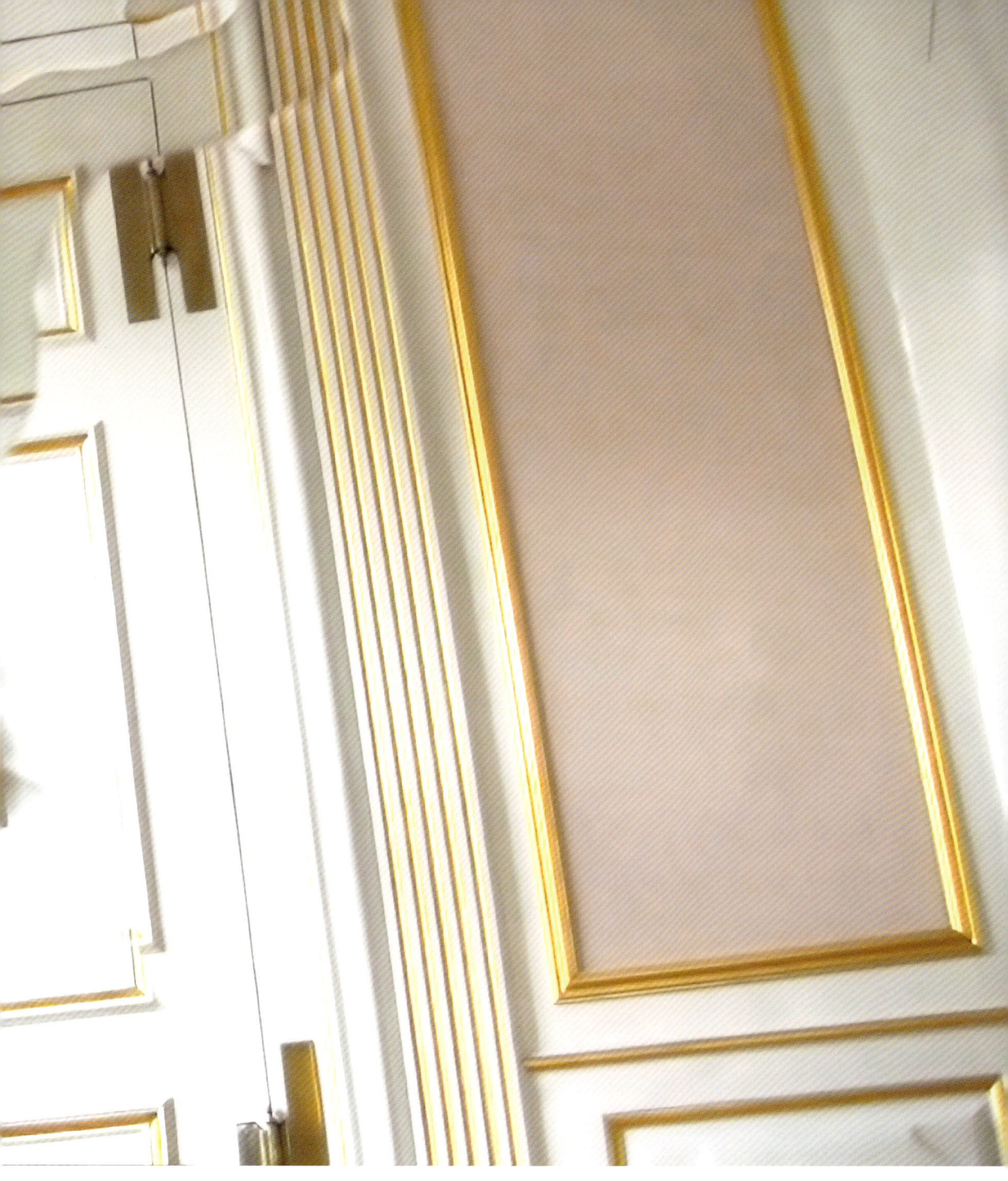

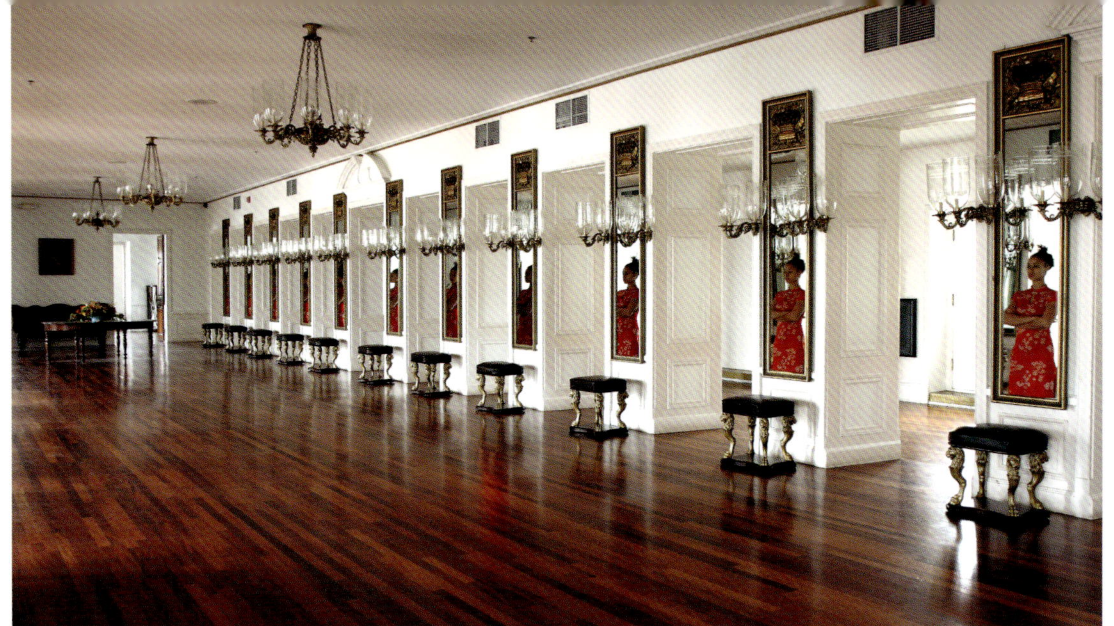

The Governor-General had no authority to abolish slavery. He came under severe attack for his decision, both by the members of the West Indian government and by slave owners. The owners had lost a large part of their wealth without knowing what compensation to expect. Peter von Scholten suffered a nervous breakdown because of the events and left the islands soon thereafter.[35]

Following up where we left off, with Jeannette Ehlers dancing through the mirrored ballroom in *Three Steps of Story*, she takes a significant step outside of colonial space to film *Speed Up That Day* (2009). In contrast to the other two videos in Ehlers's *Atlantic* series, which take place inside colonial structures, this film is shot outside Fort Frederik, where von Scholten proclaimed the emancipation of slaves in 1848. Make no mistake. This is no homage to von Scholten. Through the conscious balance between themes of visibility and invisibility, inside and outside, past and present, these three films help to set the historical records straight. Each of the films has the power to stand on its own, but when interpreted as a trilogy, the interconnected narrative is even more empowering.

Speed Up That Day begins with an excerpt from Martin Luther King Jr.'s *I Have a Dream* speech:

> . . . when we allow freedom to ring, when we let it ring from every village and every hamlet, from every state and every city, we will

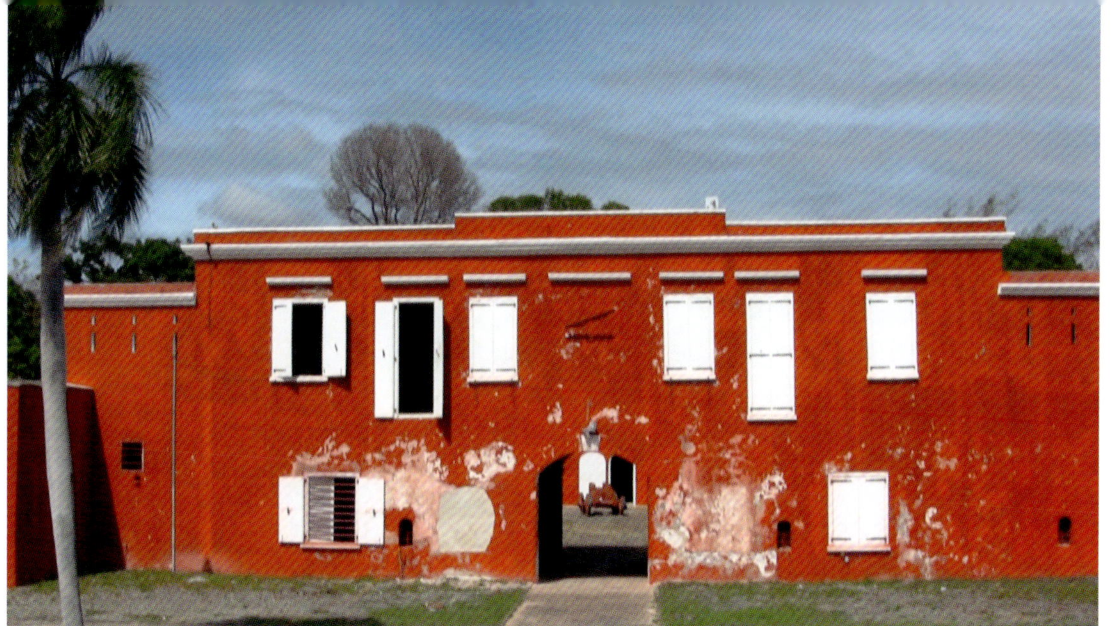

be able to speed up that day when *all* of God's children, black men and white men, Jews and Gentiles, Protestants and Catholics, will be able to join hands and sing in the words of the old Negro spiritual: Free at last! Free at last! Thank God Almighty, we are free at last![36]

The soundscape for the rest of the film features the noise from the crowd that was gathered to hear Martin Luther King Jr.'s speech. Visual markers of time include clouds passing quickly in the sky, people moving in and out of the building, and window shutters that open and close. Clearly, as with *Black Magic at the White House* and *Three Steps of Story*, what we hear is as important as what we see. Fittingly, von Scholten is completely invisible. What we do see is the outside of Fort Frederik and, by inserting an excerpt from Martin Luther King Jr.'s seminal speech into this context, Ehlers not only rewrites the colonial narrative, she also emphasizes the fact that we still have a long way to go before we are truly free from the colonial past.

Oceana James confronts Crucian colonial history in a riveting performance work that highlights the story of Venus Johannes, who has a special place in Crucian history in terms of how she freed herself from enslavement.

The Story of Venus Johannes

Oceana James confronts Crucian colonial history in a riveting performance work that highlights the story of Venus Johannes, who has a special place in Crucian history in terms of how she freed herself from enslavement. Hers is an epic story of strength and perseverance. James's site-specific performance is an abrupt wake-up call from the ignorance of colonial amnesia. As already seen in relation to Jeannette Ehlers's and La Vaughn Belle's *I Am Queen Mary*, paying homage to and honoring the enslaved Black women who fought against their colonial oppressors and bringing these women's names, faces, and experiences to life through art is a powerful act of solidarity and resistance. James's work makes an equally powerful statement about the countless Black men who continue to be murdered in today's society. As James points out, this is something that women like Venus Johannes have had to deal with since the onset of colonialism. The fact that the performance became a community engagement effort, involving locals and passersby who contributed and offered to help, really brought the town together and speaks to the genuine impact of the work.

James's *For Gowie the Deceitful Fellow* (2016) was a site-specific performance that took place at the former home of Venus Johannes in St. Croix. Johannes, who was born in Senegal, was captured as a young girl and taken to the island of Gorée where she was sold to Anne Roussine Pepin, a prominent "free-colored" woman and wife of Nicholas Pepin, who owned and built Gorée's House of Slaves with its Door of No Return. Although the headquarters of the Danish-Norwegian slave trade were located at Christiansborg Fort in present-day Ghana, Johannes arrived in the former Danish West Indies from Gorée, Senegal. Her story thereby illustrates the entanglements and overlaps between colonial rulers who were operating all along the coast of West Africa and indicates that the shipment of enslaved Africans to the former Danish West Indies was not simply limited to the ships that sailed under the Danish flag. An account of the challenges that Venus Johannes had to face throughout her lifetime is well documented by the St. Croix African Roots Project and the Danish National Archives:

[Venus Johannes] served as a domestic in the Pepin household until the arrival in 1800 of John George Maddock, captain of a slaving vessel from St. Croix.

Captain Maddock took lodgings with the Pepins, and there became so infatuated with the servant girl Venus that he offered to purchase her. Anne Roussine refused to sell Venus but agreed to take one slave in exchange if Maddock would free Venus unconditionally and go through the motions of marrying her. The following morning the arrangement was publicly validated with a traditional Gorée marriage ceremony.

Venus lived with Captain Maddock on Gorée for about 2 months. When time came for Maddock to return to St. Croix, she agreed to go with him on condition that he would give her bond to carry her back again to Gorée. Maddock consented and the signed bond was left by Venus in the hands of Nicholas Pepin.

Along with 61 enslaved Africans, Venus reached St. Croix in October 1800, with Captain Maddock. On her arrival at Frederiksted she was sold by Maddock to Jehodan Yates, daughter of his friend Captain John Yates. Venus resided with and worked for Jehodan Yates in Frederiksted between 1800 and 1815, during which time she had four children – Charlotte, Elvira, John Frederick and Rosalina.

In 1815, Venus brought her illegal enslavement to the attention of the Danish magistrate, who conducted a detailed investigation into the matter. A decision was reached whereby Venus and her youngest child Rosalina were declared free, but her other 3 children were to remain enslaved until freed either by Venus or Jehodan Yates. By 1820, they too had become free.

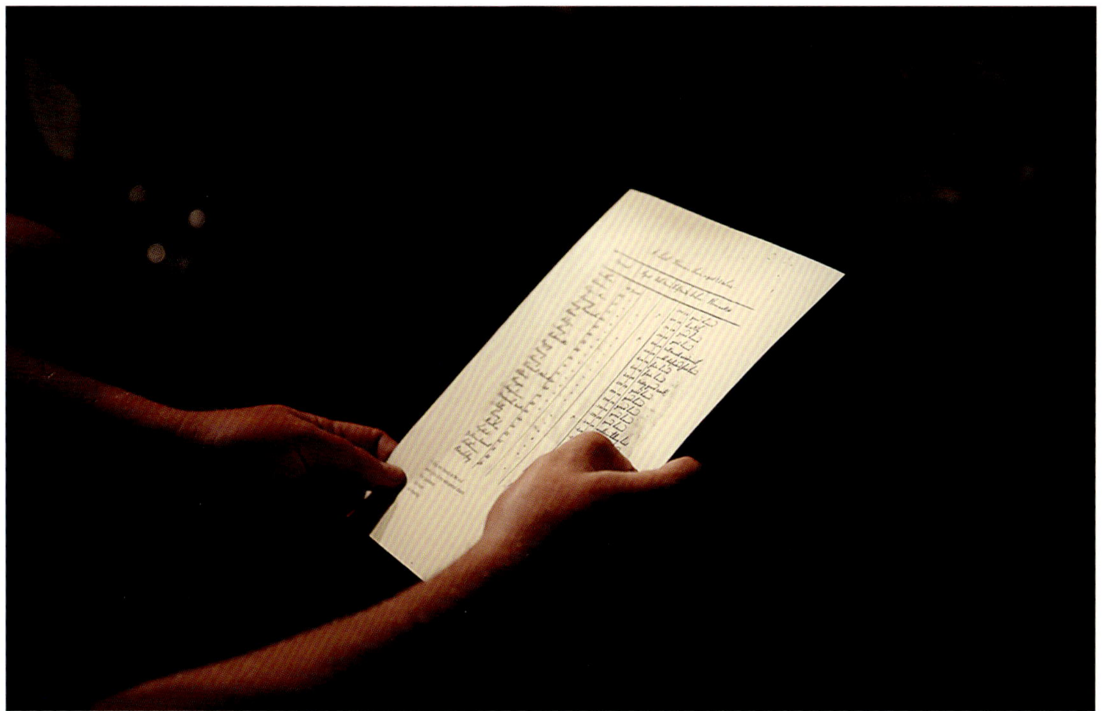

Once free, Venus married John Johannes, a barber, and they had three children—Perla, Mary Ann and John Richard. She and her family lived in a small house belonging to John Johannes located at 36B Hospital Street in Frederiksted. John Johannes died in August of 1825. Prior to his death, he and Venus gave their three children a deed of gift to the Hospital Street property. Members of Venus' family retained possession of this property until the early 20th Century.[37]

For Gowie the Deceitful Fellow is often described as a theatrical experiment, but it is so much more than that. It's a bold and radical intervention that confronts colonial history while also exposing the direct link between colonial power structures (that have yet to be dismantled) and the prevalence of racism today. Among other topics, James's performance examines how histories of enslavement have contributed to the social, cultural, and economic injustices that continue today, both in relation to colonizing nations and formerly colonized countries. James's spectacular interdisciplinary work combines movement, projections, sound, and light to convey a gripping and deeply personal story that is firmly anchored in decolonial thinking. Although the performance has also taken place in other locations,

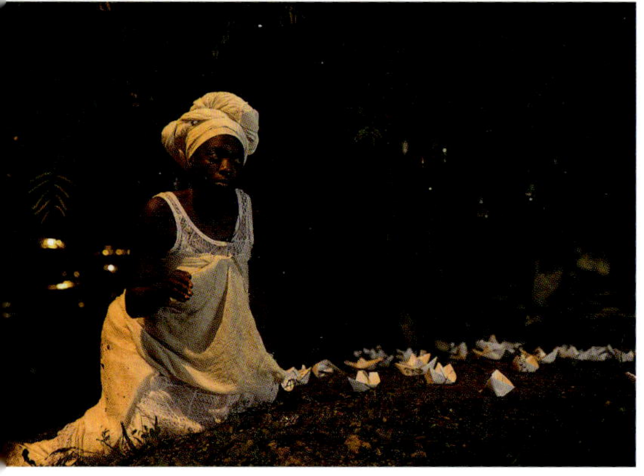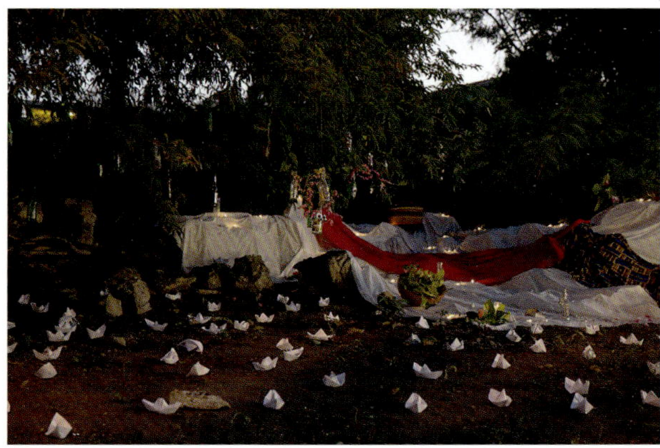

including Denmark, within this particular context my focus is on the original version which took place in St. Croix.

Dressed all in white, James used a folktale structure for her solo performance, which took place on the exact plot of land in Frederiksted once owned by Venus Johannes. Performed on the ruins of Johannes's former home, the artist conveyed a narrative about the shared history and spiritual connections between African Americans, Blacks living on St. Croix, and the larger African diaspora. Small origami boats were scattered throughout the landscape in the background, evoking a chilling visual metaphor for the slave ships that crossed the Atlantic and the enslaved Africans who were subsequently displaced and dispersed throughout the Americas and the Caribbean. A decorative shrine built to honor ancestral spirits creates a strong sense of this being a sacred site. During a particularly momentous part of the performance, James marched in front of the audience, along the street where she had written the words *love* and *rebel* repeatedly with white chalk, shouting "They were PEOPLE not slaves!" before breaking into dance. She kept rhythm with a *shekere* as she called out the names of Black Americans killed by the police and vigilante white men. In the wake of George Floyd's murder, it's horrific to think that the list of Black Americans subjected to police brutality continues to this day.

James yelled "Eric Garner was PEOPLE! Martin Luther King Jr., PEOPLE! Michael Brown, PEOPLE!" At one point an audience member called out "Renisha McBride!," to which James quickly responded "PEOPLE!," pointing her finger into the air as other names were called out. She continued her performance in an impassioned rage, "We gave birth to PEOPLE.

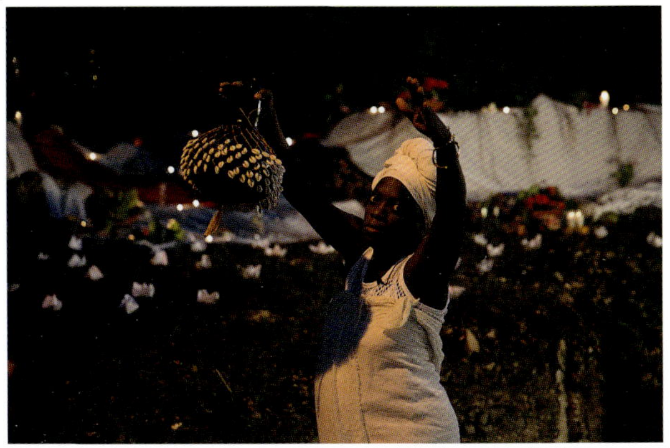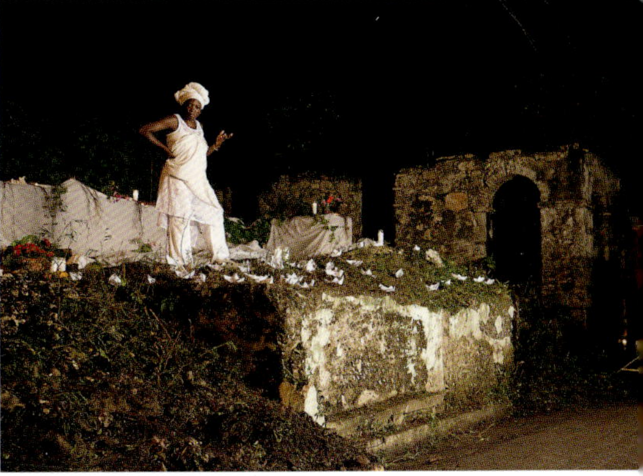

Not slaves, not slaves, not slaves! PEOPLE!" she yelled, as members of the audience cried "Ase! Ase! Ase!," thereby channeling the Yoruba philosophical concept that evokes the power to make things happen and to create change. This intense, rhythmic call and response between James and the audience represents a mesmerizing sensorial bridge between past and present. Words that began as whispers and cries in the past are transformed into earth-shattering screams in the present, only to be replaced by the piercing silence of deep, insufferable loss. At the end of the performance, James fell completely silent and handed out sheets of paper imprinted with the names of enslaved women between the ages of sixteen and sixty, with physical descriptions of each. Extending beyond the immediate framework of that very specific site and space, the performance resonates as a formidable decolonial intervention and an absolute and rightful demand for justice and respect. The implementation of her own body to help exorcise colonial demons from the site and the process of trying to heal from the trauma of the transatlantic slave trade bear significance far beyond the specifics of that particular space.

Ultimately, Oceana James brings ancestral memory and colonial history into contemporary space through a radical intervention that involves the invocation of spirits through words, sounds, rhythm, and movement. The implications of the fact that James's performance plays out on an overgrown colonial site with deep ancestral roots cannot be understated. And yet, the impact of the performance resounds both within and beyond this site. Borrowing once again from Fred Moten, "Where shriek turns speech turns song—remote from the impossible comfort of origin—lies the trace of our descent."[38]

La Vaughn Belle paints a picture of the Virgin Islands that stands as a powerful antidote to colonial erasure and whitewashing. Her paintings speak out effectively against colonial stereotypes and power structures, while also exposing the uncomfortable details of the colonial past.

Fragments of a Shared Colonial History

La Vaughn Belle is another artist whose work provides valuable insight into the colonial past of the Virgin Islands, particularly in relation to Denmark and the United States. Belle works in a variety of disciplines including painting, installation, photography, video, and public interventions. Throughout her practice, Belle finds inspiration in architecture, history, and archeology to effectively challenge colonial hierarchies and narratives, while also exposing systemic structures of invisibility. Firmly positioned at the forefront of decolonial art practice, Belle sums up some of the factors that inform her work:

> I see my art practice as an investigative tool, as a way to engage in dialogue, a platform for thinking and a means to develop knowledge. My work has evolved from figurative and symbolic explorations in painting to a variety of modes that include drawing, painting, video, performance, installation and public intervention projects. Therefore, the emphasis of my work does not lie in the medium, but in creating a space to explore social contexts and collective narratives. History, film, soap operas, fairy tales and mythology all inform my work in that they are narrative modes that I use as well as sites of investigation. I look for the narratives inscribed in various objects and places and find ways to add to them and at times subvert them. Because I live in the Virgin Islands, a place that has changed colonial hands seven times, the longest being Denmark, and the last being the United States, I am particularly interested in the colonial and neo-colonial narrative and how it shapes identity, memory and reality.[39]

Belle melds fragments of history, archaeological remnants, and references to architecture (particularly colonial architecture with its inherent power structures) into a richly interconnected visual language. In 2014, she began the ongoing body of work *Chaney (We Live in the Fragments)*. This series of paintings connects Denmark and the Virgin Islands visually, formally, and historically. These beautifully executed paintings echo the blue and white patterns of traditional Danish porcelain and the flora, fauna, and wildlife of the Virgin Islands. As Belle explains, *Chaney*, understood as a hybrid term for China and money, references the fragments of colonial plates that are still found throughout the Virgin Islands—in the gutters, on the beach, and, especially after a hard rain, as the shards are pushed up from the soil, in gardens and back yards.

Taking these fragments as a point of departure, La Vaughn Belle paints a picture of the Virgin Islands that stands as a powerful antidote to colonial erasure and whitewashing. Her paintings speak out effectively against colonial stereotypes and power structures, while also exposing the uncomfortable details of the colonial past. As objects with a very specific history, these small archaeological treasures signify a double fracture. They are physical traces of the plates, teacups, and dishes that were originally produced by colonizers and transported to the colonies to consume colonial goods. As physical fragments of colonial wealth, they are an everyday visual reminder of the fractures caused by colonialism. If these bits and pieces from the past tell only part of the narrative, Belle paints a more complete picture of the past in her decolonial narrative.

La Vaughn Belle's first visit to the Royal Copenhagen flagship store and museum is powerfully conveyed in Helle Stenum's 2017 documentary film *We Carry it Within Us: Fragments of a Shared Colonial Past*. Belle's encounter with Danish porcelain, already familiar to her from St. Croix, is conveyed in a very personal account of the historical ties between Denmark and the Virgin Islands, coupled with thoughtful reflections on the continued denial of Denmark's (and Norway's) colonial history. While it might seem like poetic justice that Belle was given the opportunity to produce the *Chaney* plate series for Royal Copenhagen, the fact is that when she approached them to do a centennial plate in 2017 using her *Chaney* designs, they turned her down because they no longer made commemorative plates. It was only later, when they invited her to design the Harald Award, that she negotiated being able to produce a limited edition of the *Chaney* plates. Belle was the first Black artist they have ever worked with and also the only

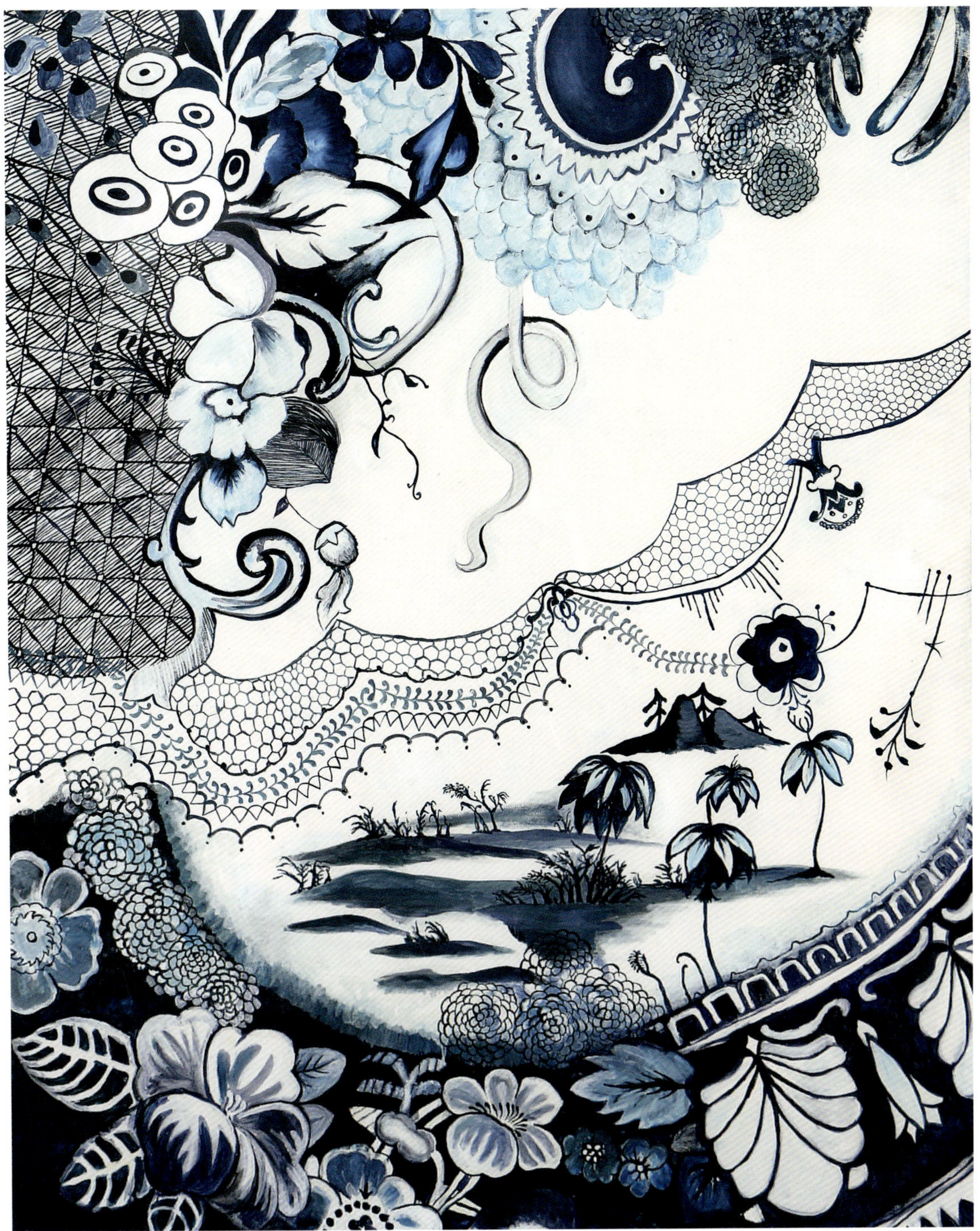

La Vaughn Belle
Chaney (We Live in the Fragments), 2015
Oil on wood
152.4 × 121.9 cm
Photo: William Stelzer

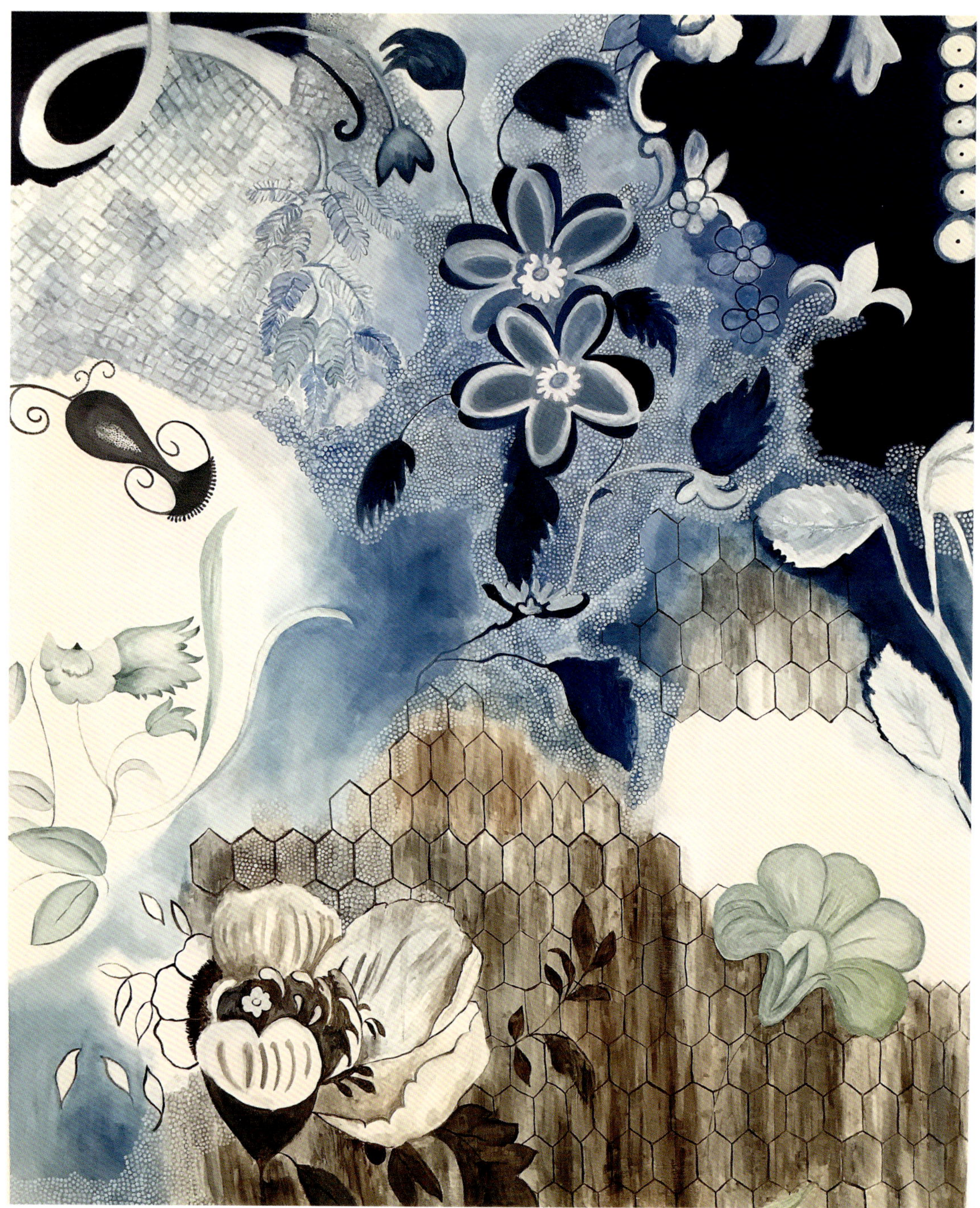

La Vaughn Belle
Chaney (We Live in the
Fragments), 2018
Oil on wood
152.4 × 121.9 cm
Photo: William Stelzer

artist from the Virgin Islands. Both the paintings and the plates are "a reminder of both the colonial past and the fragments present in Caribbean societies. These shards tell the visual stories of power and projection and how cultures reimagine themselves in this vast transatlantic narrative."[40]

Belle confronts the remnants of colonial history through works that question the implications of various objects in relation to colonialism. She makes it clear that colonial history is not something that we can dismiss as part of the past because the consequences of colonialism are ever present, as we witness today in relation to systemic racism and social injustice. As a visual storyteller who consistently exposes the link between past and present, Belle emphasizes the importance of considering who tells the narrative and who has the power to be saying what is a part of whose history. It's no secret that Denmark and Norway are wealthy countries, but the fact that much of that wealth was a direct result of Danish-Norwegian colonization and colonial trade still hasn't been adequately acknowledged. In fact, it continues to be consciously erased.

On the Service to the Kingdom (2017) addresses this kind of historical erasure and is a critical response to the fractured colonial histories that continue to be told from the colonizer's perspective. The work was inspired by the dessert plates commissioned by King Frederik VI to represent the breadth and wealth of the Kingdom of Denmark.[41] As Belle explains, there is only one plate, #75, of the eighty-one plates that depicts the former Danish West Indies, from which much of Denmark's wealth was gained. As a dessert service, the series clearly references the sugar industry, which was a vital part of the plantation economy and colonial trade. However, the image depicted on plate #75 is fictitious, it is simply a copy of a copy. The artists commissioned in 1834 to do the series had never even visited the former Danish West Indies. Instead, the artists created a composite of other paintings while adding stereotypical Caribbean signifiers such as coconut trees, a sugar mill, and an aloe plant. As such, the work explores the ideas of colonial image-making and consumption, and the resulting processes of fragmentation of identity.[42]

Beyond the sheer visual appeal of Belle's work, the numerous historical and sociopolitical references position her firmly at the forefront of decolonial aesthetics. She examines Denmark's colonial history not from the detached

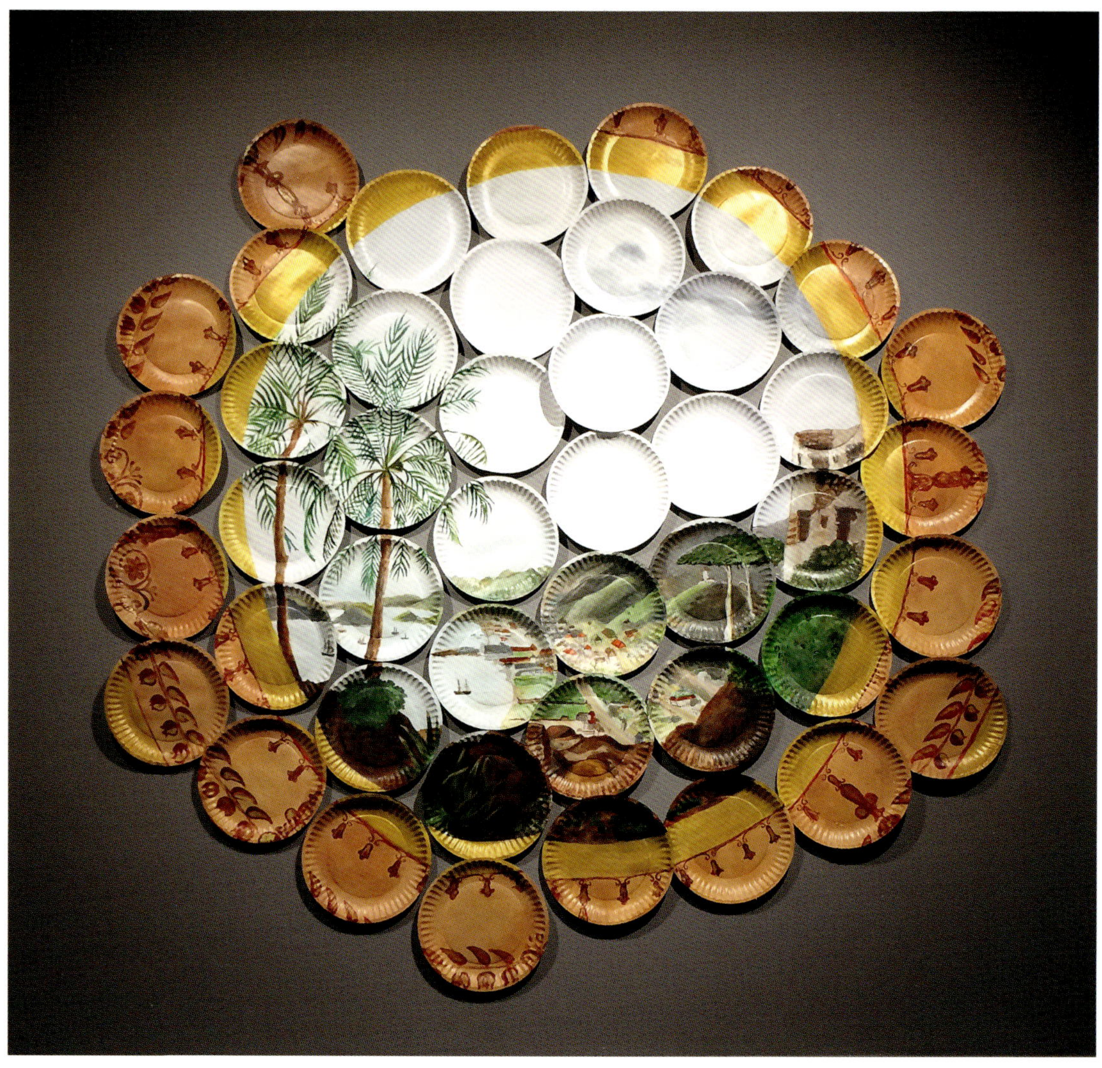

perspective of an archival researcher but with the immediacy of an archaeologist with traces of dirt on her hands. She fills in the gaping holes in Danish colonial narratives with works that reconstruct the fragments of colonial history (both physical fragments and the fragments of cultural consciousness) into a coherent, meaningful whole. Her works map out the immediate connection between history and contemporaneity. Adding to the clear historical references throughout her work, the concept of fragmentation is a vital part of her decolonial artistic strategy. Whether she weaves the implications of a found fragment of colonial history into a painted narrative or confronts the fragmentation of Caribbean identity typical of colonial image-making in a new and improved version of King Frederik's dessert service, she approaches fragmentation as one would a fracture or a

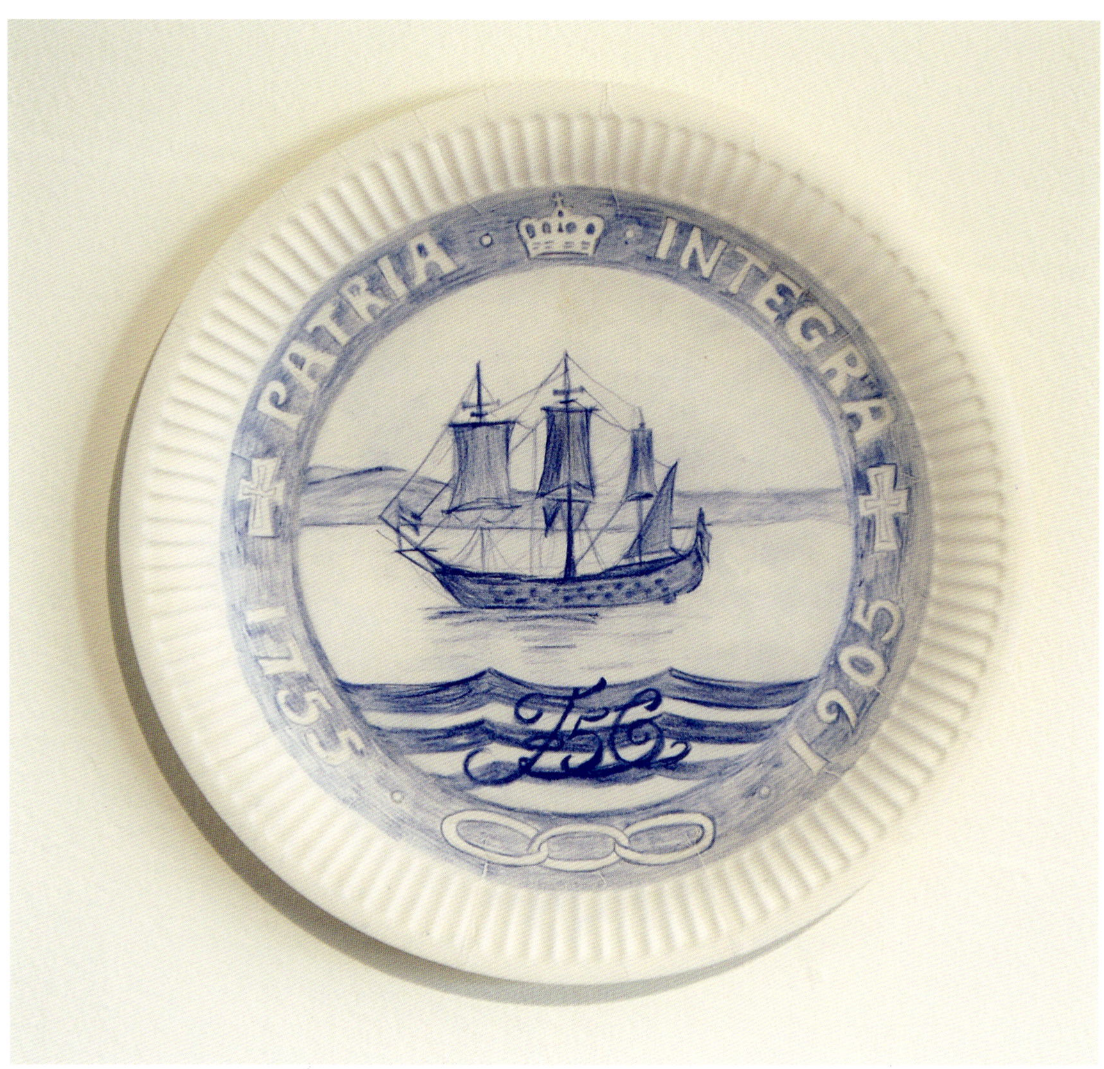

La Vaughn Belle
Collectible, 2008
Detail
Colored pencil on paper
Photo: La Vaughn Belle

wound. In the case of the dessert service, where Caribbean identity is reduced to one single plate, she takes the image from that one plate and divides it between all the plates, thereby claiming full ownership of the narrative. Similar to Belle's earlier work *Collectible* (2008), the work is comprised of everyday paper plates—the quintessential disposable object—which gives immediate associations to the fact that over the course of its tumultuous history, the Virgin Islands have been repeatedly passed along between colonizing nations.

In Michelle Eistrup's ongoing history lesson, entangled colonial histories are visualized on a borderless, interconnected cultural map. At the center of this map, the cultural ties between African Americans and Trinidadians, connected by West Africa, also come to life visually, musically, and spiritually.

Building a Bridge Across the Atlantic

Michelle Eistrup is an artist who engages directly with the physical and spiritual traces of colonialism through photography, video, installation, and performance. Her practice is fueled by in-depth artistic research and typically involves collaborations with other artists and researchers. With each new project she finds innovative ways to visualize the connections between diaspora geographies and bodies. Her work consistently reveals the visible and invisible factors that connect individuals of the African diaspora across time and between cultures. Temi Odumosu's observation regarding Eistrup's perception of the world, where "Benin is in Senegal, Senegal in Trinidad, Trinidad in Denmark,"[43] accurately describes her transcultural mindset. Similarly, Eistrup's approach to coloniality, both within a historical and contemporary context, is defined by overlaps. The past is present, and the present is defined by the past. She makes it clear that coming to terms with both is imperative in the shared journey towards the future.

Eistrup's openness to working collaboratively and between cultures has contributed to her position as a contemporary Danish Jamaican American artist who is as recognized in the Caribbean as she is in Denmark. Prime examples of her practice include her collaboration with James Muriuki on *Too Long Are Our Memories* and *Borders* (2012), *This Particular Masquerade* (2013–14), and the publication of the three-volume, eight-hundred-page book *BAT: Bridging Art + Text* (2017), which she aptly describes as connecting geographies and gaps of knowledge. For her three-channel video installation *In the Deep Underground and Up Above* (2018) she traveled to Western Australia, with its deeply imbedded colonial history, where she documented the personal stories of two indigenous women and a woman who descends from settlers. Eistrup's projects are as ambitious as they are seemingly impossible to execute—until they actually happen. For instance,

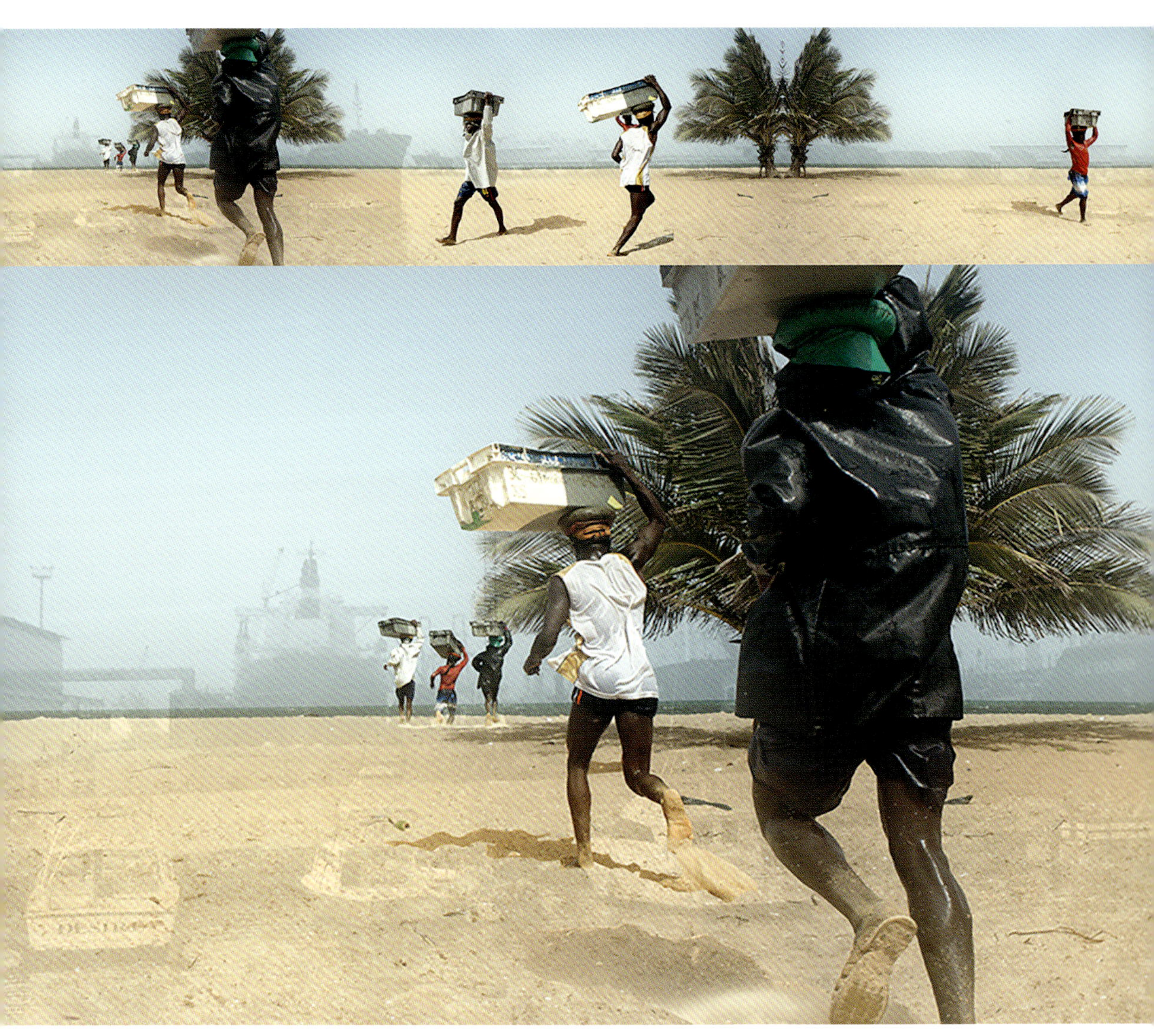

Michelle Eistrup
This Particular Masquerade 2,
Unmasked, 2013
Detail
Lambda print and Wenge
lightboxes
24.1 cm × 300 cm

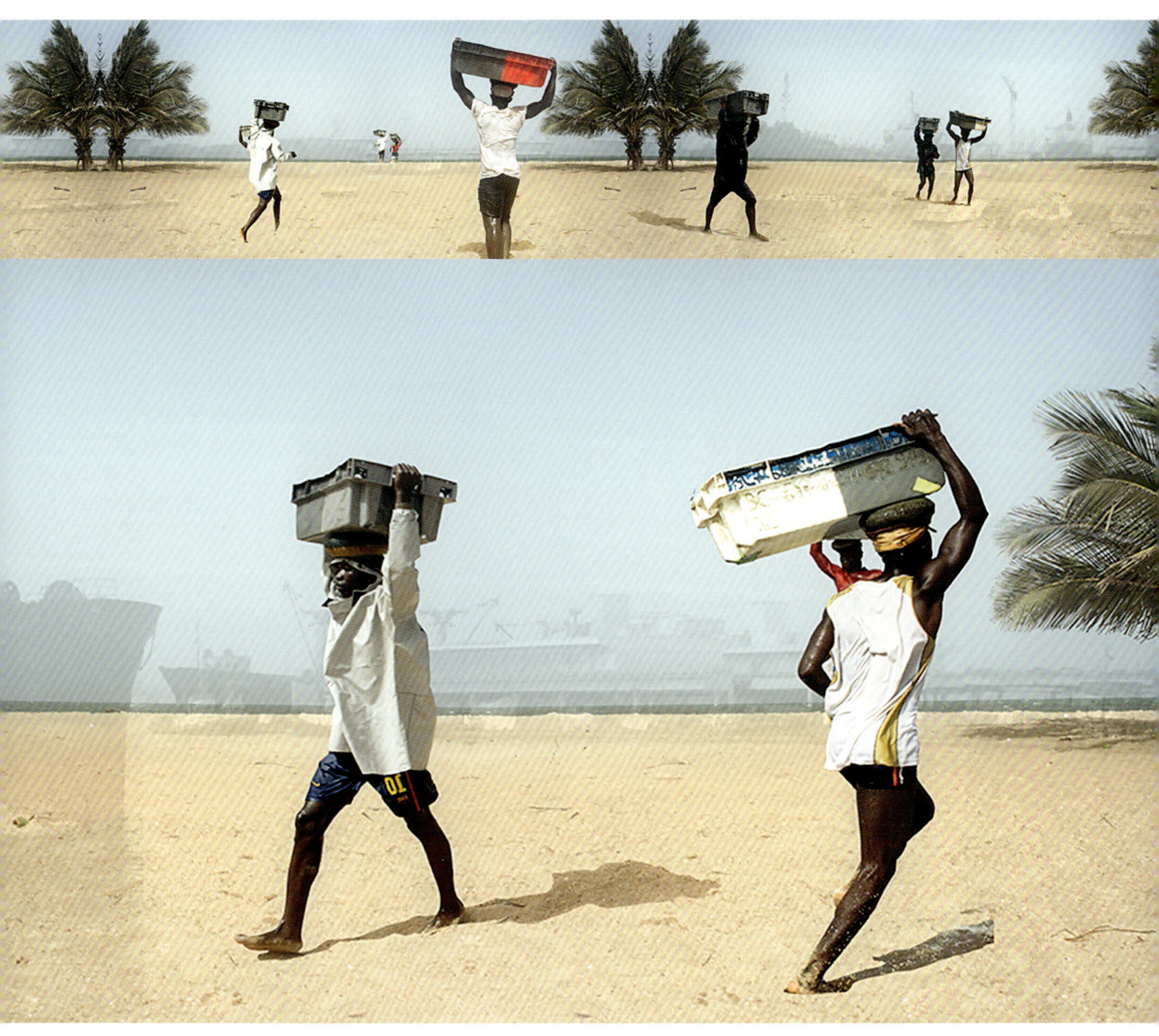

BAT: Bridging Art + Text is not only a three-volume book by and about contemporary artists of the African diaspora, it's a transcultural artistic intervention that effectively shifts the focus away from predominantly Eurocentric perspectives. From Trinidad to Senegal, Australia, Germany, or the United States she works directly with local communities and collaborates with visual artists, dancers, musicians, scholars, and institutions to connect the visible and invisible scars that connect these various locations historically and culturally.

BAT: Bridging Art + Text is the tangible result of a five-day workshop and seminar that Eistrup organized in Denmark in 2012. It's also an apt reflection of her unique approach to artistic collaboration and knowledge sharing. Her lifelong experience as a transcultural, interdisciplinary artist has contributed to an unusually keen understanding of the historical, spiritual, ancestral, geographic, and visual connections between cultures. There is reassurance and hope for the future in her inclusive approach that unites African and African diaspora individuals in a constructive dialog about the repercussions of colonial history, while also extending beyond the colonial past. With the *BAT* publication, and throughout her artistic practice, the sharing of knowledge is possibly the single most important unifying factor. She brilliantly emphasizes the importance of local knowledge by building her introductory essay around five carefully selected Jamaican proverbs. *Bambye yu all wi si* says it all—By and by, you all will understand. In a statement that captures a sense of Eistrup's transcultural diaspora experience she reveals some of the factors which define her inquisitive, knowledge-based approach to contemporary art:

> Due to the fact that cultures, ideas and artifacts have been scattered all over the globe and thus separated from their place of origin during Western colonialism and enslavement, those of us who engage in history, ancestry and beliefs, may find ourselves in all corners of the world. Bridging across the Atlantic and from north to south and being able to meet face to face can help break the sense of isolation many of us experience and provide answers to shared questions.[44]

Eistrup's newest—and possibly most ambitious—collaborative project to date, *Ntanga Zuzu* (All Suns Forever), involves the activation of Nkisi objects

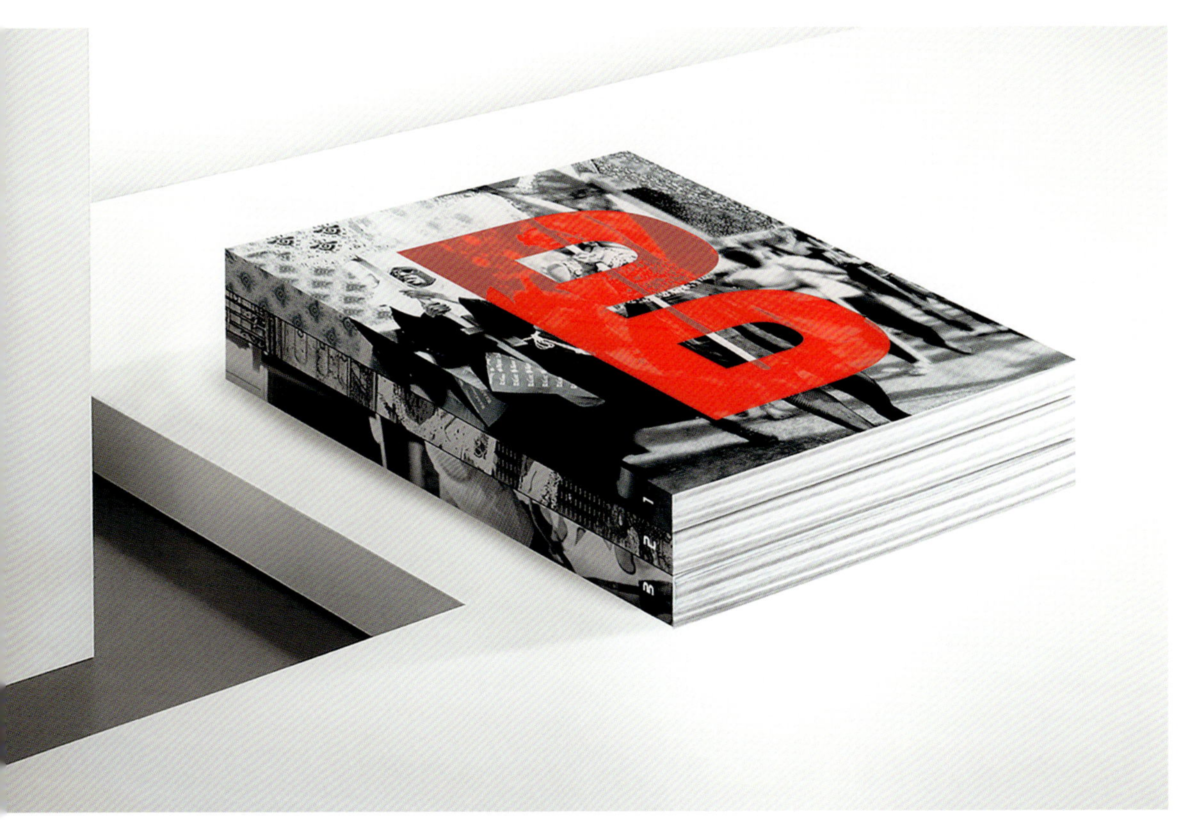

BAT: Bridging Art + Text
3 volumes, 800 pages
Copenhagen: Hurricane
Publishing, 2017
© Michelle Eistrup,
Annemari Brogaard
Clausen, writers,
and artists
Photo: Daniel Siim

that were stolen from the Kingdom of Kongo (present-day Northern Angola, the western portion of the Democratic Republic of the Congo, the Republic of the Congo, and the southern part of Gabon). This work in progress involves long-term collaborations with like-minded thinkers on both sides of the Atlantic, including Robert Farris Thompson, Professor Emeritus in the History of Art and African American Studies at Yale University, Michael Barrett, PhD in Cultural Anthropology and curator at the Museum of Ethnography, Stockholm, and dancers and musicians from the southern United States and Trinidad. Once completed, the project will feature a multi-channel video installation, a series of live dance performances conceived to initiate a dialog about and with Nkisi objects, and a series of prints.

Above all, *Ntanga Zuzu* will contribute to a long-overdue discussion about the whereabouts of stolen Nkisi artifacts. At the height of the Leopoldian regime, many European explorers participated in King Leopold's expeditions and acquired numerous treasures from the Kongo region of Africa. Espen Wæhle, former director of the Norwegian Maritime Museum, who has also worked with ethnographic and cultural history museums in Norway and

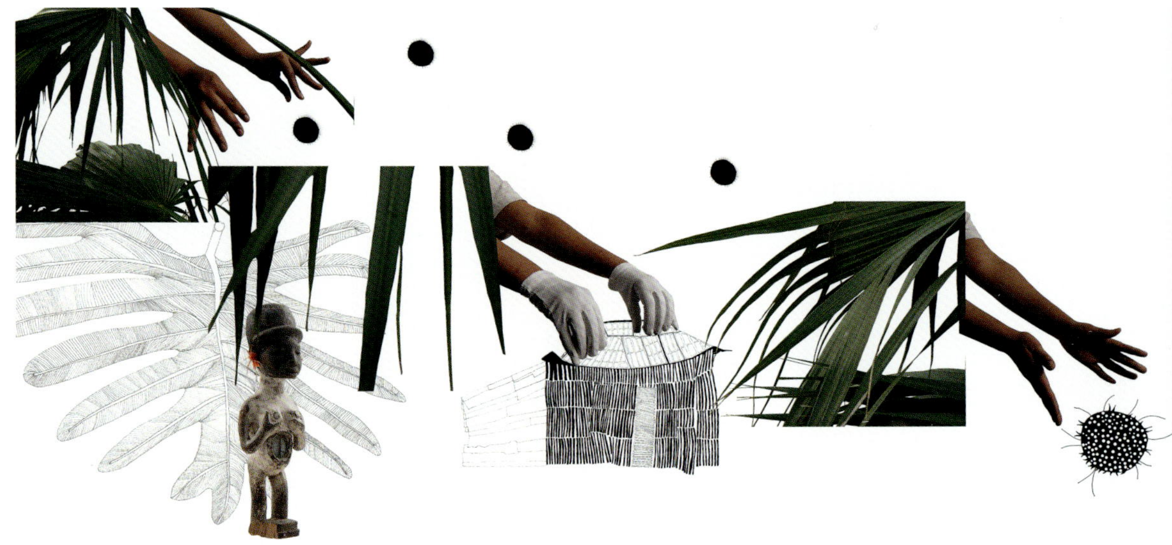

Denmark, is among those who have addressed the highly problematic acquisition of these treasures:

At least some 38,000 objects are today known in Nordic private and museum collections, internationally there are probably hundreds of thousands. The Congo collection is among the most important at the Ethnographic Museum of the University of Oslo,[45] comprising about 11% of the total collection. While many Norwegians contributed to the museum in Oslo as part of a national project (Norway became independent from the union with Sweden in 1905), some tried to make money from the colonial scramble they had been part of.

Nordic sailors made possible the colonization of the Congo. Up to 90% of those manning the ships (pilots, captains, mates, and engineers), harbours and shipyards were from Denmark, Norway, Finland and Sweden. Among the Nordic sailors two pioneers stand out: the Dane C.V.R. Schønberg Schønberg & Dane/Norwegian J.A.C. Martini (Martini was born in Norway, his parents being Danish itinerant actors, throughout his career he sometimes claimed to be Norwegian and other times Danish). They signed up for the Congo already in 1886 and manned primitive riverboats on many colonial charting expeditions and first sailings. Their book from the first years was the second book written by Scandinavians on the Congo.

Michelle Eistrup
Ntanga Zuzu, Opening in Huts, 2019
Collage comprised of photos and drawings
54.5 × 120 cm

Almost 1000 objects collected by Schønberg & Martini are still in museum collections. Their strategy to sell the large collection was unusual. They started off by arranging commercial and well-publicized Congo exhibitions at 'Tivoli' in Christiania (Oslo) and 'National' in Copenhagen. They later managed to sell most of the artefacts at a very high price (in Oslo possibly the most expensive collection ever bought by the museum).[46]

Ntanga Zuzu traces a complex colonial narrative between Scandinavia, Western Africa, the southern United States, and Trinidad. The work extends beyond simply exposing Scandinavian participation in the ethnographic scramble. Stolen from Africa and dispersed throughout ethnographic

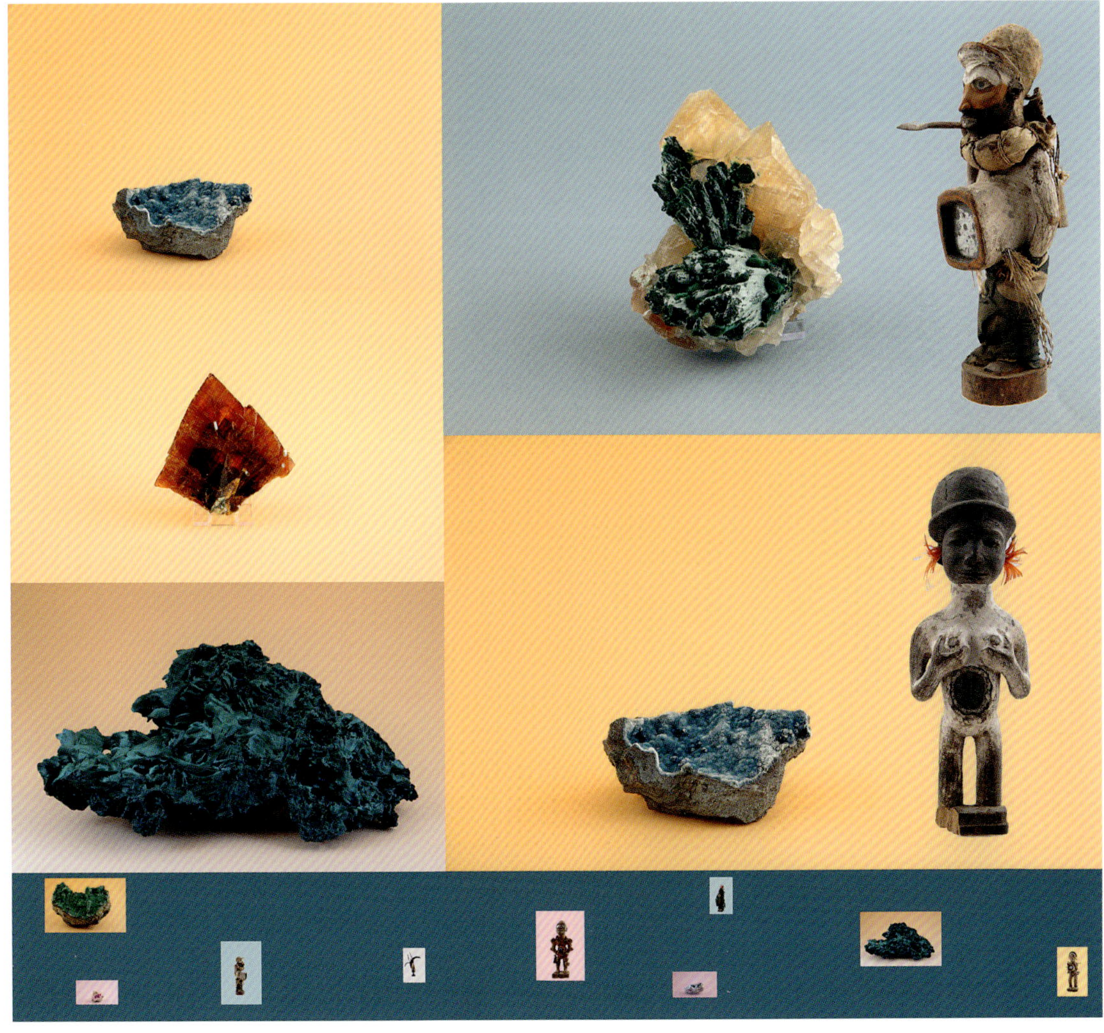

museums in Scandinavia and Europe, these artifacts are also directly connected to the stories and heritage of African Americans living in the southern United States. South Carolina in particular is inhabited by a great number of descendants of enslaved people from the Kongo region, whose ancestral and spiritual connection to these objects is honored through Eistrup's work. In her ongoing history lesson, entangled colonial histories are visualized on a borderless, interconnected cultural map. At the center of this map, the cultural ties between African Americans and Trinidadians, connected by West Africa, also come to life visually, musically, and spiritually. With dance at the core of the project, the entire concept of the movement of bodies takes on multiple layers of meaning—through history, across borders, and beyond any individual's own lifetime. Eistrup's unique interdisciplinary approach to shared cultural history involves connecting bodies through objects, movement, and sound. Above all, this multisensory work involves a crucial transition from observer (of the colonial past) to active participant (in a forceful decolonial strategy). Through movement and rhythm conceived in direct response to sacred Nkisi figures, we can expect to hear the gentle whisper of ancestral voices as an extended scream from one side of the Atlantic to the other.

As a work in progress, it's too early to write a detailed account of *Ntanga Zuzu*, but it's fairly easy to imagine how the work might develop if we take a closer look at *In the Deep Underground and Up Above* (2018). For this film, Eistrup traveled to remote Western Australia to shed light on the dark shadow of British colonial rule, told from a non-Western perspective. As Michael, the male narrator (and alter ego) states, "In the history of British colonialism we have been made to believe that certain questions can only be asked and answered by specific groups." He goes on to explain that the colonial divide and conquer mentality continues to bear repercussions, an idea which Eistrup conveys through a richly layered narrative that is punctuated by the voices of the three women who she interviewed for the film: Rebecca, Mitchella, and Tessa. Their voices are woven into a hauntingly beautiful film that says as much about colonization of culture and natural resources as it does about human nature and the struggle for survival. Mitchella's and Tessa's personal accounts of being excluded and discriminated against paint a painful picture of the experiences of indigenous people throughout the world and the ongoing struggle to come to terms with, to heal from, and to find ways to move

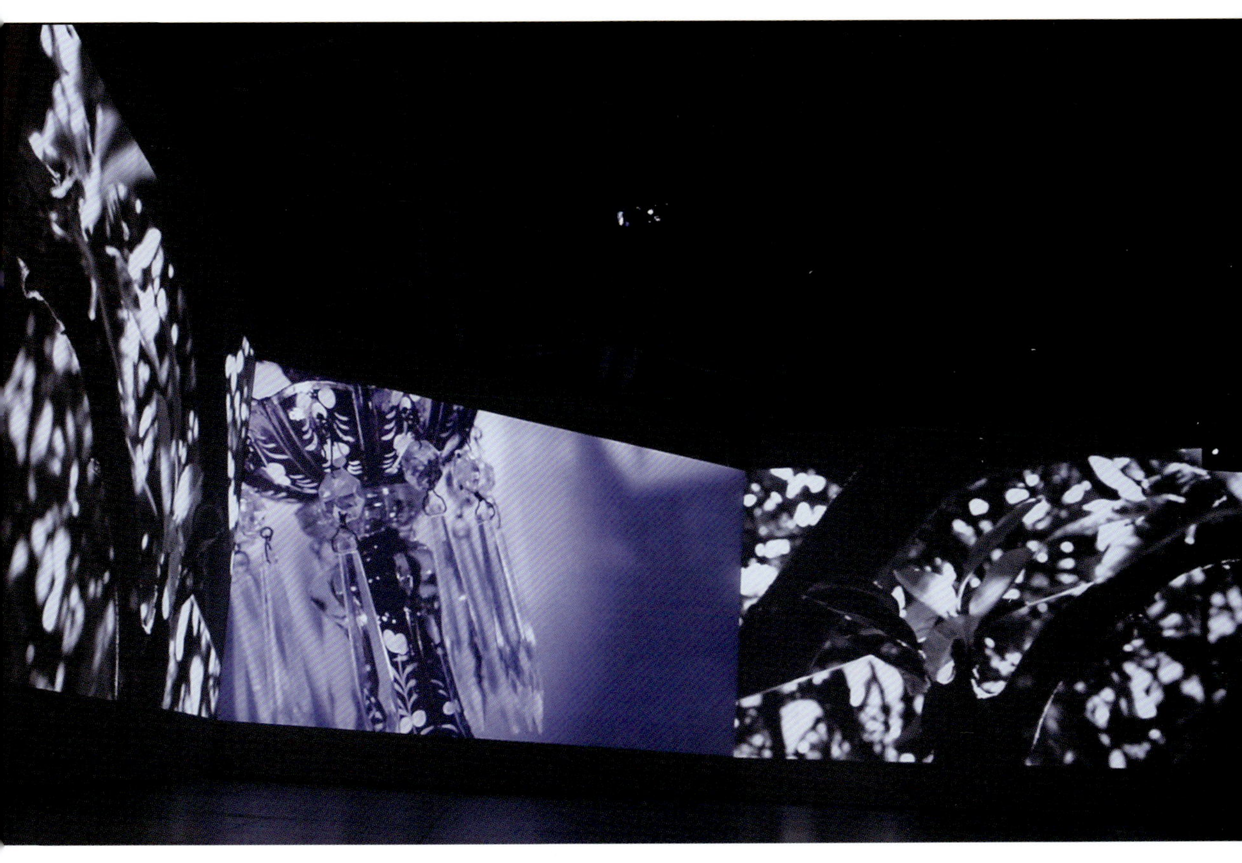

beyond the lingering impact of colonialism. Rebecca's narrative reveals how the corruption and decadence of the colonizers also continue to haunt the lives of the descendants of pioneer families. Breathtaking scenes of rugged natural surroundings are juxtaposed with interior scenes decorated with bronze statues, porcelain plates, and ornate chandeliers. As such, the film connects objects and individuals through time and geographies, while also emphasizing the fact that colonial greed and desire for riches was not limited to the invasion of geographies, cultures, and indigenous people, but also extends to the destruction and theft of natural resources through plantations, mining, and other forms of industry.

In Suchitra Mattai's work baroque ornamentation is everywhere, painted into richly detailed images of tropical flora and fauna, woven into lavish brocade fabrics, embedded in sparkling jewel-like details, and also seen in the antiques that she transforms into contemporary treasures.

The Past is Present

Suchitra Mattai employs painting, textiles, drawing, collage, video, and sculpture in works that often involve reclaiming ownership of cultural artifacts, both conceptually and through her choice of materials. She consistently challenges Eurocentric colonial narratives through artworks that address the complexities of Guyana's colonial history. References to her family history and the ancestral memory of those who traveled the Middle Passage from India to Guyana add a very personal dimension to her practice. Her work speaks clearly about processes of migration, the introduction of indentured labor as a replacement for free labor after slavery was abolished in Guyana in 1834, and other injustices connected to Guyana's plantation economy. As a Guyanese diaspora artist who has moved repeatedly within her own lifetime, her transnational background has clearly contributed to her ongoing interest in the ever-shifting definition of home.

Sugar Water (2018), featured in her solo exhibition *Sugar Bound* at Center for Visual Art, Metropolitan State University in Denver, Colorado, is among her most striking works. This large-scale installation is comprised of antique furniture and video projections. Furniture suspended by thin wires seems to float within the space while other elements are visually connected to the walls by colorful strings that create rainbow-like patterns. An ornate brocade chair with a carved gold frame lies toppled over on a plinth, a plantation-style rocking chair hangs upside down from the ceiling, and the backsides and drawers of antique dressers are used as projection screens. It's as if the entire room were in the process of exploding. *Sugar Water* effectively captures various aspects of the immigrant experience and addresses longing and nostalgia through very direct visual means. A dresser hanging from the ceiling features a video of clouds drifting in the sky. Moving images of the ocean are projected onto the three-way mirror of a

Following pages
Suchitra Mattai
Sugar Water, 2018
Mixed media installation
Center for Visual Art,
MSU Denver

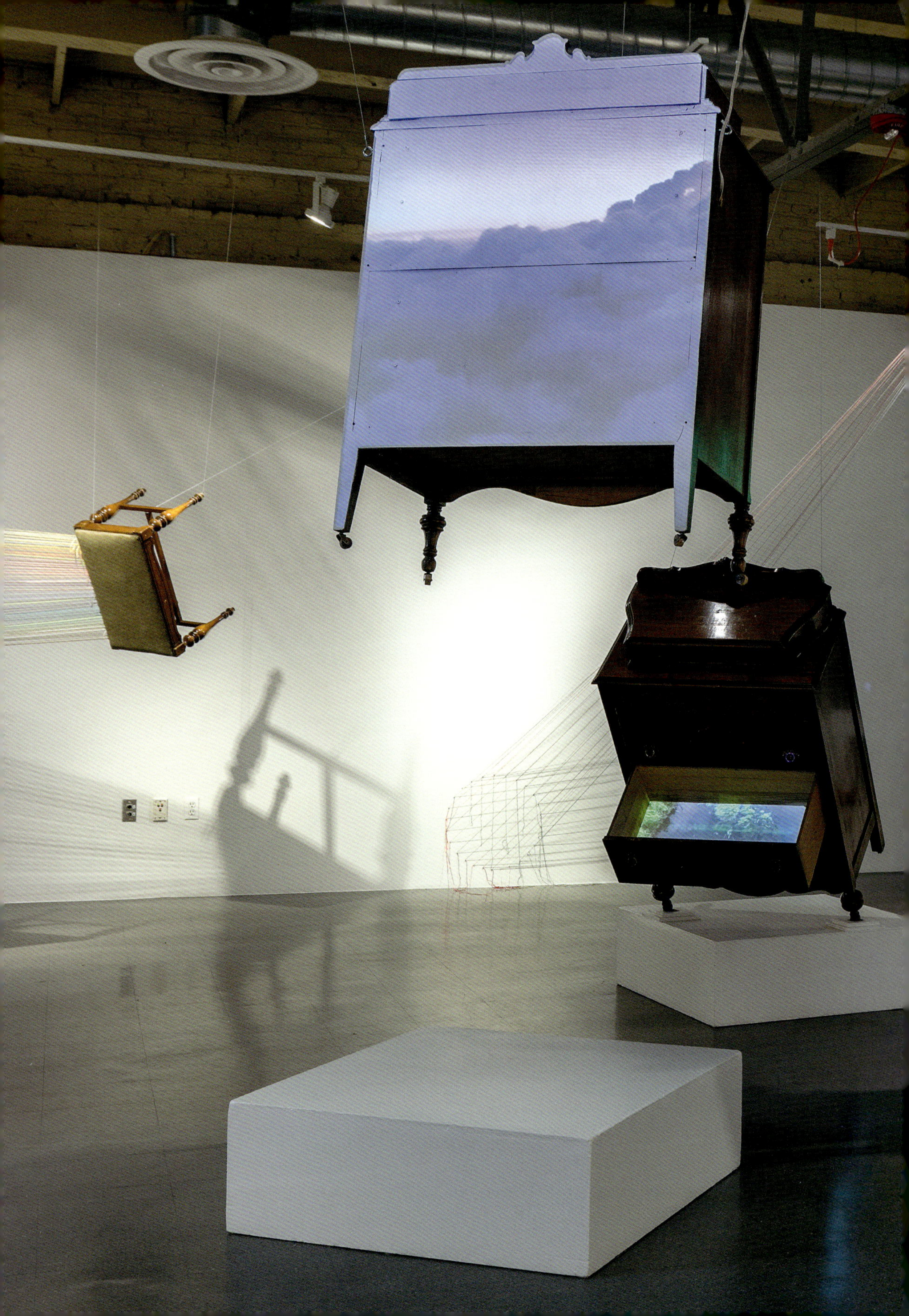

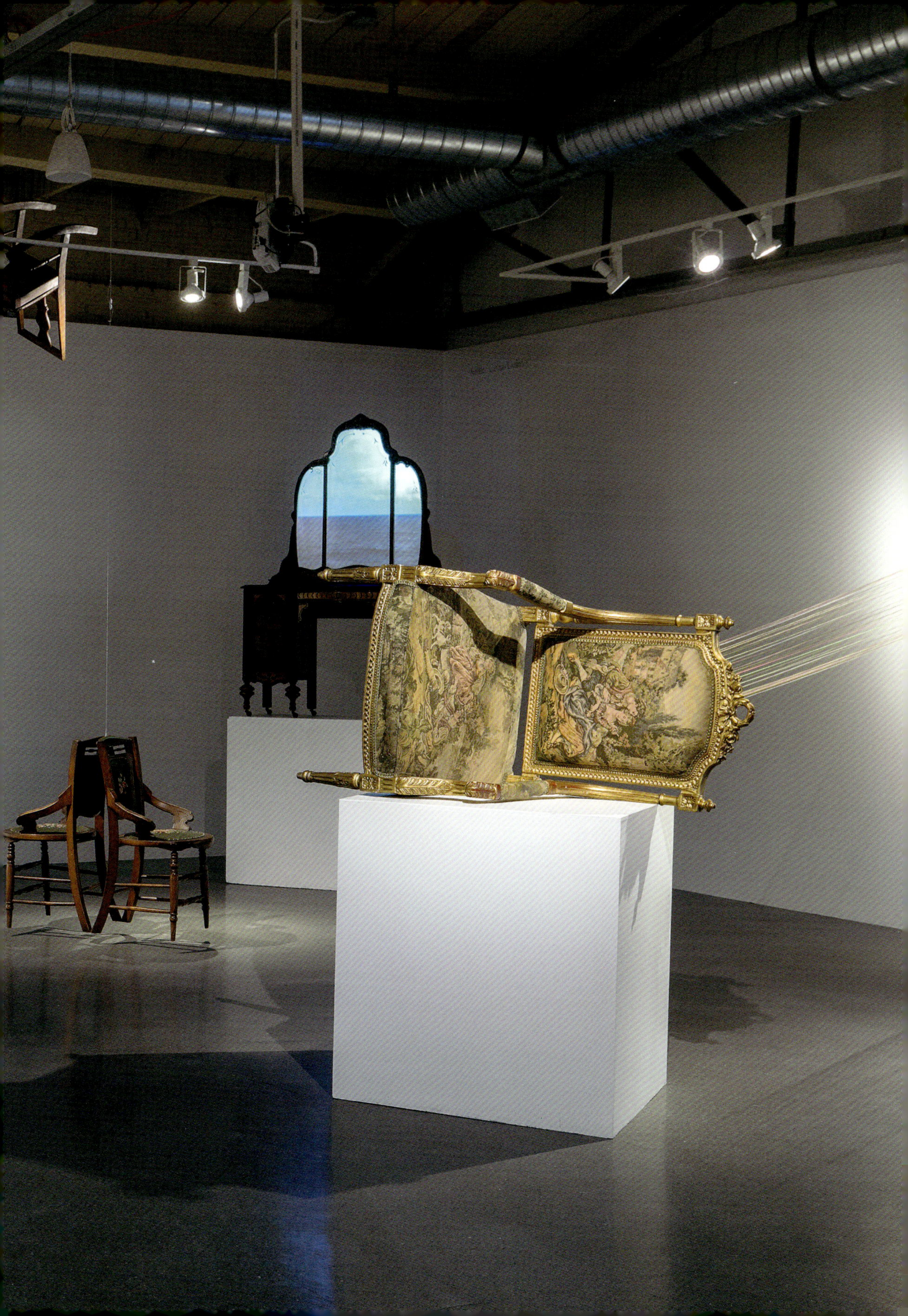

dressing vanity. A mahogany drawer is transformed into a hiding place for memories. Clearly, the chaotic placement of furniture speaks of having to move one's belongings from place to place. As such, the work evokes a strong sense of the disconnections, displacements, and disorientations experienced by people who are forced to leave their home country.

Sugar Water is among the many works by Suchitra Mattai that resonate within the framework of Édouard Glissant's thinking, particularly in terms of his concept of *chaos-monde* (a world that cannot be systematized). Overall, her works capture Glissant's interest in baroque expression and can be seen to powerfully visualize the writer's observation that "every diaspora is the passage from unity to multiplicity."[47]

Glissant's brilliant analysis of oral traditions and storytelling in *Poétique de la Relation* is quite relevant to Mattai's approach to visual storytelling; "And at stake once again in Brazilian and Hispano-American literatures: the explosion of baroque expression, the whorls of time, the mingling of centuries and jungles, the same epic voice retying into the weft of the world, beyond any imposed solitude, exaction, or oppression."[48] He elaborates on the topic of baroque sensibility in *Traité du Tout-Monde* (Treatise on the Whole World):

> The baroque is willingly the order (or disorder) of orality. This is encountered in the Americas in the beauty of crossbreeding and creolization, where the angels are Indians, the Madonna is black, the cathedrals like landscapes of stone, and this echoes the word of the storyteller, which also extends into the tropical night, accumulated, repeated. The storyteller is Creole, Quechua, Navajo, or Cajun. In the Americas, baroque is naturalized.[49]

In other words, in the Americas, and in this case Guyana, a baroque sensibility is intrinsic to the surroundings. In Suchitra Mattai's work baroque ornamentation is everywhere, painted into richly detailed images of tropical flora and fauna, woven into lavish brocade fabrics, embedded in sparkling jewel-like details, and also seen in the antiques that she transforms into contemporary treasures. Most importantly, her practice involves a critical questioning of coloniality, migration, and diaspora identity. She combines references to colonial history and recent history in visually captivating collages and installations, often implementing needle and thread in ways that emphasize the decolonial message. From small, intimate works executed on found needlepoint to massive mixed media installations, the intricate details consistently mirror the complexity of the issues she addresses.

The Past is Present (2017) is a perfect example of Mattai's distinctive approach, which often includes many elements that are integrated into a comprehensive whole. Consisting of a collage of mixed media works set against a backdrop of printed vinyl and tape, the work is an excellent visualization of Glissant's concept of baroque sensibility. The centerpiece of the work, *Castaway*, is a repurposed needlepoint. Mattai effectively rewrites the colonial narrative embedded in its dusty threads. Sewing rays of light around the young boy at the center of the composition turns him into the absolute focal point of the work. *Castaway* is surrounded by a selection of vintage landscapes and fussy images of white colonizers, all beautifully repurposed by Mattai. With every colorful stitch she deconstructs and rewrites the colonial narrative. In a clever reframing of the colonial gaze, she pokes holes in the eyes of the oppressors. The printed vinyl background unifies the various elements, while the neon-colored tape echoes the linear patterns that are sewn into each of the small landscapes and portraits. The background image is a digital print of *Castaway*, blown up to the point of abstraction, to the extent that the details are completely blurred and erased. Ultimately, past and present are woven into a new narrative that creates order out of colonial chaos.

Speaking in reference to Mattai's participation in Sharjah Biennial 14 (SB14), curator Grace Aneiza Ali pinpoints the importance of her work: "Suchitra Mattai is weaving saris together to create these beautiful landscapes that speak to her own personal migratory paths, and to the history of migration she embodies as a woman of the Indian diaspora whose ancestors came from India to Guyana through the system of indentured labor to work sugar and rice plantations."[50] Mattai's participation in SB14 included the large-scale installation *Imperfect Isometry* (2019), comprised of vintage saris from India, Sharjah, and her own Indo-Guyanese family. The saris were woven into a large-scale work that speaks powerfully about entangled colonial histories and contemporary migration. Mattai explains:

> The work connects diasporic communities of South Asians across
> the globe, giving voice to generations of women while also probing

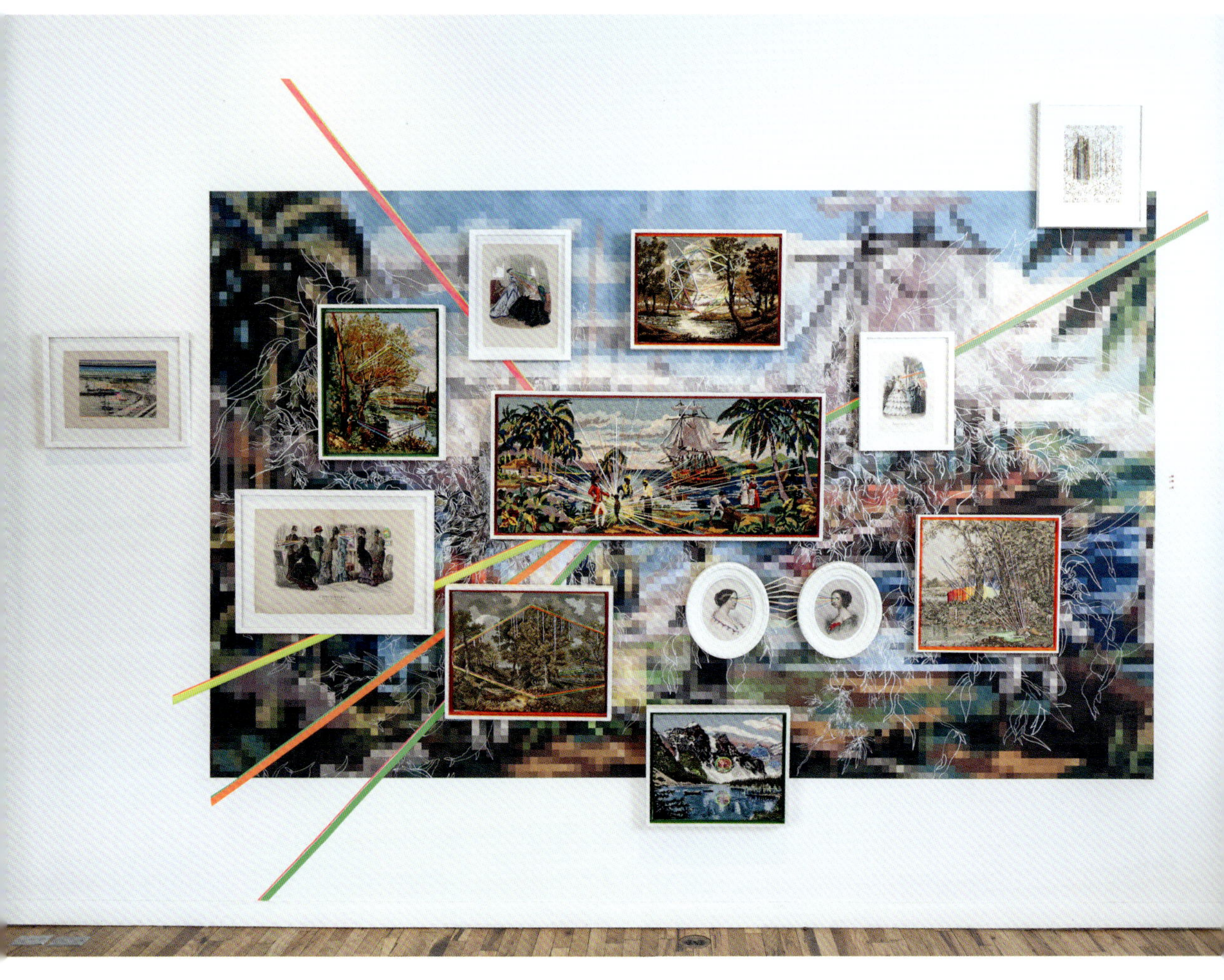

Suchitra Mattai
The Past is Present,
2017
Mixed media installation
Dimensions variable

questions of displacement resulting from European colonization. Many South Asians left India in the nineteenth and early twentieth centuries to work as indentured laborers around the world, including the Caribbean, South America, Fiji, Mauritius, Uganda, etc. Focusing on this period is both a means of tracing my family's history in Guyana and of fostering discussion around contemporary issues surrounding labor and gender.[51]

Imperfect Isometry was presented outdoors in the Bait Obaid Al Shamsi courtyard along with an abandoned merry-go-round found in a former kindergarten, which effectively symbolizes the continuous cycle of historical and contemporary displacement and movement between people and cultures. The installation also includes a video featuring images of border walls between Israel and Palestine, the United States and Mexico, and a prison wall. In contrast to the vibrant textiles that are woven into visual patterns of migration, the predominantly beige and sand colors in the film reflect a more austere sensibility in a narrative that addresses the absolute prevention of mobility. The seamless melding of a prison wall with border walls makes a compelling statement about the social and political injustice of closed borders in contemporary society. It's important to keep in mind that these works not only reference migration and mobility, they are created from the traces of actual garments. As symbols of a shared identity, these fabrics connect Indian and Indian diaspora women visually and metaphorically. Having first been dispersed throughout the world, Mattai weaves these delicate garments into monumental installations that really claim their presence in the space. If the varying colors and patterns of each sari corresponds to a single individual in India, Sharjah, Guyana, or elsewhere, here they are unified into a comprehensive whole in rich, sumptuous, undulating tapestries that effectively visualize themes of diversity and unity while also conveying a sense of overlapping histories and experiences.

Suchitra Mattai
Castaway, 2017
Repurposed needlework
Detail of *The Past
is Present*

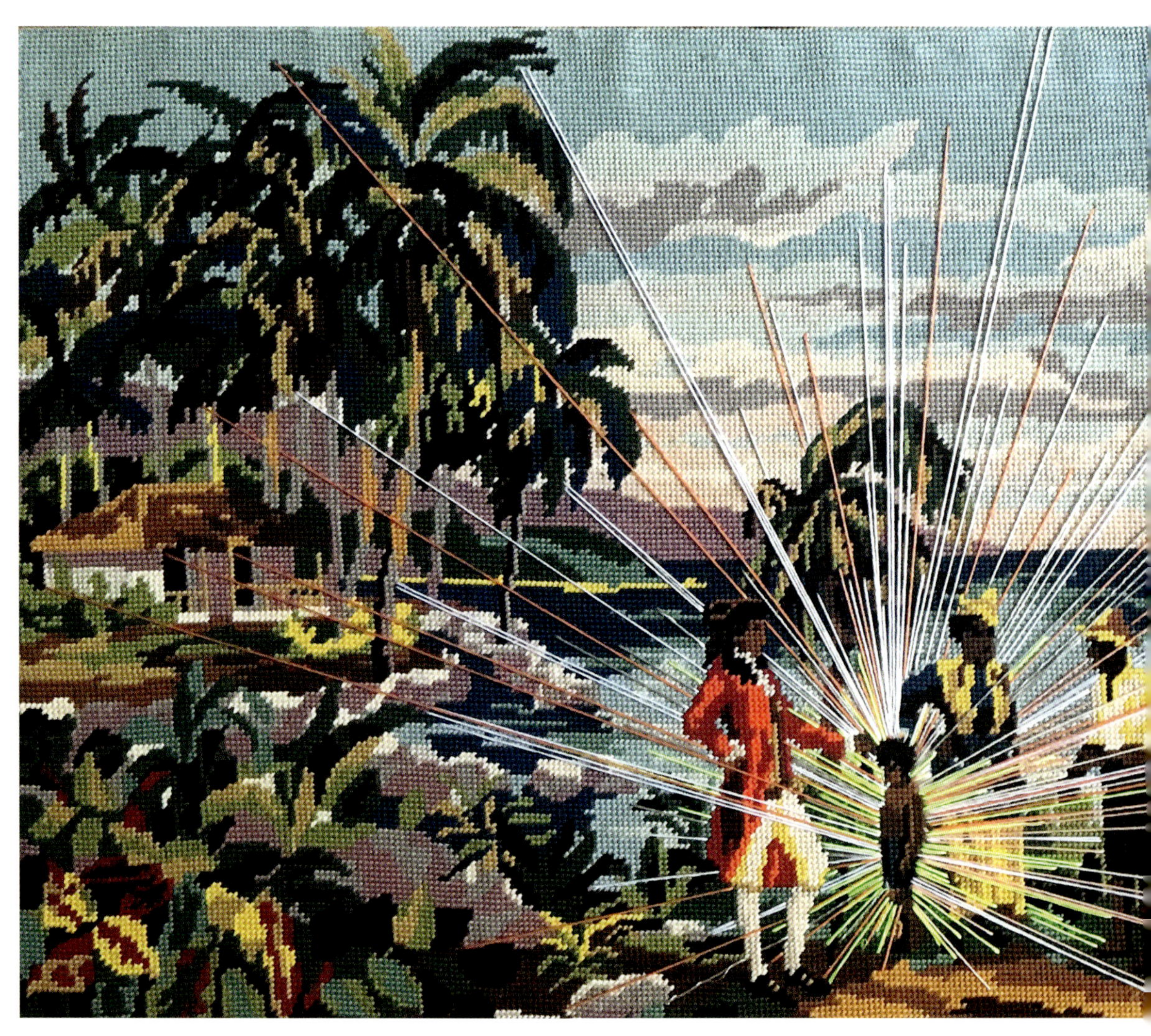

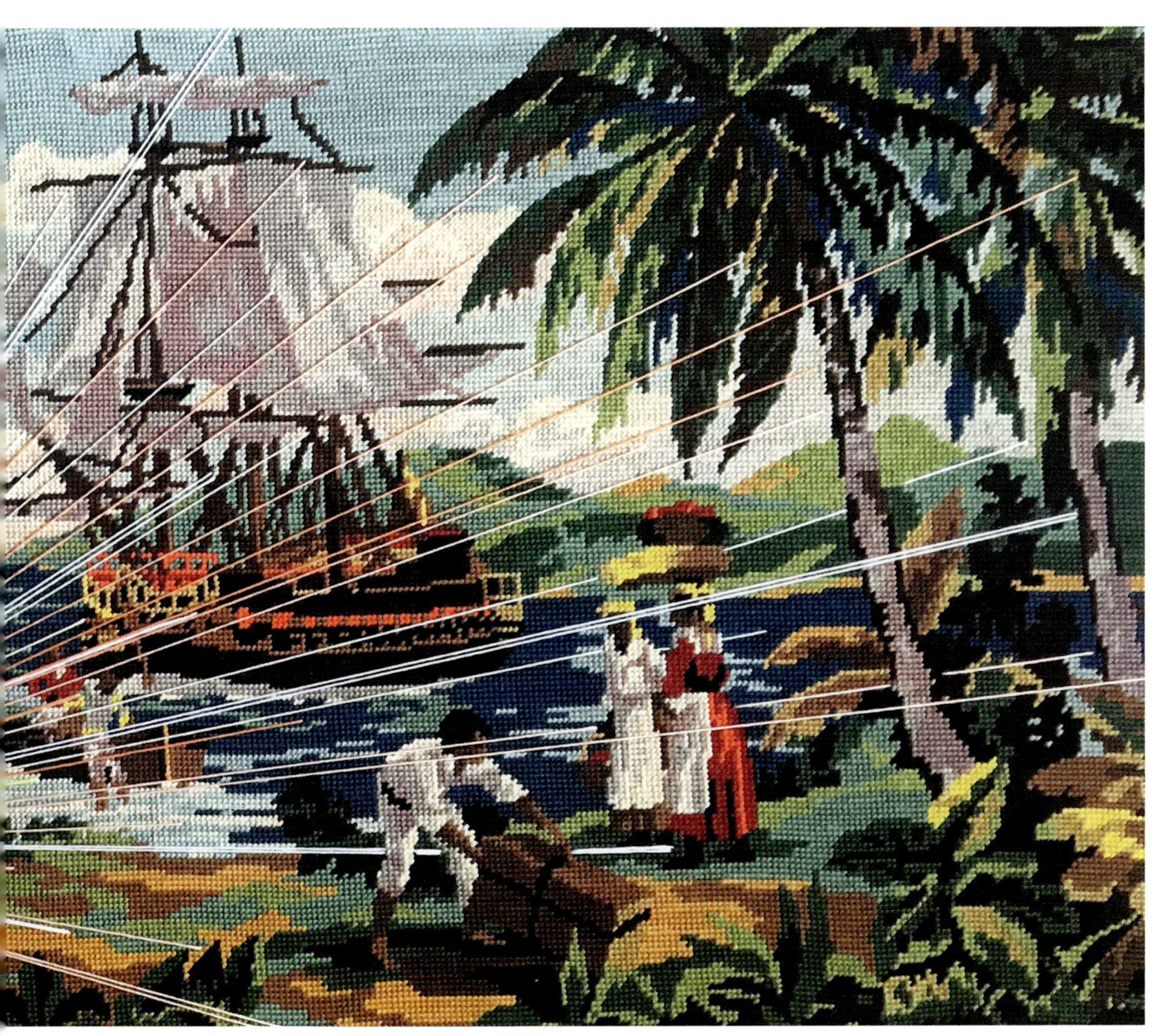

Suchitra Mattai
Imperfect Isometry, 2019
Installation and video
Mixed media
Sharjah Art Foundation

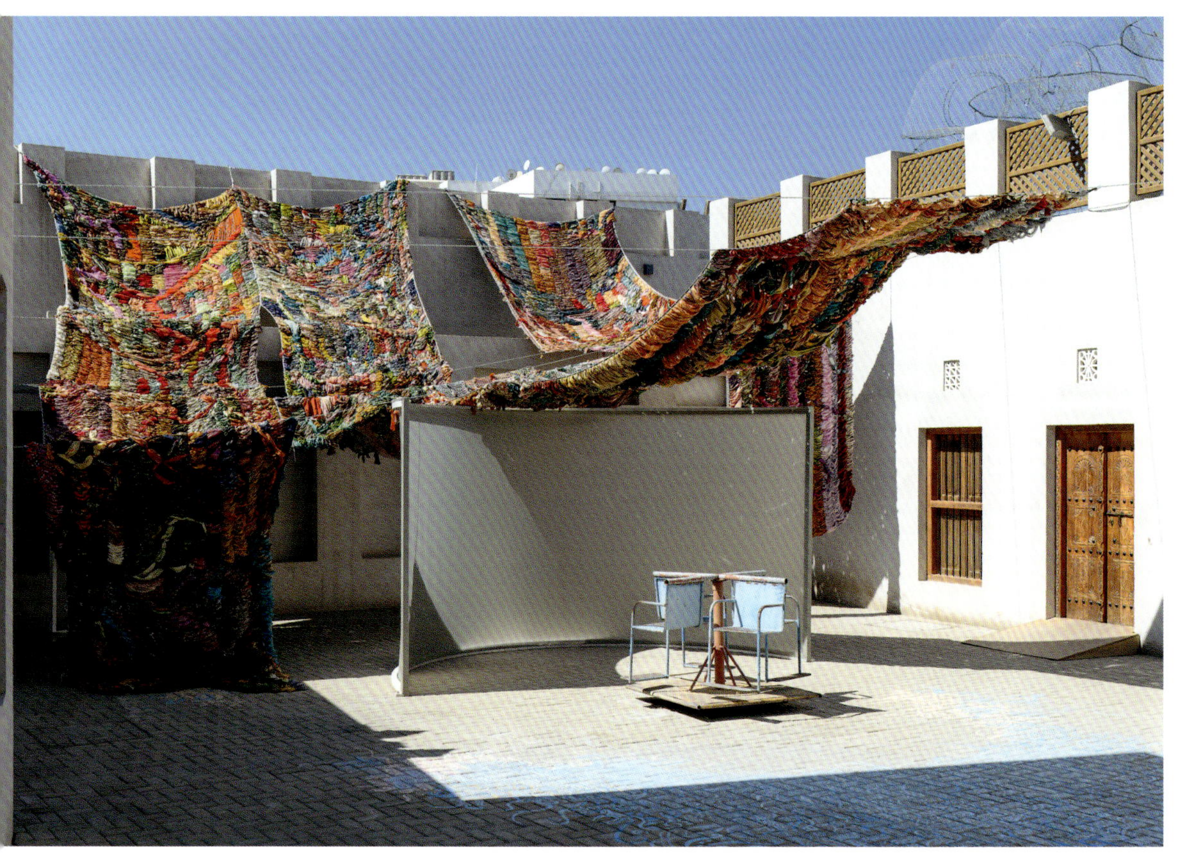

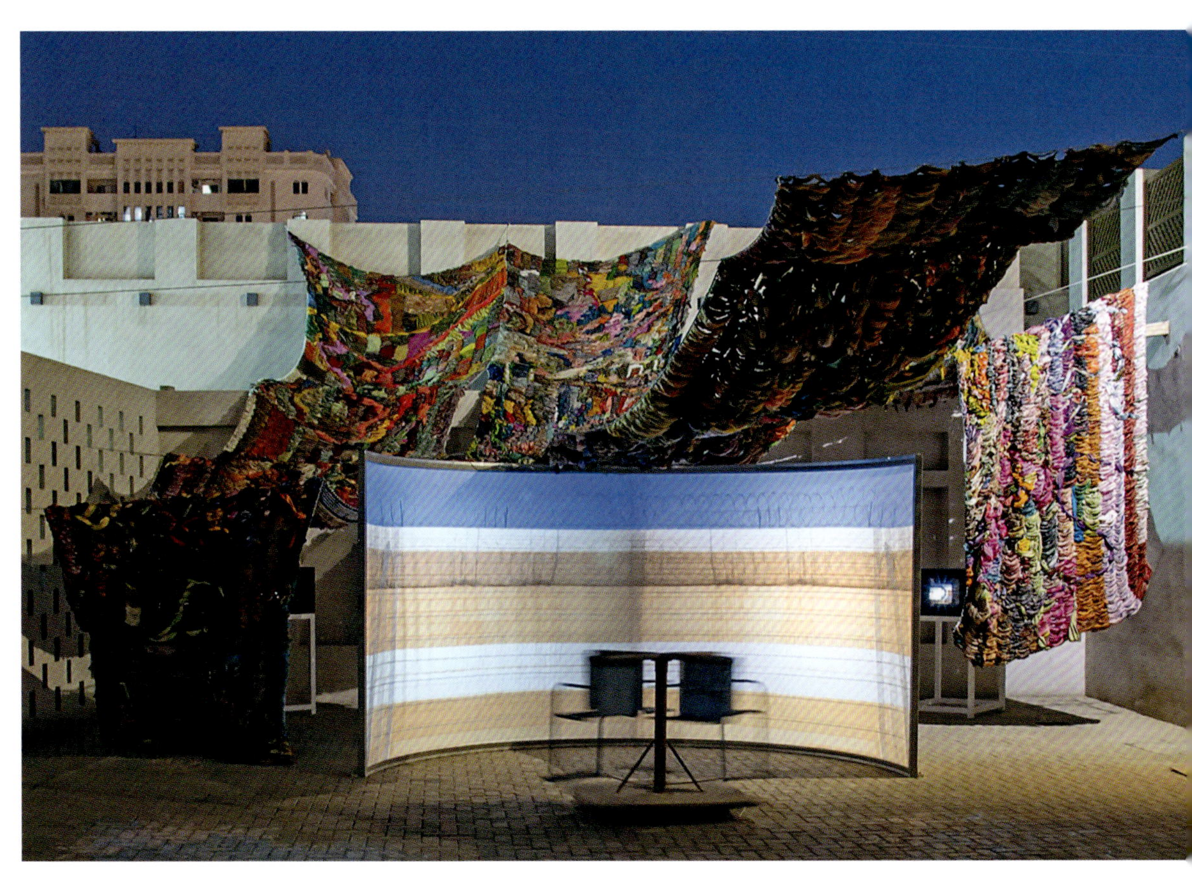

Amnesia is often thought of as a temporary condition, but as Whittle makes clear, colonial amnesia has been going on for centuries.

The Sound of the Black Atlantic

Alberta Whittle's artistic practice is carefully built around the deconstruction of colonial amnesia. Throughout her performances and videos, she mixes sonic and visual elements in an interconnected narrative that extends through time and across continents. Shared histories and personal memories are melded into a rich visual language that features its own decolonial sound system. She eliminates white noise so that we can hear stories of resistance against the continued effects of colonialism. Whittle samples sound and music with the steady hand of a DJ whose conscious remix helps to set the historical record straight. In her 2017 video *You Can Never Touch the Same Water Twice* we hear ambient sounds of the Atlantic, wind chimes, a lone saxophone player, and words that are repeated once, twice, even three or four times, just like history.

How long will we have to wait for an appropriate response to her insistent call for justice? These are the deep blues that Glissant and Du Bois knew all about—the kind of blues that spread from shantytowns and plantations. She says it outright: hers is the tongue of a selector mixing tunes of shanties and riddims. Her works ask us to rise up against the continued aftermath of colonialism. While we wait for a suitable response from the powers that be, there is sonic justice and empowerment in her use of the active voice. This is the voice of someone who refuses to wait any longer. She is ringing the alarm. She is waking the town. She is telling the people. She is taking back what was stolen from her ancestors and what is rightfully hers. She is calling for reparations and will not give up until that has happened. Listen to her voice:

My tongue lives in exile. It's origins unknown. Memories of ancestors have been lost through my creolized tongue, but my body

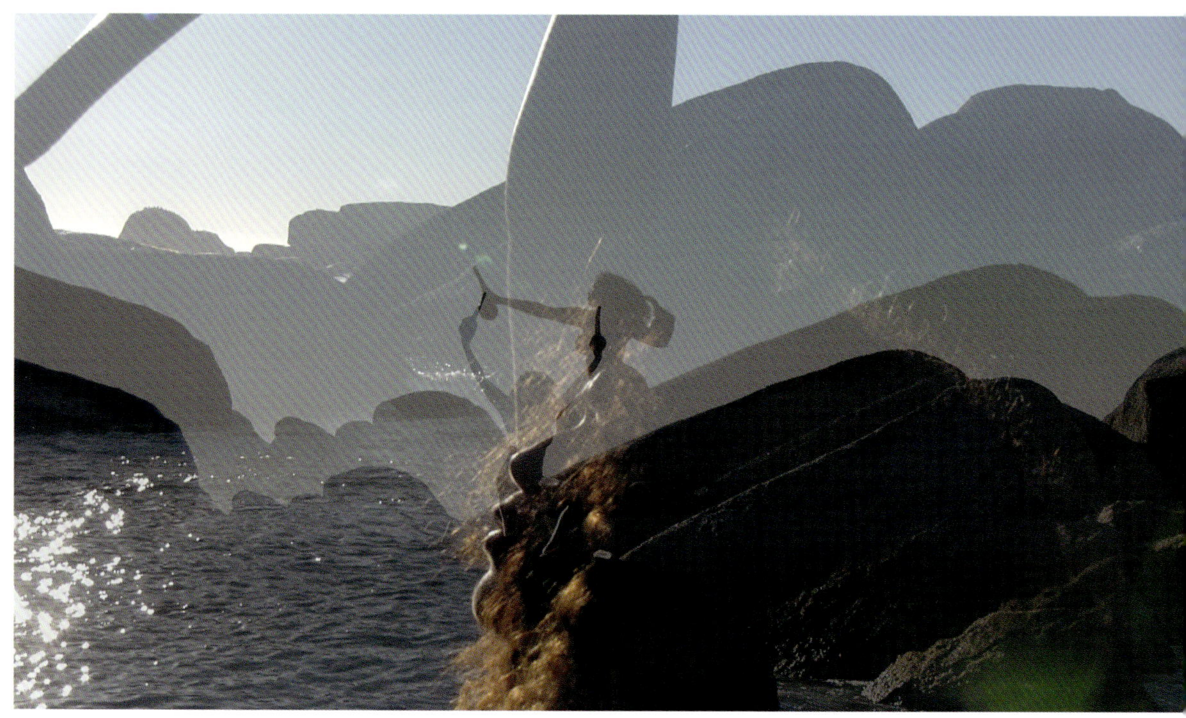

remembers the journey across the Atlantic, in the swollen belly of a ship whose name has been long forgotten. Water, water, water . . . everywhere, everywhere, and not a drop to drink. The sea is a graveyard, and the slave ship is a coffin. Are we still playing dead to survive? My tongue is not swollen like a corpse, nor is it gagged, and I prevented from speaking the truth. My tongue is a selector mixing tunes of shanties and riddims . . .[52]

Whittle weaves an intricate narrative that exposes the immediate connection between the crimes carried out during colonial rule and the injustices that continue today. She implores us to be conscious of and to take action against colonial amnesia. In a critical questioning of the power structures that continue to keep colonial thinking in place, Whittle addresses Scotland's colonial history in relation to the Caribbean. Her works expose the continued impact of colonial history on contemporary society, most evident in terms of poverty, forced migration, systemic and everyday racism. She speaks forcibly about the urgency for reparations, while also shedding light on current events such as the deportation crisis in the UK, the Grenfell Tower fire in London, and the dire aftermath of Hurricane Dorian on individuals throughout the Caribbean.

In her 2019 work *What Sound Does the Black Atlantic Make?* Whittle compellingly addresses the 2018 Windrush Scandal. Before delving into the intricate details of this work, it's worthwhile to provide a very brief historical background. As a result of the 1948 British Nationality Act, colonial British subjects were included under a single definition of British citizenship and thereby given the right to enter the UK. Subsequently, hundreds of thousands of individuals migrated from the Caribbean to the UK and helped rebuild the country after World War II.[53] The term Windrush generation comes from the *Empire Windrush*, which was one of the first ships that brought immigrants from the West Indies to the UK in 1948. During the Windrush Scandal people from the Windrush generation were illegally detained, denied legal rights, threatened with deportation, and, in numerous cases, were actually deported from the UK by the British Home Office.[54] The fact that many of these individuals had come to know the UK as their only home adds insult to injury.

Whittle shapes these topics into an intricate narrative about overlapping colonial histories. *What Sound Does the Black Atlantic Make?* begins with an introduction to the four basic steps in rubber production, offset by the soothing sound of wind chimes and a saxophone playing in the background. Notice the use of the present tense in her critical questioning of the sounds that the Black Atlantic makes. Once again, she effectively brings the past into the present through sound. We are back in Glissantian territory where jazz and blues are understood as a response to suffering. The four basic steps of rubber production are clearly defined through images and words, including mastication.[55] This creates a haunting metaphor for the bodies that were forced into the bellies of the slave ships, reduced to a pulp (like rubber) and spit out on the other side of the Atlantic. Historical footage includes scenes from Queen Elizabeth II's visit to Barbados as part of her royal tour of the Crown colonies of the Caribbean in 1966. Whittle spells out what no amount of pomp and circumstance could possibly hide: respectability will not save you. It certainly hasn't saved the West Indians who travelled to the "mother country" at their own expense to help fight against the Germans in World War II, and who helped rebuild the UK after the war.

Alberta Whittle is keenly aware of the power of implementing sound to bring history and memory into contemporary space. Her most riveting performances play out in historical sites that are somehow connected to slavery. Her soundscapes feature everything from delicate musical instruments and

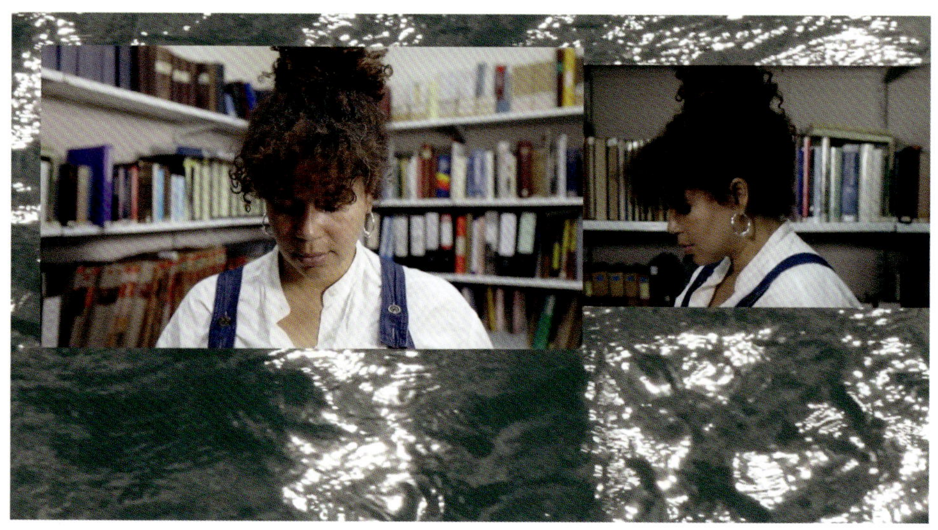

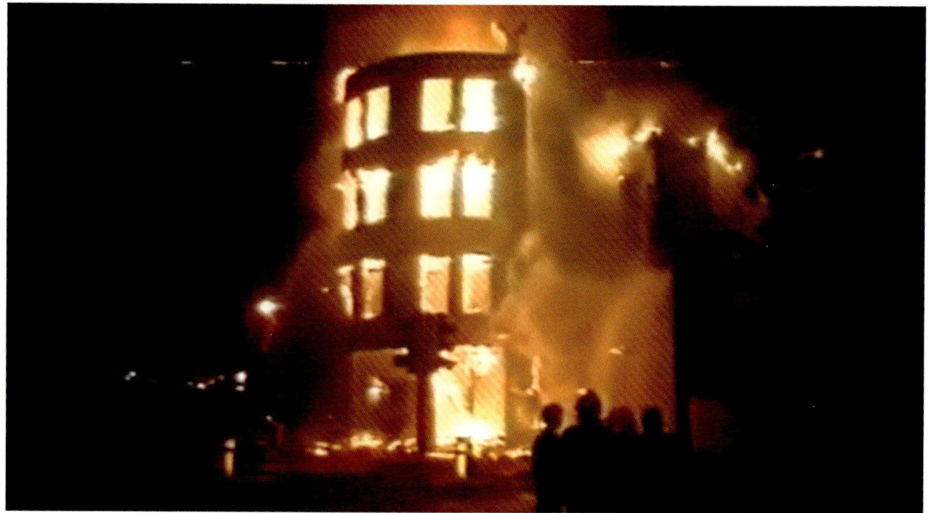

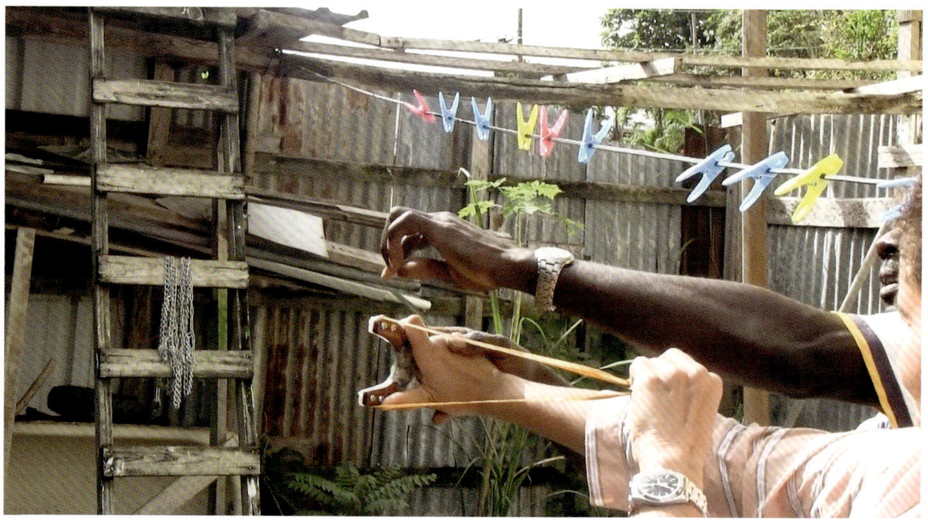

subtle sounds from nature to the spoken word, poetry, lullabies, and politically imbued adaptations of pop songs. She hums, sings, groans, and screams for our attention. In her 2016 performance *Impossibility of Return (Ghana)*, which takes place at the slave fort in the Jamestown neighborhood of Accra, she rips open the wounds of her own ancestral memories. Wondering aloud what she might be able to claim as her own memory, she makes it clear that the ancestral memory of crossing the Atlantic is always carried in her body:

Where does a memory go? Through how many generations can a memory travel?

Arriving in Accra, Ghana, my skin prickled with the sensations of memory. An insistent niggle under the skin tells me that I have left something behind. I am haunted by memories that have no name, unquantifiable and shape shifting, forever squirming beyond my reach. Without reason, I felt an unassailable conviction that even though uncountable seconds and hours, days and decades have passed, I knew, without question that I had walked this land before. Some part of me tells me that I am 'returning', but to what exactly I do not know. Half-baked tales of brothers and sisters from the Americas 'returning', seeking out a Mother in Africa remind me that this is impossible. Africa does not remember her kin, instead we metamorphosis into the tribe of 'how are you'.

How can I grasp this memory that remains out of reach? Hoping to transform my body into a conduit, I set my self in motion.

I have no hard-edged memory fuh sure of Accra being a location where my ancestors toiled, laughed and loved before their capture and eventual sale into slavery. There is no blood, no skin, no semen, nor torn clothing to be found. Everything that speaks of that is gone.

Grasp as I might, through the entrails of my mind, there is nothing but indistinct facts of a past ripped from history books. Footnotes on some page, which write of miscegenation, rape, bodies being sold, families destroyed but who somehow survive. But the how and the why press down upon me now that I stand before the slave fort in Jamestown. This place has seen boats swelling

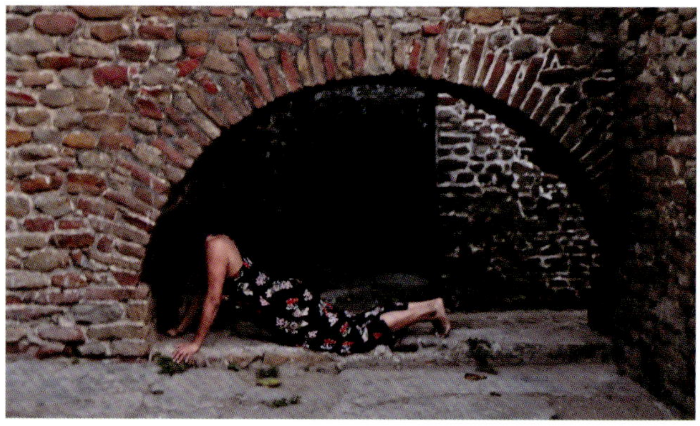

Alberta Whittle
*Impossibility of Return
(Ghana)*, 2016
Site-specific
performance
Accra, Ghana

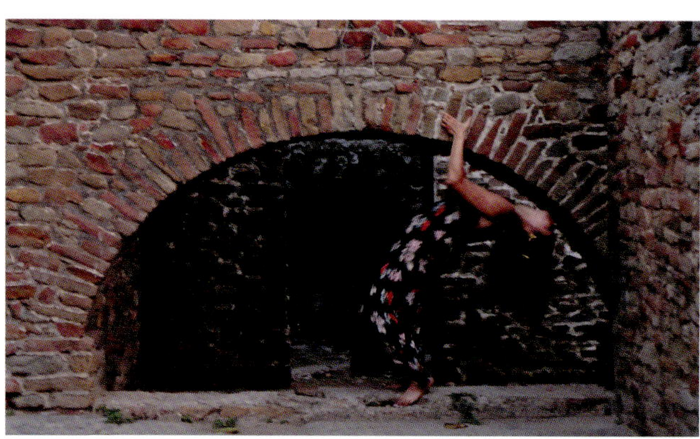

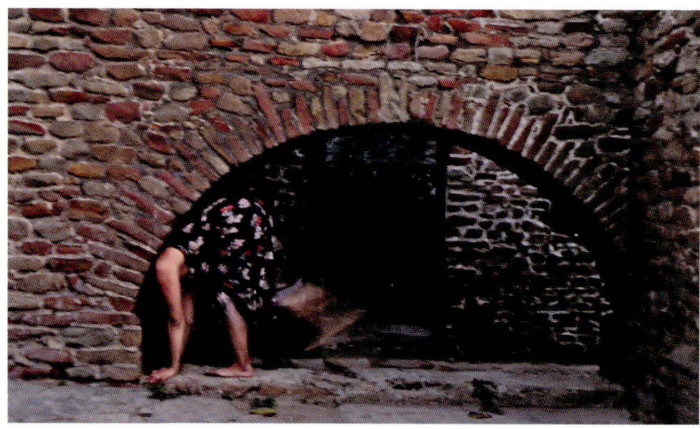

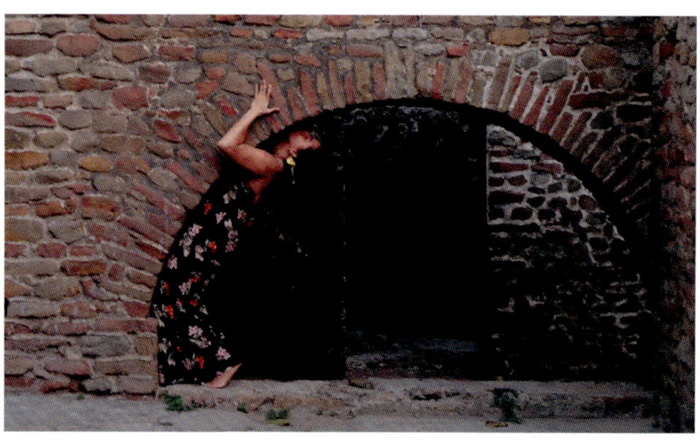

with cargo of humans and today still swells full of life, uncontainable and inexhaustible life.

Those living lives in Jamestown do not remember me. There is no mirror image here, waiting for me to see myself as I may have once been, that self is lost to me forever. My skin has grown smudged with new lines, my veins filled with the bloodlines of Massa, shards of forgotten features leaving me unrecognizable to Mother Africa.

Accra makes me think of the Caribbean. The land seems similar. Like many early British colonial outposts, we are named for King James and bear the name Jamestown. Architecture of the colonies is fortified by plantations, forts, and slave lodges pockmarking the landscape, haunted by Massa and slave. Walking through these crumbling effigies, I feel a pull from my navel to connect with my ancestors, to retrieve someone I have left behind. Maybe that someone is I.

Stones holding up the remains of these monuments to slavery are crumbling, but life perseveres, finding ways to survive amongst the rubble. Families live in the structures that may once have held their kin, chickens amble by in search of grubs. Washing hangs on lines above tunnels, and girls find quiet spots to do their make-up before an assignation.

I felt a pull to press myself into the bones of the building, forcing my DNA into the stones and the dust. Leaning backward, pressing into, fitting my chinks into the crevasses of buildings, which had no right to survive. I tried again, willing my fingers, toes, hips and spine to arch against gravity and touch the curves of the buildings that once held slaves. Tracing ancestors in the buildings that had once held them captive, I felt the imprint of their presence in the hair, skin and blood that had long since turned to dust and was now all they had left behind in the slave fort.

Finding my ancestors in the dust, I connected with the detritus of life.[56]

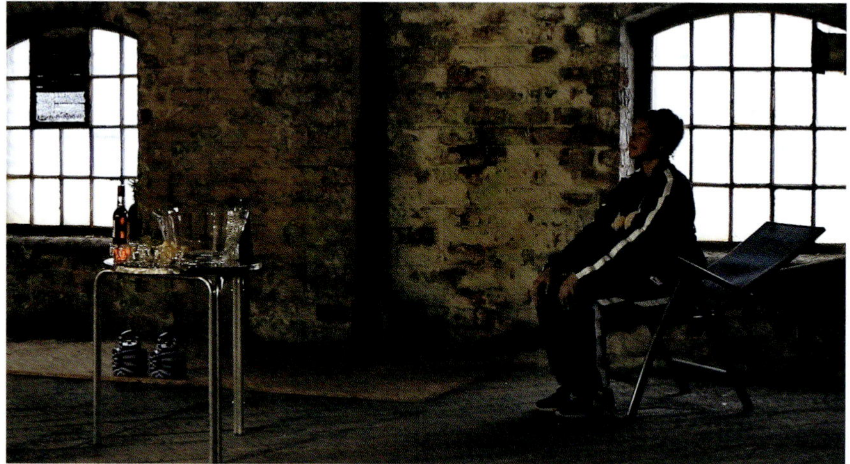

The fact that this performance takes place at a former slave fort is itself a powerful act of resistance and empowerment. Similar to how Jeannette Ehlers inserts herself into colonial space, thereby reversing the power structures connected to colonial space, Alberta Whittle also responds not only to but also against a colonial site. Now *she* is calling the shots, as she points out in *A Recipe for Planters Punch* (2016). Similar to *Impossibility of Return (Ghana)*, this work was also conceived as a meditation on slavery and memory. The performance took place in the former Tobacco Warehouse in Greenock, Scotland. Whittle explains: "At the height of trade to the port, Greenock received up to 400 ships from the Caribbean annually arriving with sugar and tobacco."[57] The work also directs the viewer's attention at what she describes as the "luxury of amnesia," which involves the ability to forget colonial histories shared between Scotland and the Caribbean. This is comparable to the prevalence of colonial amnesia witnessed not only in Scotland, but throughout Europe and Scandinavia, as conveyed by all the artists featured in this book. Again, Whittle uses sonic politics to get her messages across. Here, she manipulates the lyrics to Rihanna's *Bitch Better Have My Money (BBHMM)* to full effect, transforming it into a call for reparations.

Whittle's eloquent description of the work brings the politicism of her performance to life:

> During my performance, I dissected the original lyrics from BBHMM and sang them to the audience, 'I call out all the shots', 'Don't act like you forgot' and finally 'Bitch Better Have My Money'. Shifting the tone of my voice to engage with the audience,

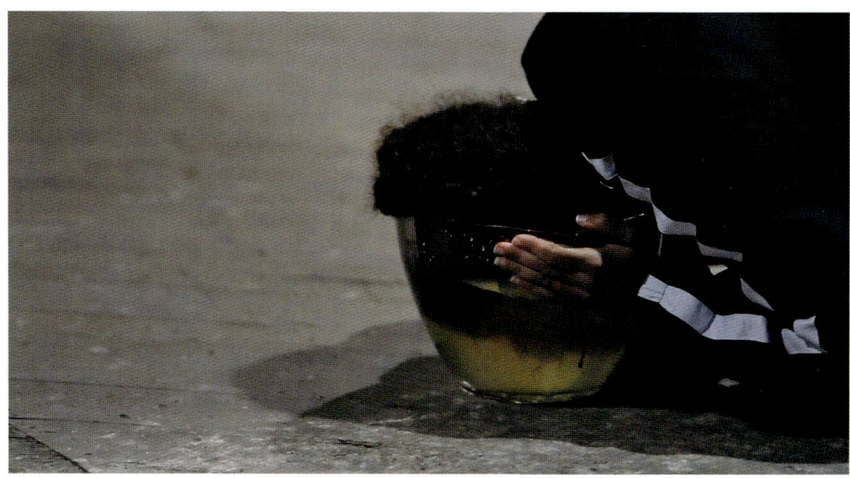

I sang the lyrics as part lament, part demand. Throughout my singing, I move between the audience placing key ingredients for the rum punch in their hands and instructing them to pour them into a punch bowl.

After each ingredient was added to the rum punch, I would sing 'Don't act like you forgot' before placing my head into the punch bowl and attempting to sing these lyrics, whilst my face was submerged under the liquid, holding my breath and singing as long as I could underwater. The shift between the labor of preparing the ingredients for the punch—cutting and squeezing limes, grating nutmeg, pouring sugar syrup, bitters, rum and sea water—and the act of drowning myself, created a tension between myself and the audience where their presence and role in communally preparing the rum punch, witnessing my submergence in the punch, implicated them in this process and the shared history of making and consuming this drink, associated with conviviality and revelry, not slavery.[58]

At the end of the performance Whittle leaves the room in a rage. She leaves the filthy bowl of planter's punch behind, which appears to be mixed with blood instead of Grenadine. As she explains towards the end of her performance, this is the blood of her ancestors washed clean by the sugar that they made. In keeping with the double-entendres throughout her work, washing functions as a compelling metaphor for erasure, or a washing away of the secrets of the colonial past. Amnesia is often thought of as a temporary condition, but as Whittle makes clear, colonial amnesia has been going on for centuries.

The stories of each of these women unite them as one, over millennia, between continents, and across oceans. In an interconnected narrative that extends from Africa to the Caribbean and Latin America, Queen Nanny and Queen Nzinga are joined by Escrava Anastácia who is also given an honorary seat at the table.

A Seat at the Table

Patricia Kaersenhout's socially engaged art practice involves an ongoing inquiry of African and African diasporic movements in correlation with feminism, sexuality, racism, and the history of slavery. She is an important contributor to decolonial discourse, is a frequent lecturer at the Decolonial Summer School in Middelburg, and is also a participant and contributor to BE.BOP. (Black Europe Body Politics).[59] Kaersenhout is dedicated to honoring the countless Black women whose importance has long been erased from Eurocentric historical narratives. Through empowering, radical artistic gestures she exposes the hidden and secret histories of colonial history.

The Soul of Salt, which Kaersenhout exhibited in 2018 at Manifesta 12 in Palermo, is among her most iconic works. She explains its powerful symbolism and how it relates to the history of enslaved people:

> The sea salt refers to the salt which enslaved people refrained from eating so they could fly back to Africa. But it also stands as a symbol for mental and physical liberation. It refers to slaves crossing the saltwater of the Atlantic Ocean on their way to plantations. It's the salt of all the tears shed during slavery and colonialism.

> The mountain of 8000 kilos of sea salt depicts the suffering, but also the hopes and dreams of people. With this work I wanted to commemorate the past, and also transcend it.

> Indigenous people believe that history lies before us because we can visualize the past. A group of refugee girls sing the slave song *Many Thousand Gone*. This way the past is connected to the current humanitarian crisis of bodies crossing the sea.

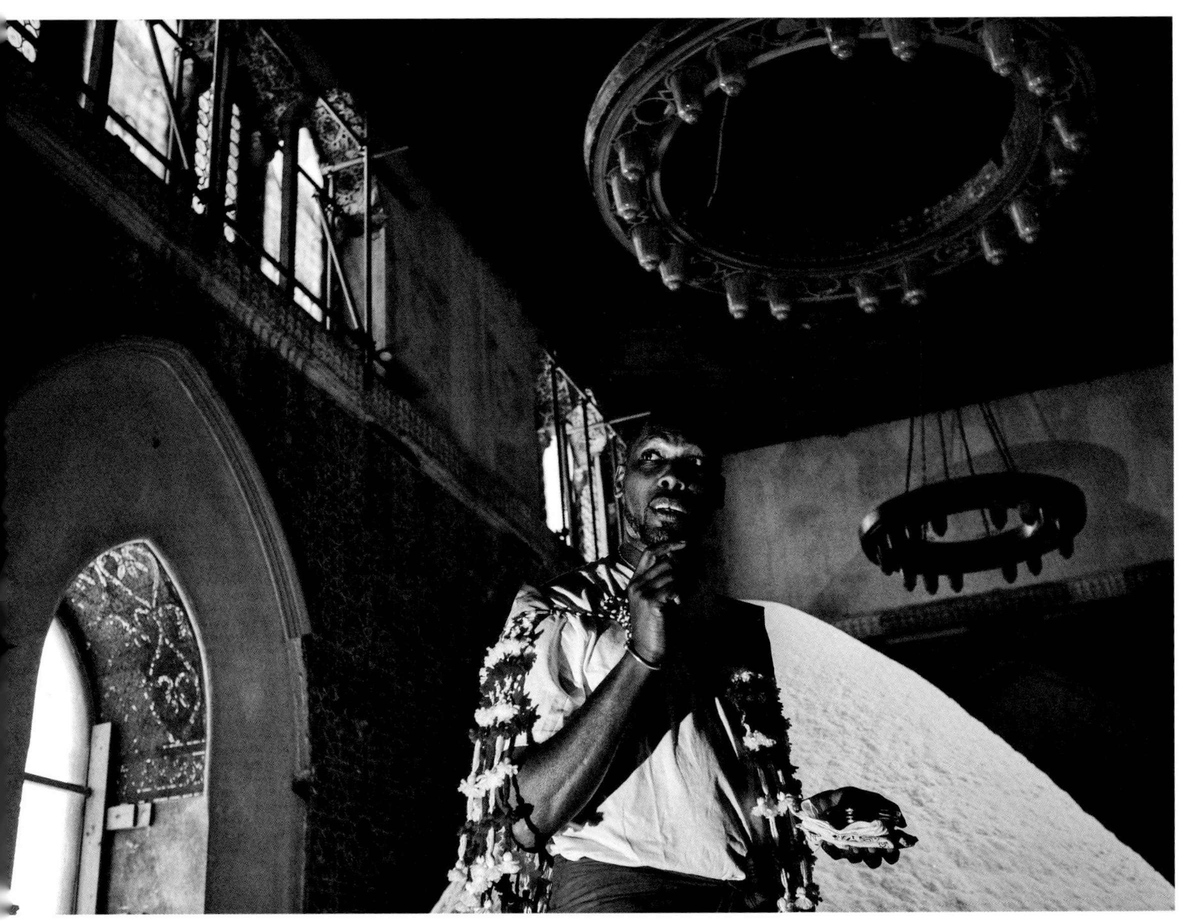

The public is asked to dig into the mountain and to bring home some salt which has been blessed by a Winti priest (Winti is a nature religion from Suriname). Together with family members, they can dissolve the salt in water, as a symbol for solving the pain of the past and thus giving rest to the souls of their own ancestors. With the excavation of the mountain, we dig a path into the future, which is behind us because we can't see it. Digging together creates a connection and hopefully we can leave the shared wounds of a painful past behind us, without forgetting, but with forgiveness.[60]

Patricia Kaersenhout
The Soul of Salt,
2016–18
Performance with blessed salt in Palermo during the opening weekend of Manifesta 12
Commissioned by Manifesta 12 and supported by Mondriaan Fonds
Courtesy the artist and Wilfried Lentz Rotterdam
Photo: Francesco Bellini

Throughout the Caribbean, the legend of "flying Africans" has been kept alive both through oral storytelling and literature. According to the legend, which varies slightly from island to island, enslaved Africans who were forced to work on Caribbean plantations were said to avoid eating salt so as to become light enough to fly back to Africa. The common thread between the

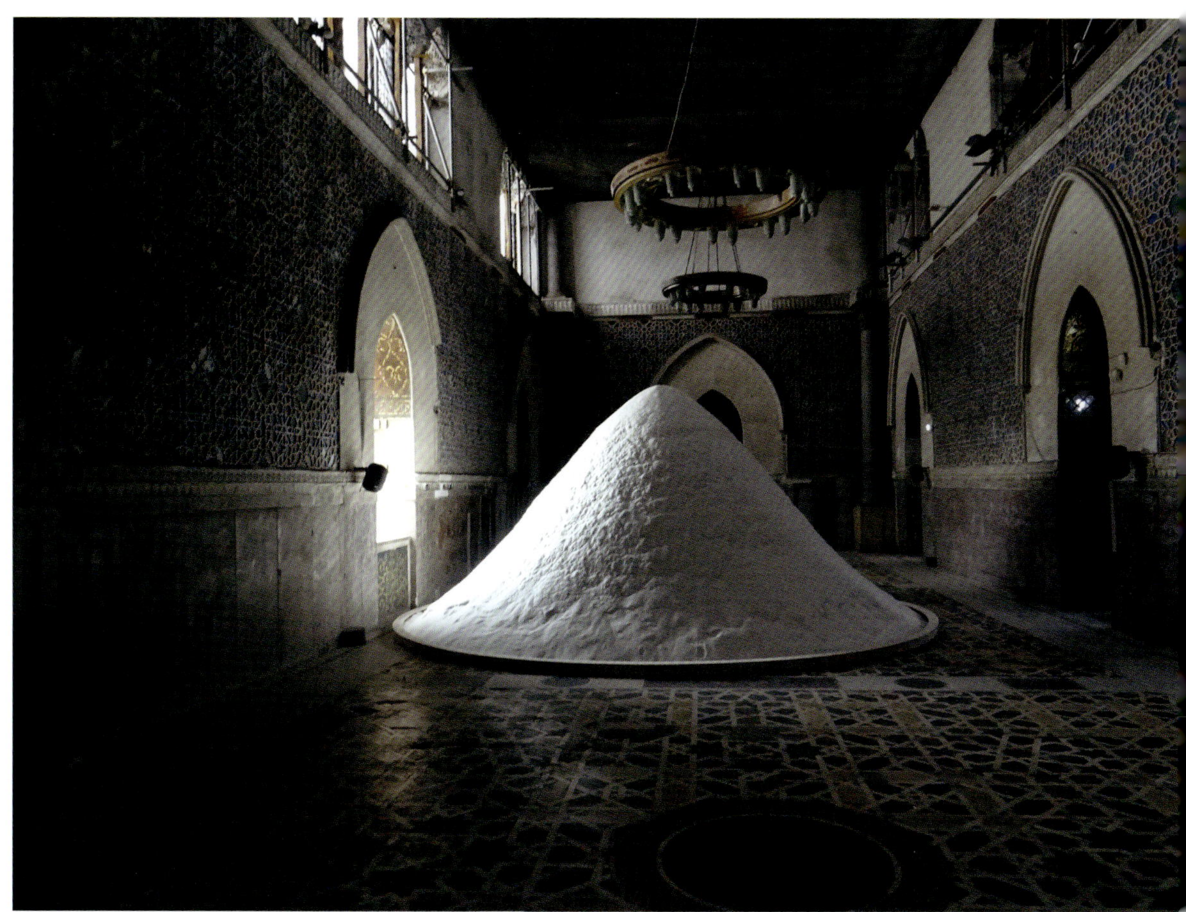

various versions of the legend is the shared experience of enslaved Africans who endured the transatlantic passage and who longed to return to Africa throughout their lifetime. The legend figures prominently in African American and Caribbean literature, conveyed in books ranging from Toni Morrison's *Song of Solomon* (1977) to Kei Miller's *Augustown* (2016). The legend is also conveyed through music, and perhaps nowhere more memorably than in the lyrics of Bob Marley's *Rastaman Chant*: "I say fly away home to Zion (fly away home) One bright morning when my work is over Man will fly away home."

The Soul of Salt installation is accompanied by a video recording, which documents the highly significant gesture of Kaersenhout flying part of the blessed salt back to the island of Gorée in Senegal, where she releases it back to the sea near the Door of No Return. For Kaersenhout this was a way of providing peace to the souls of the enslaved ancestors, while the transport of the salt stands as a thought-provoking symbol of the migration of Black bodies. Kaersenhout still has a reserve of salt that was blessed in Palermo that she intends to fly to the Dutch Caribbean and release into the sea. Again, she will make a short video recording of the intervention and invite local activists to talk about the current neocolonial situation on their islands as part of the documentation.

Kaersenhout has a keen sensibility for bringing memory into contemporary space through sound. Her specific choice of *Many Thousand Gone*, a popular African American spiritual which was sung by enslaved individuals who fled from plantations during the Civil War, couldn't be more appropriate. In fact, this was one of the songs that the Fisk Jubilee Singers sang on their international concert tour.[61] As Du Bois put it, "the world listened only half credulously until the Fisk Jubilee Singers sang the slave songs so deeply into the world's heart that it can never wholly forget them again."[62] And yet, as unforgettable as these songs were, and still are, cultural amnesia still persists. Here, this is witnessed and heard in the song of refugees. It's as deceptively simple as that. Kaersenhout effectively combines song and salt to connect the past to the current humanitarian crisis of bodies crossing the sea. She doesn't stop there. She cuts a clear path to the future by inviting the audience to dig into the mountain of salt. By engaging the audience in the work, she offers an opportunity to acknowledge and come to terms with the wounds of the past through a potentially healing gesture.

Similar to how Jeannette Ehlers and La Vaughn Belle have honored the Crucian freedom fighter Mary Thomas in their collaborative monument *I Am Queen Mary*, Patricia Kaersenhout's installation *Guess Who's Coming to Dinner Too?* conveys the stories of heroines who have been left out of the Eurocentric colonial narrative. In response to Judy Chicago's seminal work *The Dinner Party* (1974–79), Kaersenhout was interested in a more inclusive list of invitees, as a counterpoint to Chicago's dinner party to which few Black, Brown, or Indigenous women were invited.[63] In fact, Sojourner Truth[64] was the only African American woman with a seat at the table. It's worth noting that Chicago included Susan B. Anthony,[65] activist and leader of the American suffragist movement, as "Queen of the Table." Kaersenhout's table is set up in the same triangular shape as Judy Chicago's installation, but the similarities stop there. Kaersenhout's installation celebrates and honors thirty-eight Black, Brown, and Indigenous women who were never granted their rightful and deserved seat at the table. The invitees represent a timespan that extends over millennia, while their experiences and accomplishments unite cultures and continents, from West and East Africa to Australia, Asia, the Caribbean, and Latin America.

Narratives of leadership and rebellion turn Kaersenhout's dinner party into a long overdue celebration of these women's contributions to history. She elaborates on the implications of the title, which is vital to an overall appreciation of the work:

> The title *Guess Who's Coming to Dinner Too?* can be dually interpreted. On the one hand, it is a nod to Chicago's *The Dinner Party*. However, this time the invited guests are the previously uninvited, absent black women and women of color. On the other hand, it serves as a reference to the famous film *Guess Who's Coming to Dinner?* (1967) with Sidney Poitier in the leading role. In this film, Poitier's character is in an interracial relationship with a white woman. He is invited to have dinner with his future in-laws but remains the uninvited guest throughout the evening. He is deprived of any agency, as not once do we get to see his perspective of this complicated situation. This exemplifies what Sara Ahmed, feminist writer and independent scholar, wrote: "Whiteness is produced as host, as that which is already in place or at home. To be welcomed is to be positioned as the one who is not at home."[66]

Among the numerous historical figures, Kaersenhout also includes several contemporary heroines to serve as "a reminder that the battle against racism, inequality and oppression is by no means overcome and still remains today."[67] Among the heroines who are honored in Kaersenhout's installation, there are three women whose fight against colonialism and slavery are particularly relevant within the context of this book: Queen Nanny of the Maroons, Queen Nzinga, and Escrava Anastácia.

Queen Nanny (1686–1733) most likely came from the Asante tribe of present-day Ghana, West Africa. After escaping slavery, she became a Maroon leader in Jamaica around the early eighteenth century. Maroons were enslaved people in the Americas who escaped and formed independent settlements.

Following pages:
Patricia Kaersenhout
Guess Who's Coming to Dinner Too?, 2017–19
Installation view at de Appel, Amsterdam, 2019
Triangular table, 39 table runners, 36 napkins, approximately 60 glass vessels, rods, and vases, a bamboo grid hanging from the ceiling, 2 bamboo tables, with 6 limited edition publications with biographies of 38 Black women, and 38 Adinkra symbols (felt on cotton)
Photo: Aatjan Renders
Courtesy the artist and Wilfried Lentz Rotterdam

The installation is financially supported by Mondriaan Fonds, AFK, Stichting Doen

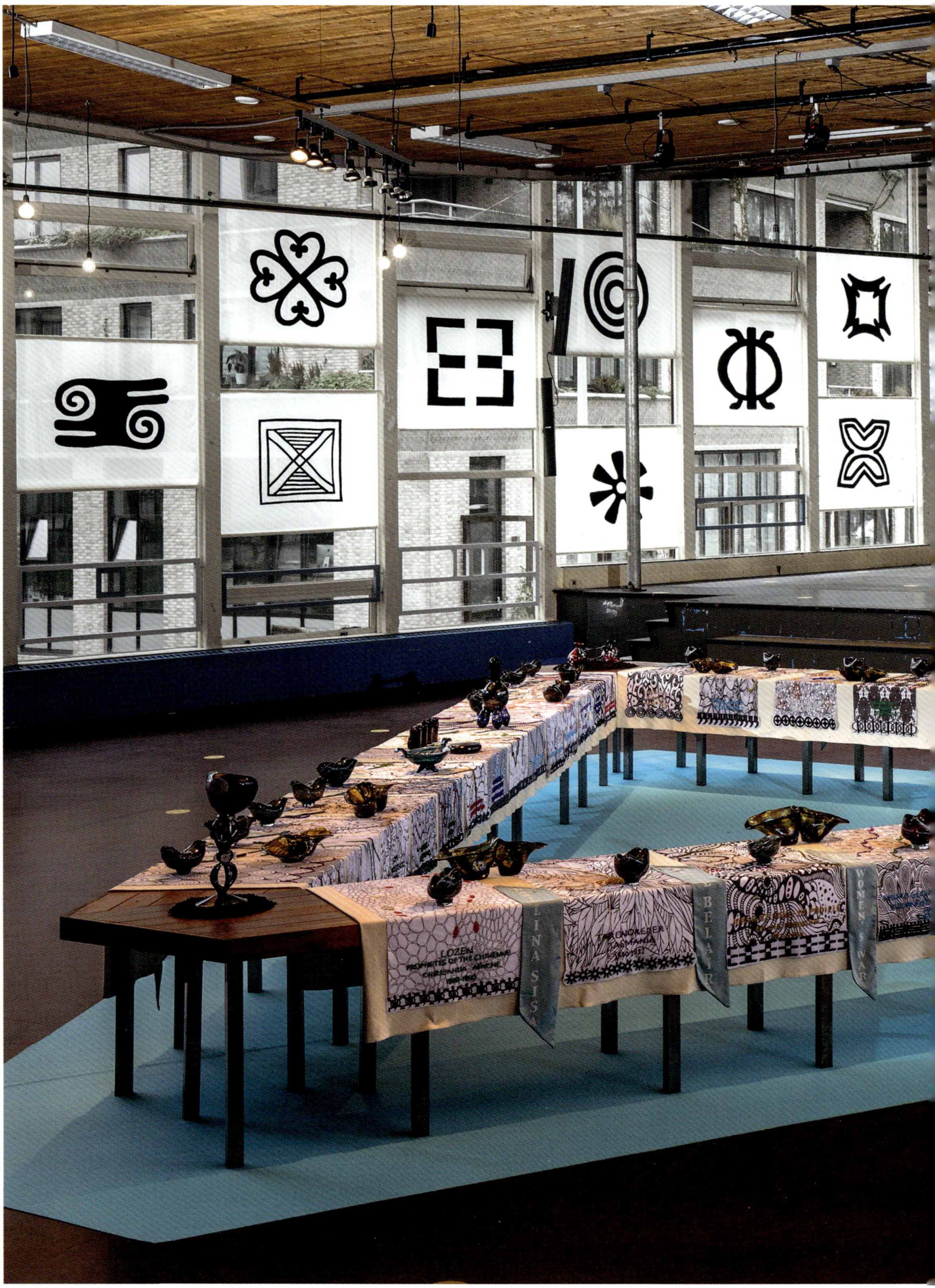

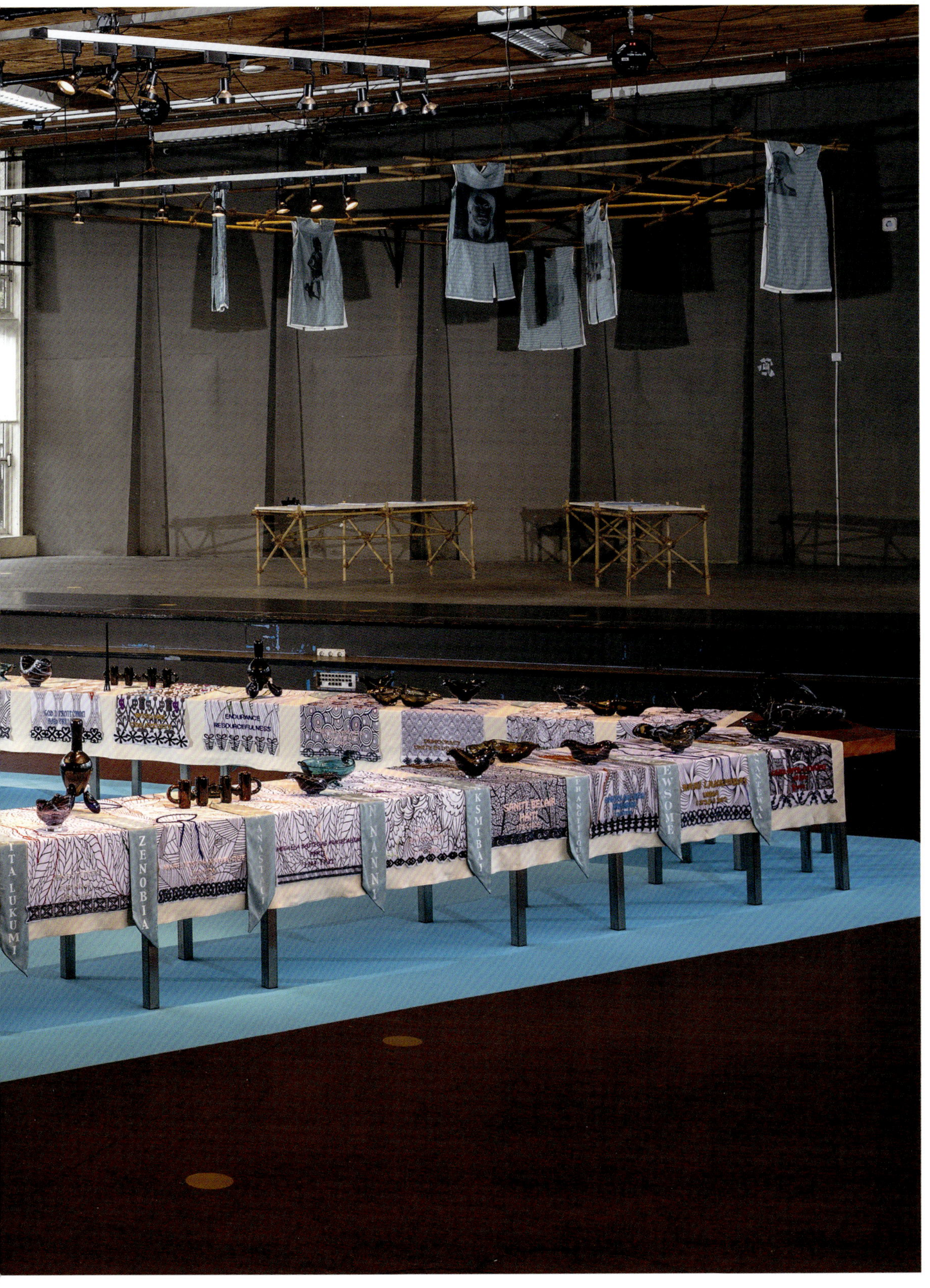
ITA LUKUMI
ZENOBIA
ANASTA
NANN
KSMIBAY
SAINT-BELAIR
EWSOME
ENDURANCE
RESOURCEFULNESS

Nanny and her four brothers (all of whom became Maroon leaders) escaped from their plantations into the mountains and jungles of Jamaica. Nanny and one brother, Quao, founded a village in the Blue Mountains that became known as Nanny Town. Nanny has been described as a practitioner of Obeah, a term used in the Caribbean to describe spirituality and religion based on West African influences.

Nanny Town, placed as it was in the mountains away from European settlements and difficult to assault, thrived. Nanny preferred to farm and trade peacefully with her neighbors and limited her attacks on European settlements. She did however organize successful raids to free enslaved people held on plantations and it has been widely accepted that her efforts contributed to the escape of almost a thousand people.

Threatened by the successes of the Maroons, the British colonial administration employed soldiers, militiamen, and mercenaries to scour the Jamaican jungles. Nanny is said to have been killed in 1733 by Captain William Cuffee, during one of many bloody engagements. After her death, many of the Windward Maroons moved across the island to the more sparsely inhabited Western (or Leeward) side of Jamaica. Nanny Town was eventually captured by the British and destroyed in 1734.

Nanny is known as one of the earliest leaders of resistance against slavery in the Americas.[68]

Queen Nanny of the Maroons is among the most well-known freedom fighters who has also been a source of inspiration for other contemporary artists. Most notably, Jamaican artist Renée Cox was among the first contemporary artists to pay homage to Queen Nanny in her 2004 photographic series *Queen Nanny of the Maroons*. *Redcoat* is among the most iconic images in this series and stands out as a harbinger of decolonial strategies in portraiture. The entire series, and this portrait in particular, makes a powerful statement about the military prowess of Queen Nanny and effectively depicts her as a symbol of unity and strength. Cox succinctly sums up Queen Nanny's importance to Jamaican history:

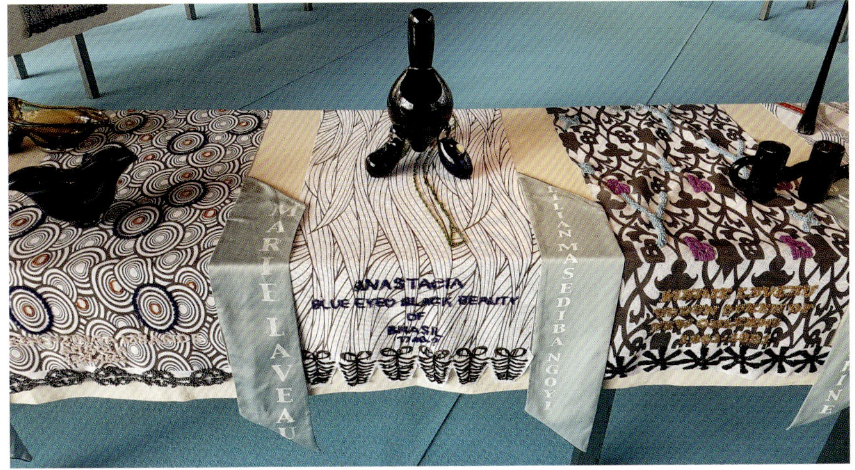

"Throughout time, the legend and spirit of Nanny of the Maroons, the only female among Jamaica's national heroes, continues to inspire those with a desire for independence and the spirit to achieve it."[69] Another contemporary artist who has paid homage to Queen Nanny is Senegalese photographer Omar Victor Diop, whose *Liberty* series commemorates slave revolts, the fight for social justice, and the events that sparked these uprisings. Diop plays every male role of the *Liberty* series, and in one of the photographs he appears as Queen Nanny's brother Quao.

Returning to Kaersenhout's dinner celebration, it's time to tribute Queen Nzinga:

> Queen Nzinga was a ruthless and powerful seventeenth-century African ruler of the Ndongo and Matamba Kingdoms (modern-day Angola). Nzinga fearlessly and cleverly fought for the freedom and stature of her kingdoms against the Portuguese colonizers.

> In 1622 the Portuguese invited King Ngola Mbande to attend a peace conference to end the hostilities. Mbande sent his sister Nzinga as his representative, who convinced the Portuguese governor she was her brother's equal. When the governor refused to give her the single chair in the room, she signaled one of her assistants who fell on her hands and knees and served as a chair for Nzinga during the meeting. Her servant knew that as a queen, Nzinga had to sit at least at equal height, or higher, as her collocutor.

Unlike other rulers at the time, Nzinga was easily able to adapt to the fluctuations in power around her. Her determination and resilience towards the Portuguese transformed her kingdom into a strong, wealthy state. To fortify her kingdom's martial power, Nzinga offered sanctuary to fugitive slaves and African soldiers. She stirred up rebellion among the people still left in Ndongo, ruled by the Portuguese. Nzinga also reached out to the Dutch colonists, who by that time had seized the city of Luanda and invited them to join troops with her. However, even their combined forces were not enough to drive the Portuguese out, and after retreating to Matamba again, Nzinga started to focus on developing Matamba as a trading power and the gateway to Central Africa.

By the time of Nzinga's death in 1661, at the age of 81, Matamba was on equal footing with the Portuguese colony. The Portuguese eventually came to respect Queen Nzinga for her intelligence and determinateness.[70]

Kaersenhout's installation not only pays homage to Black female rebels, warriors, and divine spirits, it unites these women through time and place. Kaersenhout invites us to celebrate the achievements of women, who, despite consistently having been left out of Eurocentric narratives, have each played a crucial role in changing history. The stories of each of these women unite them as one, over millennia, between continents, and across oceans. In an interconnected narrative that extends from Africa to the Caribbean and Latin America, Queen Nanny and Queen Nzinga are joined by Escrava Anastácia who is also given an honorary seat at the table.

Within Rio de Janeiro, the legendary 18th century blue-eyed black beauty Anastácia is revered as a saint and considered one of the most important women in Brazil's Black history. Like all legends, nobody knows who Anastácia actually was. Although her story has many versions, all of them recount her beauty as well as her profound strength in enduring the hardship of enslavement and patriarchal violence.

A common legend holds that she was the child of an enslaved woman from West Africa who was raped by her white slave-owner.

From this violence Anastácia was conceived, becoming the first black child born with blue eyes in Brazil. The brutality is said to have continued when Anastácia's later slave-owner became enchanted by her piercing beauty and was infuriated when she refused his advances. In punishment, and to hide her face from all the world, Anastácia was condemned to wear an iron mask for the rest of her life, only removing it once a day to eat. In this legend she lived for some years before she died from the toxic consequences of wearing an iron mask.

However, there is another story in which Anastácia was a 17th century African queen, enslaved and transported to a sugar plantation. In this account she is held to have taught other enslaved people to worship their African gods, until she was discovered and imprisoned. Forced to wear an iron mask to prevent her from speaking, she became the concubine of a guard who secretly loved her. In this legend Anastácia practices powers of traditional healing. However, she is once again said to have died soon after from the effects of the iron mask, this time of gangrene.

Yet another story proposes that Anastácia had been able to fend off attacks by the slave-owner, inspiring women today to defy abusive husbands.

Whichever story is true, Anastácia took on the status of a saint, especially among Afro-Brazilian women during the Brazilian black-consciousness movement of the 1980s. Nurses revered her for her self-healing, and her image proliferated within black beauty salons. In response to the growing power of Anastácia's memory, in 1987 the Catholic Church declared her to be merely legend rather than a legitimate historical figure and removed her image from Church-owned properties. This, however, does not deny her power, as her legend is considered an amalgam of the many enslaved women who have inspired healing, beauty and hope.[71]

Kilomba's groundbreaking work as a writer and theorist not only informs her own practice as an interdisciplinary artist; it's equally relevant to the work of each of the artists featured in this book.

Plantation Memories

Anastácia also figures prominently in Grada Kilomba's three-channel video installation *The Desire Project* (2016), the details of which I shall return to. As a writer, theorist, and interdisciplinary artist whose work investigates memory, trauma, gender, racism, and coloniality, Kilomba's contribution to decolonial thinking cannot be understated. There are three overriding questions that she addresses throughout her practice: Who can speak? What can we speak about?, and What happens when we speak? She consistently combines theory and practice in a perfect melding of academic and artistic languages. Storytelling is a central element in her unique interdisciplinary approach, which often involves visual, oral, and textual interpretations of her own texts. Her wide-ranging creative practice, which she describes as "performing knowledge," includes publications, performances, staged readings, installations, films, text collages, sound and video installations.

If the past is ever-present throughout Kilomba's work, it's "because we all know that we are still inhabiting geographies of the past."[72] Among the most important topics that she addresses is the fact that colonial history is restaged through everyday racism, as documented in her seminal book *Plantation Memories: Episodes of Everyday Racism* (2008), a compilation of episodes of everyday racism written in the form of short psychoanalytical stories. Her book relays first-hand experiences of trauma and the traumatic history of racism told by women of the African diaspora. *Plantation Memories* has also been adapted into a series of staged readings, which are powerful decolonial interventions in their own right. The book is beautifully complemented by her installation *The Desire Project*, which she describes as an experimental video that enabled her to "explore how thoughts can be associated not only with theory, but especially with sounds, movement and emotions."[73]

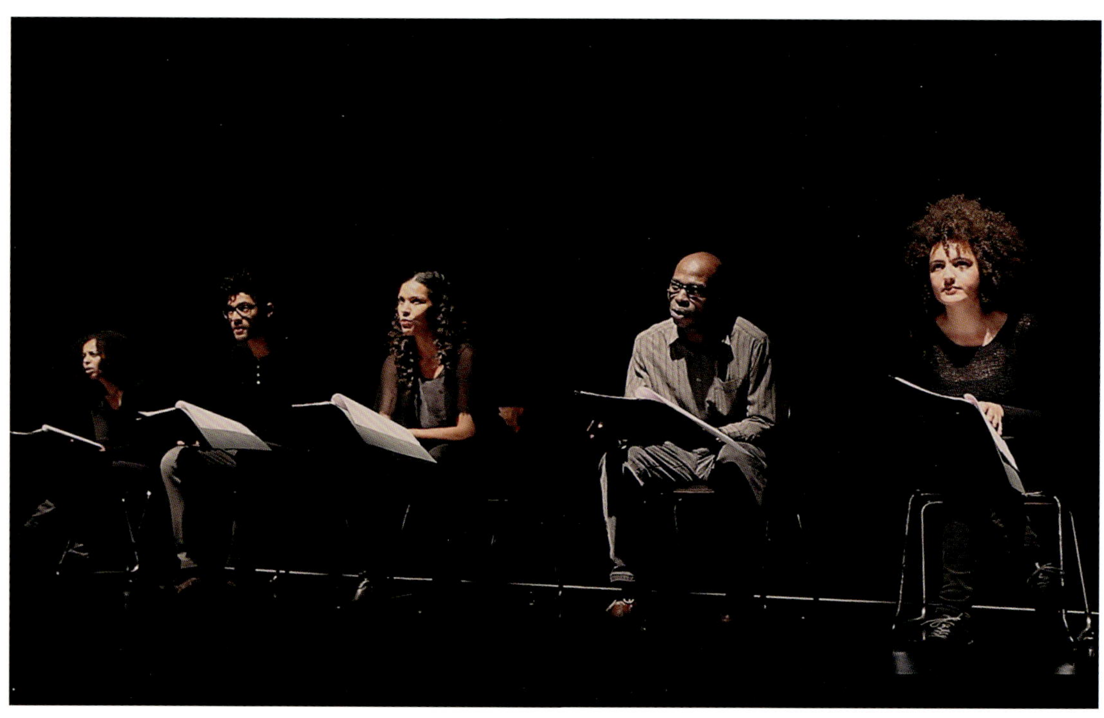

Grada Kilomba
Plantation Memories,
2018
Single-channel video
installation of staged
reading, HD in color,
sound
14 minutes 14 seconds
on loop
Courtesy the artist
and Goodman Gallery

Grada Kilomba
The Desire Project, 2016
Stills from Act III
While I Write
Courtesy the artist
and Goodman Gallery

Grada Kilomba
The Desire Project, 2016
Three-channel video
installation, HD in black
and white, sound, two
printed impressions,
and shrine
2 minutes 46 seconds
on loop
Installation view at
Goodman Gallery,
Johannesburg, 2018
Photo: Anthea Pokroy
Courtesy the artist
and Goodman Gallery

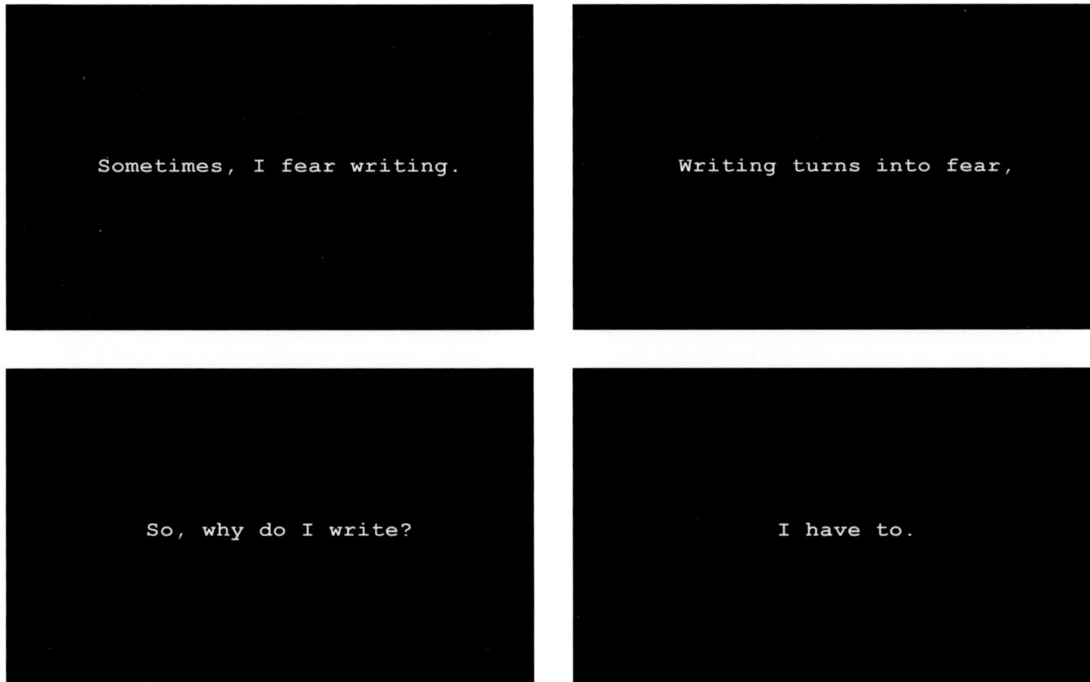

Sometimes, I fear writing.

Writing turns into fear,

So, why do I write?

I have to.

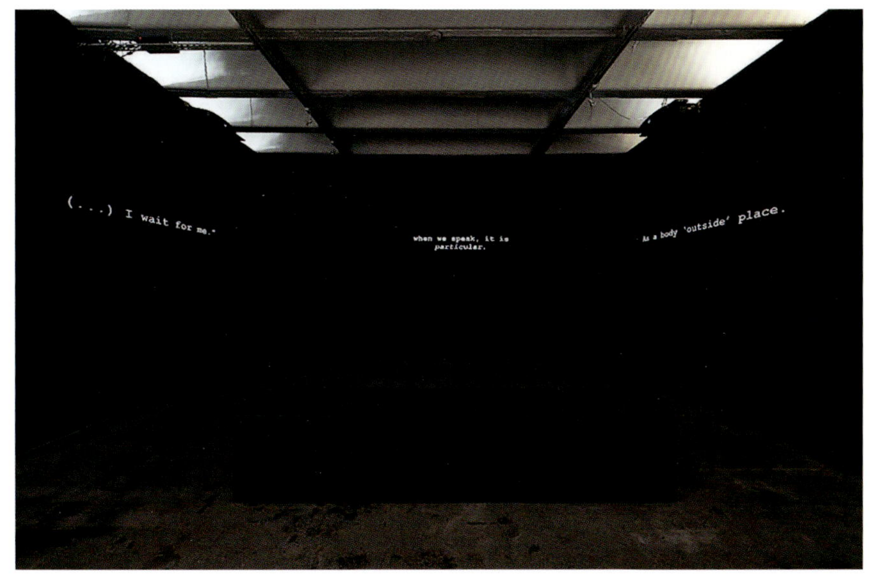

(...) I wait for me.·

when we speak, it is
particular.

As a body 'outside' place.

The Desire Project is a perfect example of Kilomba's ability to shift effortlessly between textual, visual, and sonic forms of expression. The installation features a video divided into three acts: *While I Walk*, *While I Speak*, and *While I Write*, presented along with a shrine to Anastácia. The three films, each projected on its own screen, convey how everyday racism is experienced in public space, through speech, and through language. The indiscernible clamor of voices at the beginning of each film is gradually replaced by the insistent and rhythmic beat of a drum, which heightens the overall impact and helps to punctuate the texts that appear in carefully coordinated succession on the screens. At times, it's as if the words were dancing to the beat of the drum. Suddenly there is complete silence. While the work speaks clearly about the question of who gets to *speak*, the perfectly timed silences invite us to also consider who is *silenced*. The formal details of the work consistently mirror what Kilomba is saying textually, visually, and sonically. Text and music not only replace image and speech, text and music *become* image and speech. This transformative act of *becoming* is particularly important here because it speaks about *becoming* empowered. As Kilomba repeatedly makes clear, whether empowerment is achieved through language, speech, music, art, text, or interventions it involves taking full control of the narrative and telling one's own stories.

The Desire Project started with the video Kilomba created for the 32nd São Paulo Biennial (2016), *While I Write*. She subsequently filmed *While I Speak* and *While I Walk*, which are included in the full version of *The Desire Project* along with the shrine. It's best described in her own words:

It speaks precisely about the narratives that were silenced and how we got our voice back, how we gave voice to our history, or how we recollected our history, which is fragmented. There are three different moments that refer to it, and in each moment the audience will sit, watch the video, go to the next video, view it again, and then move to the third video, watch it again. For me, this is a spiritual and reflective journey, because I want to work with rhythm, voices, music and text and it's something that is felt at the corporeal level and also on the emotional level.[74]

In an interview with psychoanalyst and cultural critic Suely Rolnik for Goethe-Institut's *Episodes of the South Magazine*, Kilomba describes the implications of the narratives conveyed in the work: "They are silenced narratives acquiring voice to make themselves heard, to tell their story. This is the path: the three moments explore this idea of someone who wants to come to voice. This is *The Desire Project*: what I want, what I desire, what it takes, how I want to tell my story."[75]

As previously mentioned, *The Desire Project* also features a shrine dedicated to Anastácia. Extending beyond the importance of Anastácia's role in Brazilian history and her elevation to saint status, more specifically, Kilomba examines the implications of the mask Anastácia was forced to wear during enslavement. In chapter two of *Plantation Memories*, "The Mask: Colonialism, Memory, Trauma and Decolonization," Kilomba explains the symbolism of the mask in relation to colonialism, exposing its function as "a brutal mask of speechlessness":

> This mask was a very concrete piece, a real instrument, which became a part of the European colonial project for more than three hundred years. It was composed of a bit placed inside the mouth of the Black subject, clamped between the tongue and the jaw, and fixed behind the head with two strings, one surrounding the chin and the other surrounding the nose and forehead. Formally, the mask was used by *white* masters to prevent enslaved Africans from eating sugar cane or cocoa beans while working on the plantations, but its primary function was to implement a sense of speechlessness and fear, inasmuch as the mouth was a place of both muteness and torture.

> In this sense, the mask represents colonialism as a whole. It symbolizes the sadistic politics of conquest and its cruel regimes of silencing the so-called 'Others.'[76]

She elaborates on this in a subsequent passage:

> The mask, therefore, raises many questions: Why must the mouth of the Black subject be fastened? Why must she or he be silenced? What could the Black subject say if her or his mouth were not sealed? And what would the *white* subject have to listen to? There is an apprehensive fear that if the colonial subject speaks, the

Grada Kilomba
The Desire Project, 2016
Three-channel video
installation, HD in black
and white, sound, two
printed impressions,
and shrine
2 minutes 46 seconds
on loop

Detail of shrine to
Anastácia
Installation view at the
32nd São Paulo Biennial,
2016
Photo: Leo Eloy
Courtesy the artist
and Goodman Gallery

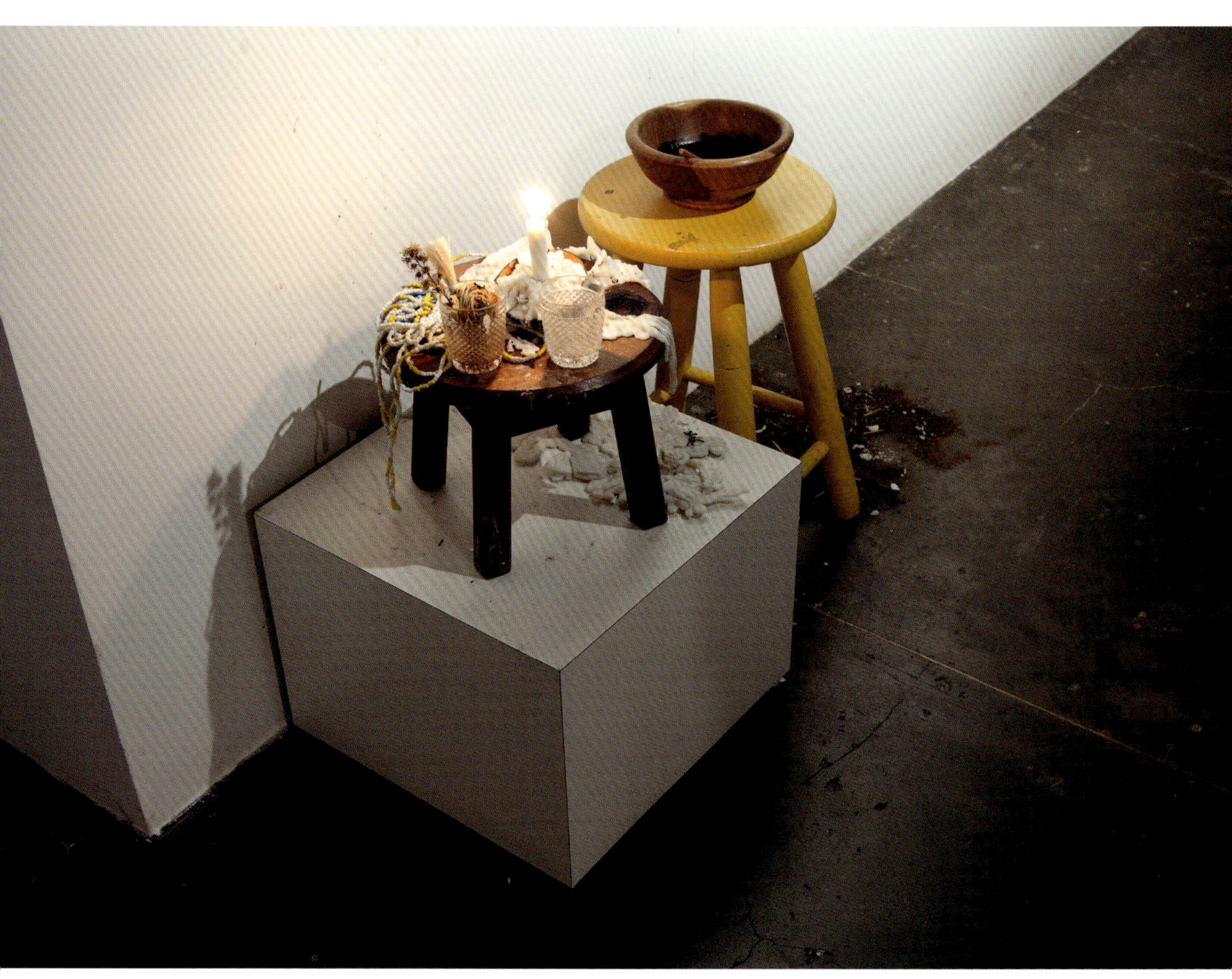

Grada Kilomba
The Desire Project, 2016
Detail of shrine prints
Installation view at the
32nd São Paulo Biennial,
2016
Photo: Leo Eloy
Courtesy the artist
and Goodman Gallery

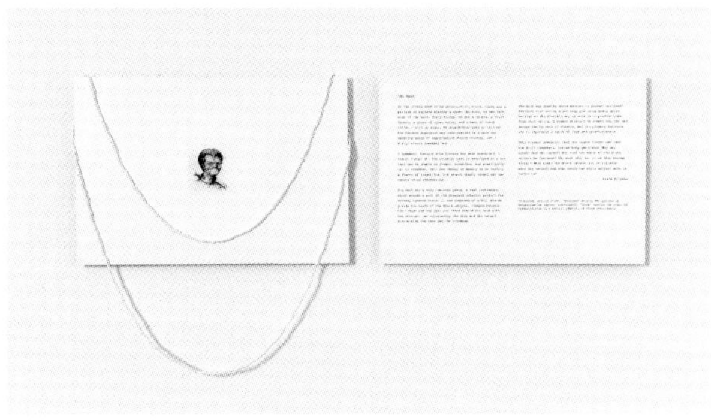

THE MASK

In the living room of my grandmother's house, there was a picture of Escrava Anastácia above the sofa, on the left side of the wall. Every Friday, we put a candle, a white flower, a glass of clean water, and a bowl of fresh coffee – with no sugar. My grandmother used to tell me how Escrava Anastácia was incarcerated in a mask for speaking words of emancipation during slavery, and I should always remember her.

I remember, because this history has been memorised. I cannot forget it. The colonial past is memorised in a way that one is unable to forget. Sometimes, one would prefer not to remember. But, the theory of memory is in reality a theory of forgetting. One cannot simply forget and one cannot avoid remembering.

The mask was a very concrete piece, a real instrument, which became a part of the European colonial project for several hundred years. It was composed of a bit, placed inside the mouth of the Black subject, clamped between the tongue and the jaw, and fixed behind the head with two strings: one surrounding the chin and the second surrounding the nose and the forehead.

The mask was used by *white* masters to prevent enslaved* Africans from eating sugar cane and cocoa beans while working on the plantations, as well as to prevent them from *dirt eating*, a common practice to commit suicide and escape the horrors of slavery, but its primary function was to implement a sense of fear and speechlessness.

This violent scenario, that one cannot forget and that one still remembers, raises many questions: Who can speak? And who cannot? Why must the mouth of the Black subject be fastened? Why must she, he, it or they become silent? What could the Black subject say if its mouth were not sealed? And what would the *white* subject have to listen to?

Grada Kilomba

enslaved, and not slave. 'Enslaved' recalls the process of dehumanisation against individuals; 'Slave' recalls the state of dehumanisation as a natural identity of these individuals.

Following pages
Grada Kilomba
Table of Goods, 2017
Installation with soil, sugar, coffee beans, ground coffee, cocoa, dark chocolate, and candles
Dimensions variable
Installation view at MAAT, Lisbon, 2017
Photo: Bruno Lopes
Courtesy the artist
and Goodman Gallery

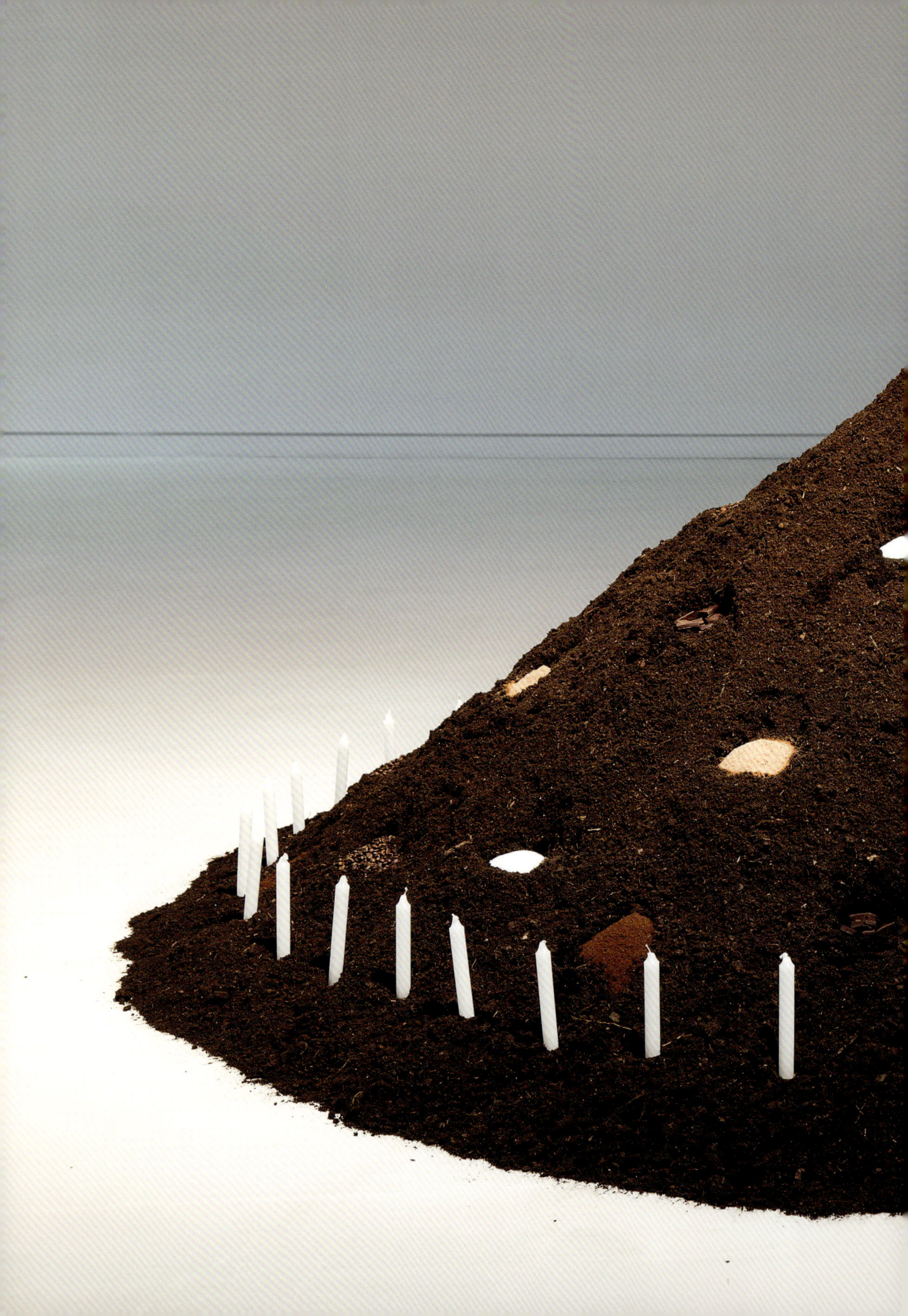

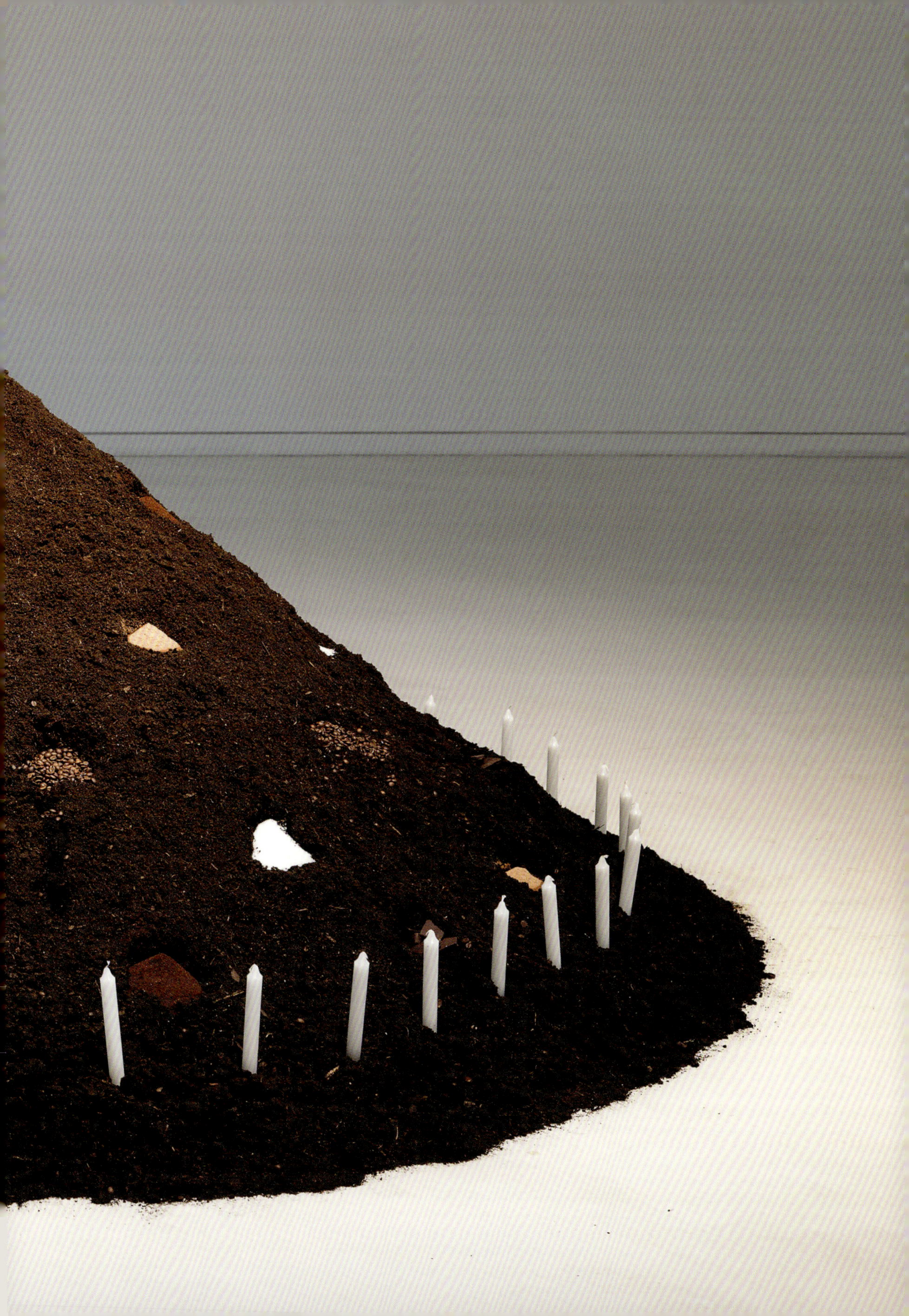

colonizer will have to listen. She/he would be forced into an uncomfortable confrontation with 'Other' truths. Truths that have been denied, repressed and kept quiet, as secrets. I do like this phrase 'quiet as it's kept.' It's an expression of the African Diasporic people that announces how someone is about to reveal what is presumed to be a secret. Secrets like slavery. Secrets like colonialism. Secrets like racism.[77]

Clearly inspired by her shrine to Anastácia, Kilomba created *Table of Goods* (2017). Comprised of soil, sugar, coffee, cocoa, dark chocolate, and wax candles, *Table of Goods* is a powerful visual reminder that the exchange of goods within our global, capitalist system is inextricably linked to the plantation economy. Turning goods that were an integral part of the slave trade into an art installation is a compelling visualization of Kilomba's observation that "the pleasures of the West are the horrors of the rest." The work expresses clearly how wealth was achieved at the cost of enslaved Africans. The candles bring to mind spiritual votives which are lit to honor ancestors, and in this case to recognize and pay homage to the enslaved individuals whose hard labor working the soil of the plantations contributed to the wealth and fortune of colonial oppressors. Kilomba's decolonial shrine is a brilliant reversal of the plantation economy. It can hardly go unnoticed that she recommodified colonial goods (sugar, coffee, cocoa, and chocolate) to create a contemporary artwork, available for sale in a limited edition of three—for the one percent.

Kilomba's groundbreaking work as a writer and theorist not only informs her own practice as an interdisciplinary artist; it's equally relevant to the work of each of the artists featured in this book. Her ongoing fight to give voice to those who have been historically silenced, her acute observations about the direct correlation between colonial history and contemporary racism, her insistence on reclaiming ownership of colonial narratives, her dismantling of still-existing colonial power structures, and every empowering step that she takes is a significant step towards completely decolonizing the future.

Writing in reference to Paul Gilroy's description of the five different ego defense mechanisms that the white subject goes through before being able to really listen, Kilomba explains that the fifth stage—reparation—is only achieved after denial, guilt, shame, and recognition have been confronted: "Reparation then means the negotiation of recognition. One negotiates reality. In this sense, it's an act of repairing the harm caused by racism by changing structures, agendas, spaces, positions, dynamics, subjective relations, vocabulary, that is, giving up privileges."[78] Perhaps most important, Kilomba doesn't discuss colonialism and racism from a detached perspective. To the contrary, her ongoing academic research involves the crucial transition from objecthood to subjecthood, an act of empowerment that ultimately provides an opportunity for the descendants of the enslaved and the millions of individuals who continue to be oppressed to find ways to heal and move forward. Digging beneath the surface of psychoanalytic theory she opens the deepest colonial wounds in an ongoing decolonial process that has the ability to change the dynamics of power both now and in the future.

The dramatic contrast between shadows and light results in intricate, undulating patterns that play cleverly with notions of visibility and invisibility. Staples are the perfect punctuation in a visual language that speaks of erasures and reversals.

Shooting as a Radical Decolonial Gesture

Sasha Huber addresses the immediate connection between the social injustices of colonial history and contemporary society through performance-based interventions, video, photography, and stapled mixed media works. Among her most iconic works is the ongoing *Shooting* series, which involves the use of an air staple gun, a tool that has clear implications as a potential weapon. This extensive body of work involves a radical decolonial gesture which effectively challenges the legitimacy of colonial power structures, while also exposing how they persist today. The series includes portraits and other images on wood and various repurposed objects, which forcefully challenges all forms of discrimination and racism. In its entirety, these works are part of an interconnected ongoing narrative that began in the past and is still being experienced in the present.

Formally speaking, variations in how light plays against the staples creates fascinating visual patterns throughout. The dramatic contrast between shadows and light results in intricate, undulating patterns that play cleverly with notions of visibility and invisibility. Staples are the perfect punctuation in a visual language that speaks of erasures and reversals. The staple-based images, particularly those executed on dark backgrounds, are reminiscent of photographic negatives, in itself a symbolic reversal. Similar to how a photographic negative is the foundation for all analog photography, yet typically tucked away in a drawer once the photograph has been printed, many of the individuals of the African diaspora who Huber pays homage to throughout her work have typically been overlooked, brushed aside, even consciously erased from Eurocentric narratives of colonial history. Here, these individuals are highly visible yet also partially hidden, thereby emphasizing the perpetuation of social imbalances that have been inherited from colonialism. These grayscale works also bring to mind the portraits of

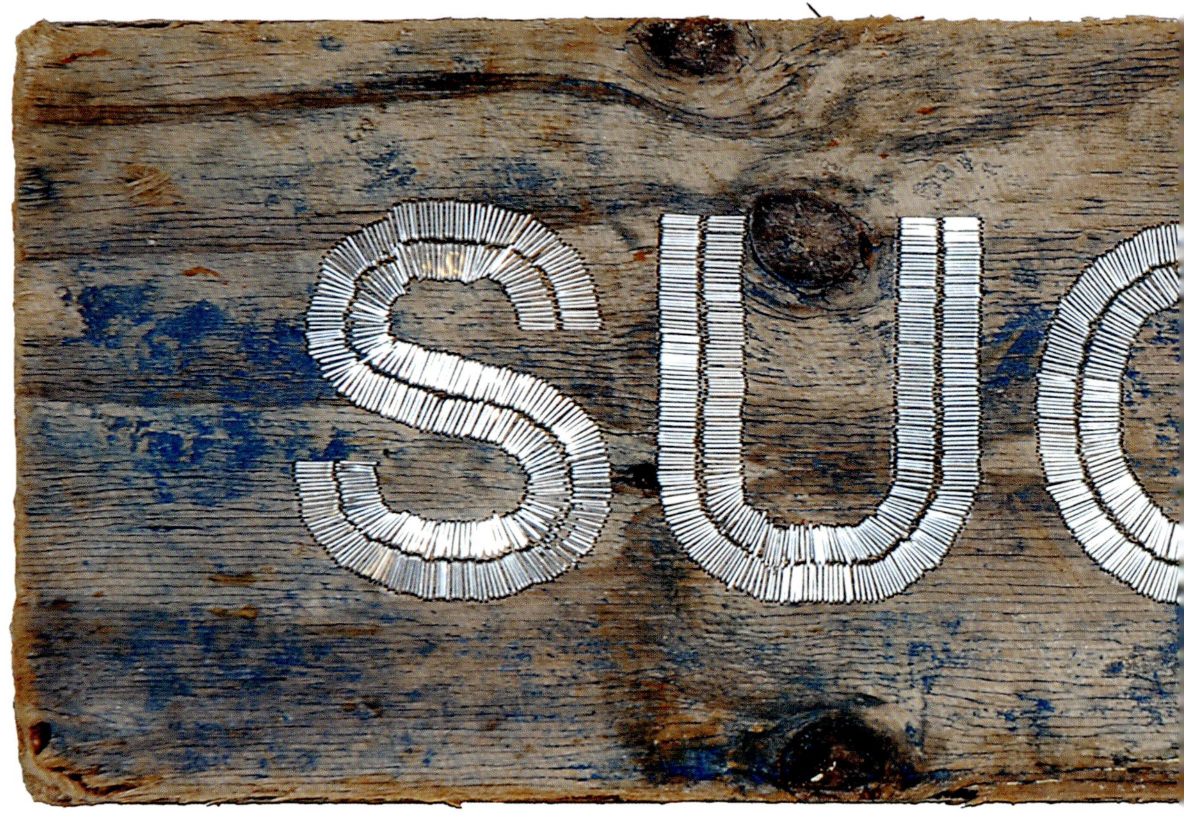

African American painter Amy Sherald, who describes her own implementation of grayscale as a measure to "exclude the idea of color as race."

As one of Sasha Huber's first works that responded to colonial history directly, her description of *Shooting Back – Reflections on Haitian Roots* provides valuable insight into her practice:

> The primary incentive for my artistic work has been the exploration of my Swiss-Haitian roots and identity via colonial history. This approach has broadened out considerably to include a range of histories and postcolonial realities. As an artist my first critical reaction to history and colonialism was to make the portrait series *Shooting Back – Reflections on Haitian Roots* (2004) depicting Christopher Columbus (1451–1506) and the Haitian dictators François 'Papa Doc' Duvalier (1907–1971) and Jean-Claude 'Baby Doc' Duvalier (1951–2014). I 'shot' their portraits on discarded plywood using a compressed-air staple gun, aware of its symbolic significance as a weapon.[79]

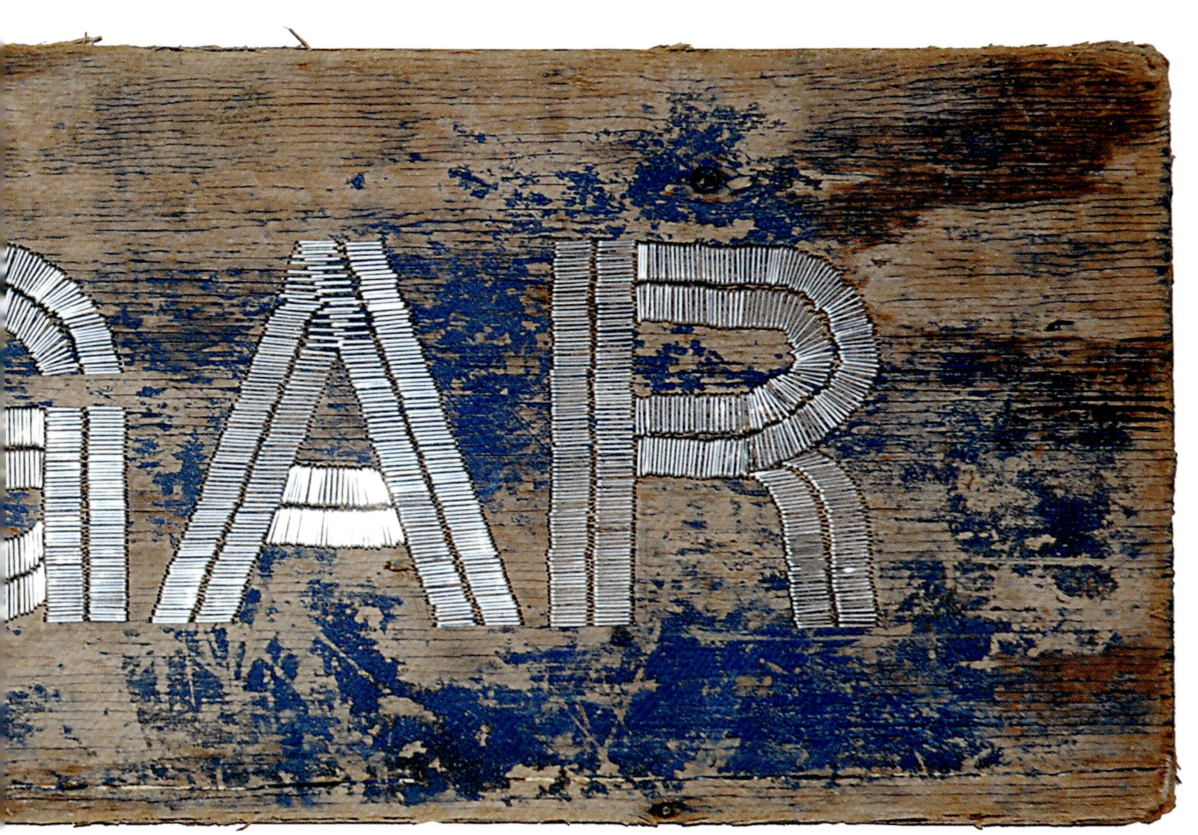

Sasha Huber
Sugar, 2007
Metal staples on
driftwood from Barbados
24 × 73.5 × 2 cm
Private Collection,
Switzerland
Photo: Sasha Huber

Following pages
Sasha Huber
Sea of the Lost, 2016
Metal staples on wood
120 × 355 cm
The Saastomoinen
Foundation Art
Collection
Photo: Ari Karttunen/
EMMA

There is a clear and logical development between *Shooting Back – Reflections on Haitian Roots* (2004) and her ongoing body of staple-based works. Both formally and thematically, it's significant that many of these works are executed on found and repurposed objects, including abandoned bits of plywood picked up on the streets of Helsinki for *Shooting Back*; a piece of driftwood from Crane Beach, Barbados for *Sugar* (2007); the in-situ window shutter of the chalet where James Baldwin spent time in Leukerbad, Switzerland for *The Firsts: James Baldwin* (2018), and a pair of burnt Dutch clogs for *Free Zwarte Piet* (2019), to name only a few examples. Huber's transformation of found objects into exquisite works of art mirrors her ongoing effort to bring hidden and untold narratives to the fore. She honors the countless individuals of the African diaspora who, despite often being left out of Eurocentric historical narratives, have played a crucial role in history.

Sea of the Lost (2016) really stands out in terms of expressing the atrocity of the Middle Passage through visual means. The nearly two hundred thousand staples required to create *Sea of the Lost* symbolize what Huber

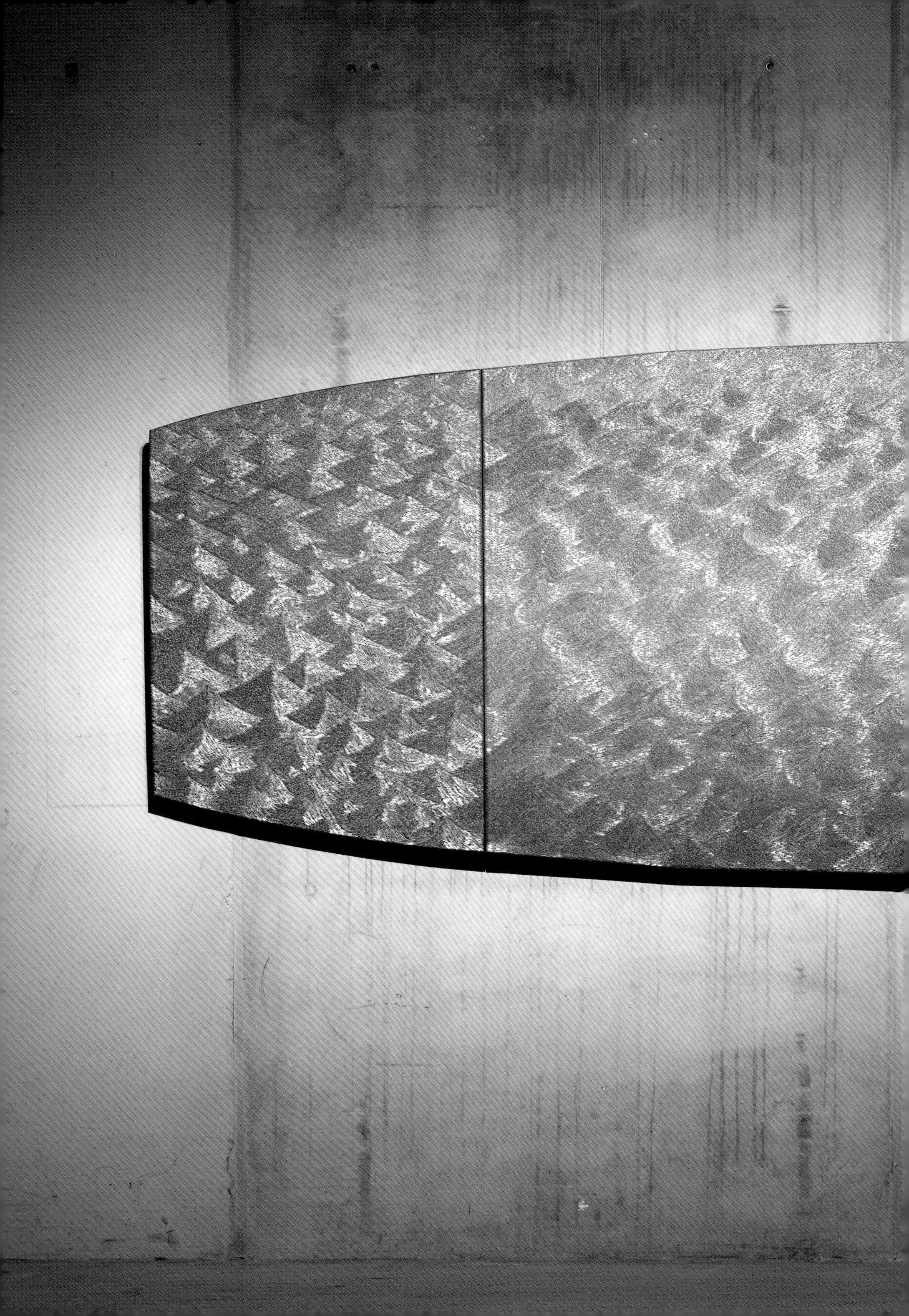

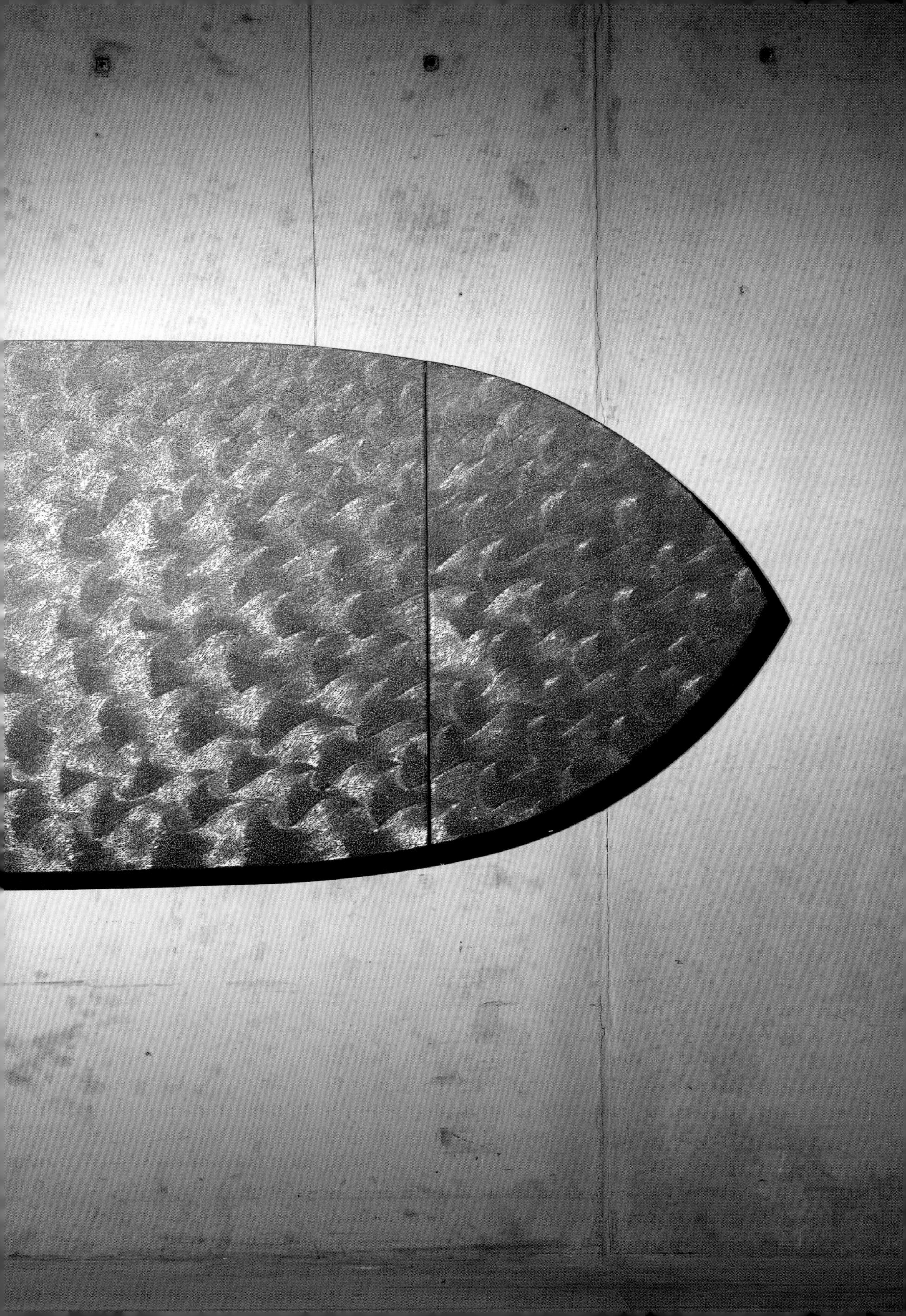

describes as "marks that go under the skin, binding a traumatic past to the present." The staples are shaped into a seemingly endless wave-like pattern that covers the entire surface, which is shaped like a ship. This gives immediate associations to the Atlantic Ocean and the Mediterranean Sea, and in turn, the topic of forced migration over these bodies of water, both past and present. Huber elaborates on some the most important details and the specifics of the accompanying portraits:

> The work commemorates the almost two million lives lost out of more than 15 million uprooted Africans who did not survive the tragic transatlantic Middle Passage. It also commemorates the thousands fleeing war-torn home countries today by crossing the Mediterranean Sea in precarious circumstances, earning it a comparison to the Middle Passage. The fleeing mothers, fathers, young adults and children are not slaves, but the precarious journey they have to go through to reach Europe resembles the undignified transit made by those who were forced to migrate during the era of the slave trade.

> As a symbol of how the life of a fleeing person who survives the passage can continue, I decided to portray the teenager and professional swimmer Yusra Mardini from Damascus, Syria. Through special circumstances I got to meet her in Berlin in June 2016. In August 2015 she and her sister Sarah decided to flee after their home was destroyed. They reached Turkey via Lebanon. In Turkey they embarked alongside 16 others on a rubber boat that was made for a maximum of seven persons. Soon after their departure the motor stopped, and the boat started to fill with water. Yusra, her sister and two other passengers who could swim decided to get into the water to push the boat. After 3.5 hours they reached Greece safely. The entire journey took them through six countries altogether and they eventually reached Berlin. Soon afterwards Yusra took up swimming again and joined a Swim club. Her dream of participating in the Olympics at some time in her life came true sooner than expected in the summer of 2016, after the Olympic committee announced the first ever Refugee Olympic Athletes Team, which she qualified to join.[80]

Sasha Huber
The Firsts: James Baldwin (1924-1987),
2018
Metal staples on window shutter
69 × 49 cm
Leukerbad, Switzerland
Photo: Siro Micheroli

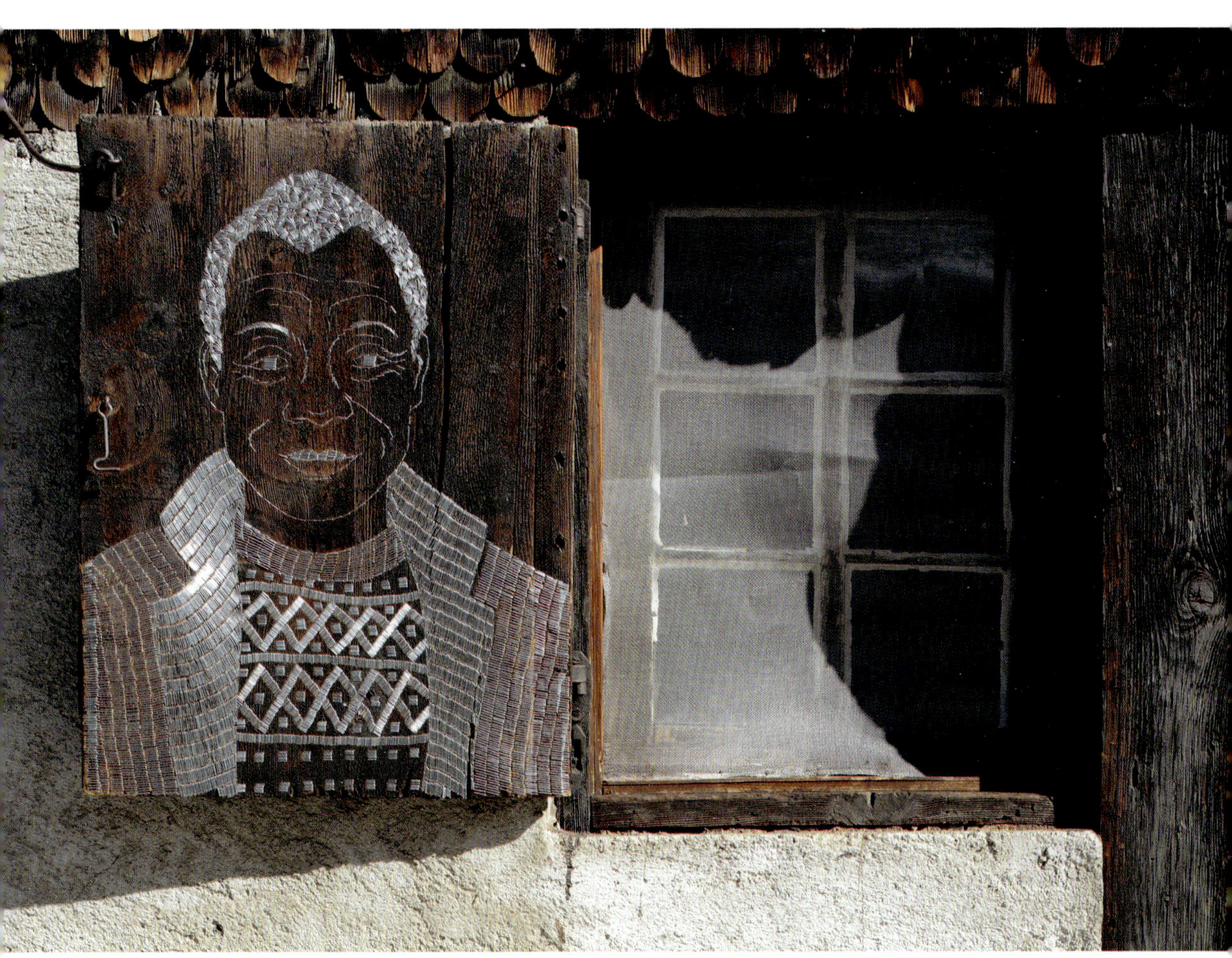

Sasha Huber
The Firsts: Rosa Emilia Clay, 2017
Metal staples on black painted acoustic board
100 × 100 cm
Private Collection
Photo: Kai Kuusisto

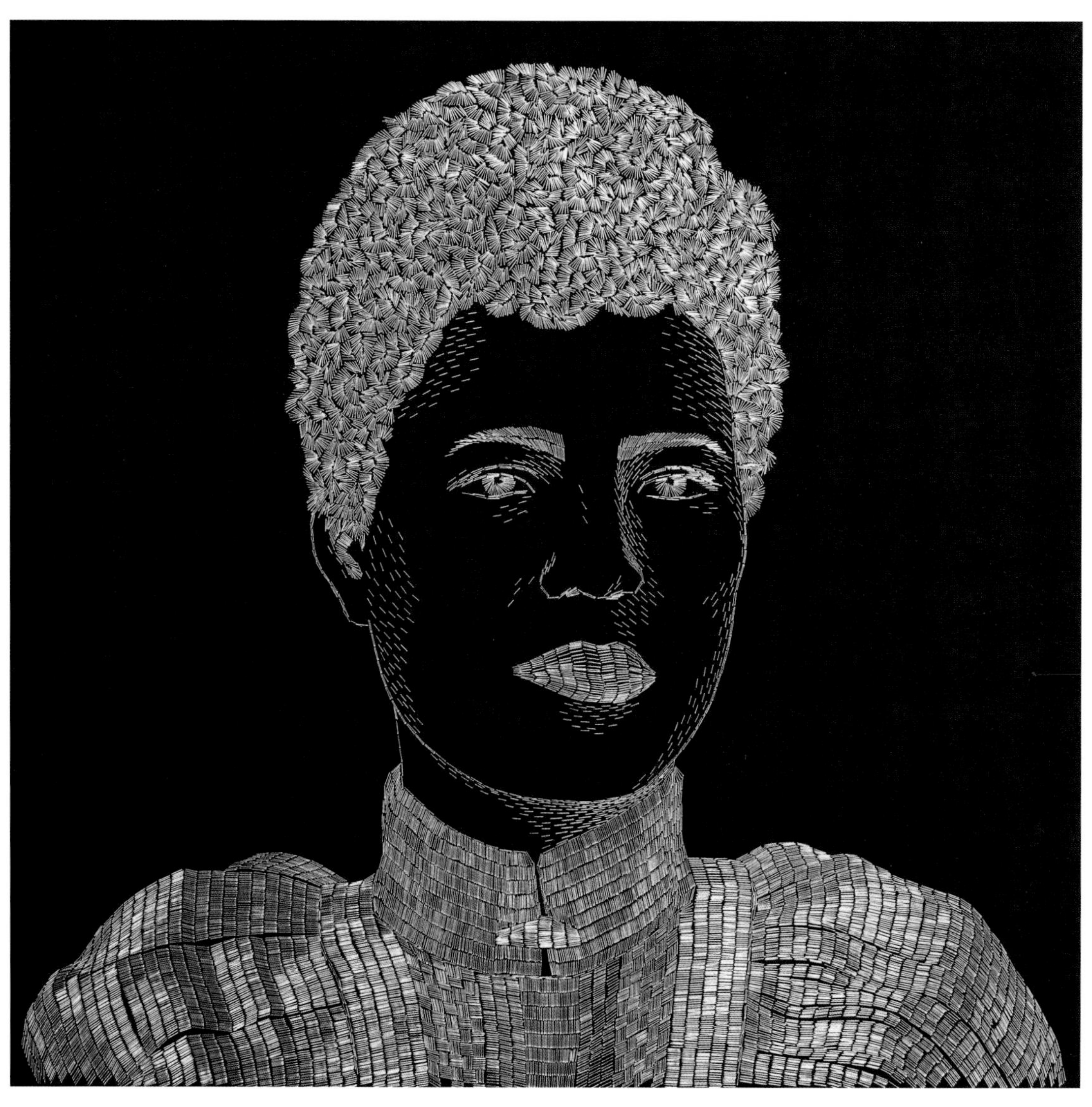

Sasha Huber
The Firsts: Edmonia Lewis, 2019
Metal staples on black painted acoustic board
100 × 100 cm
Photo: Petri Saarikko

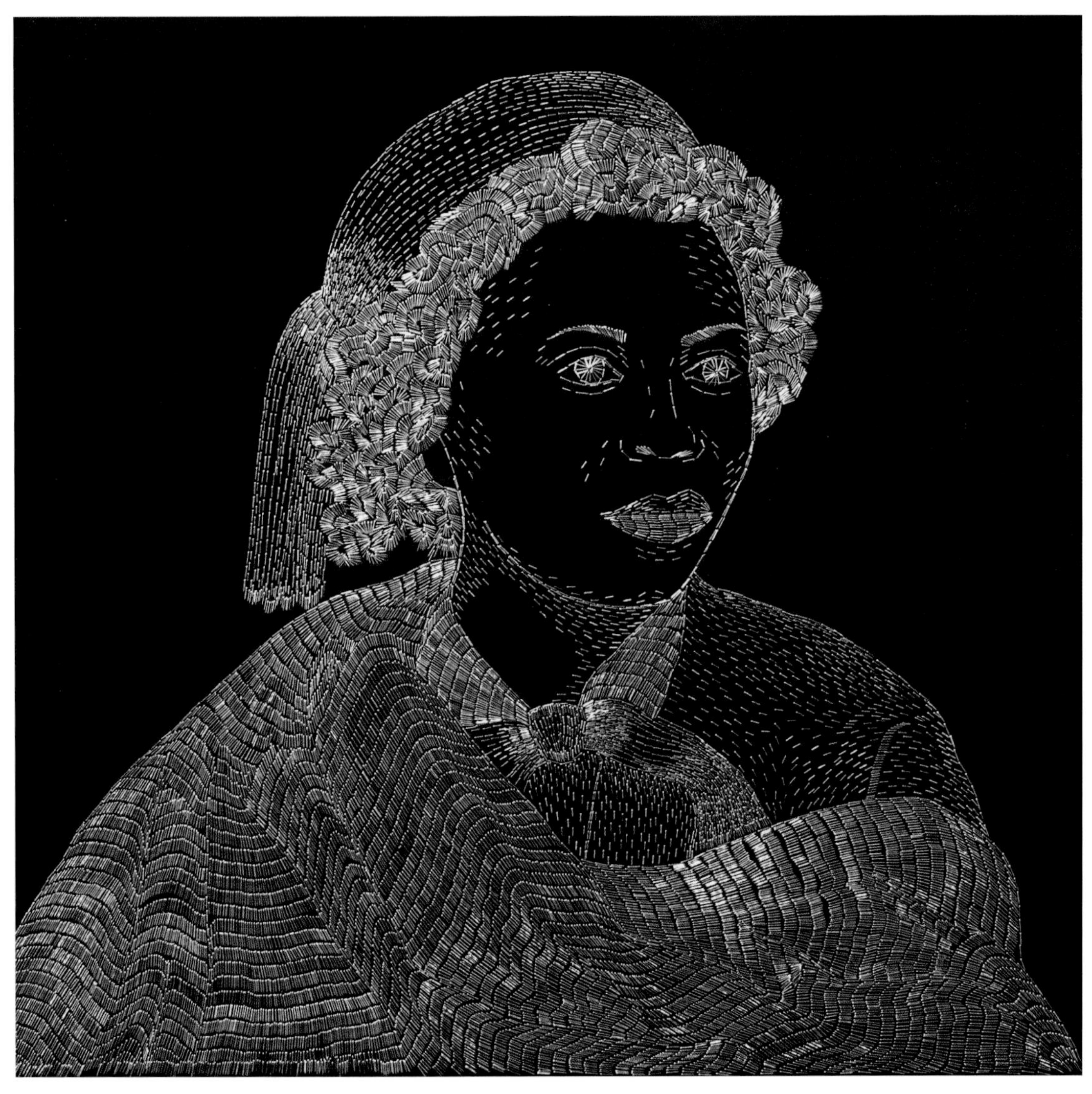

While the reference to forced migration over deep and treacherous waters is captivatingly conveyed in the wave-like patterns of the staples in *Sea of the Lost*, the work also features a series of works on paper, which are highly significant in their own right. Both the Middle Passage and the journey of migrants today involve a violent erasure of life and the loss of Black bodies in particular. While the combined symbolism of a ship and the sea, executed with metal staples on wood, evokes a clear sense of the movement of water and the journey of a ship over massive bodies of water, the rubbings are imbued with a dual symbolism as physical traces of the traces of the past. If the ship and the sea symbolize a geographic location where the atrocities of colonialism were carried out, the still unhealed wounds of colonialism—the actual burns, cuts, and scars inflicted on human beings—are hauntingly conveyed in the graphite rubbings on paper which give immediate associations to the physical marking of enslaved individuals. While the historical implications can never be erased, the sheer beauty of these decorative, abstract patterns, and the artistic process of executing these works signals a healing, memorial gesture.

In her ongoing series *The Firsts*, Huber researches historical and contemporary racism and its dehumanizing effect on individuals of the African diaspora community, with particular focus on the underrepresentation of women throughout history. As Huber describes it, this kind of suppression and silencing has come in the way of equitable societal and economic developments, which are linked directly to white supremacist thought and action.[81] *The Firsts* confronts these issues directly, and questions why it's still possible today "to be the first black person to achieve specific goals across many fields of practice."[82] *The Firsts* is also dedicated to the first individuals from the African diaspora who migrated to various European countries in the nineteenth and twentieth century. The very first portrait, completed in 2017, is of the teacher Rosa Emilia Clay (1875–1959) who migrated to Finland from Ovamboland (present-day Namibia) in 1888 with a family of missionaries. In 1899 she became the first person from the African continent to be granted Finnish citizenship. Clay ended up moving to the United States in 1904, where she became an active director of the American Community Choir and Theater, a teacher of Finnish language, and a cultural activist for the labor movement.

To date, there are three additional works in this series: *The Firsts: James Baldwin* (2018), *The Firsts: Jani Toivola* (2019), and *The Firsts: Edmonia*

Lewis (2019). Jani Toivola was Finland's first Black parliamentarian who served between 2011 and 2019, and Edmonia Lewis (1844–1907) was the first Black woman in Rome to become an internationally renowned artist. While all four portraits are noteworthy, the site-specificity of the James Baldwin portrait is particularly interesting within the wider framework of Huber's artistic practice. As hard as it might be to imagine today, Baldwin was the first Black visitor to Leukerbad, Switzerland, a small village in the Valais Alps, where he spent periods of time between 1951–53 writing his semi-autobiographical novel *Go Tell It on the Mountain*. In 2016, when Sasha Huber visited Leukerbad for the first time, she met the owner of the chalet where Baldwin had stayed and asked for permission to memorialize James Baldwin on one of the chalet's antique wooden window shutters, to which he agreed. Following approval from the James Baldwin Estate in New York, she was also allowed to bring the shutter home to her studio in Helsinki, where she completed the work before returning to Leukerbad to install the work in 2018.

Huber's beautifully executed portrait, a permanent shrine to James Baldwin, was inspired by the ubiquitous image of Baldwin accessible worldwide in photographs and films. With an unusually keen eye for meaningful details, Huber chose to portray Baldwin wearing a hand-knit wool sweater that he actually bought in Leukerbad. The geometric patterns on his sweater, the compact rows of staples which make his jacket appear three dimensional, and the delicate play of light on his curls create a stunning contrast to the weather-worn wood of the chalet. If the artistic process itself involved sweeping away the cobwebs of a sleepy alpine village, it also represents a reckoning with the ghosts of the colonial past.

Throughout John Akomfrah's films the sea is understood as the repository for all the crimes of Empire: ranging from enslaved Africans who were subjected to the Middle Passage to the contemporary version of the Middle Passage—forced migration across treacherous seas to escape dire political, social, and economic circumstances.

The Unfinished Conversation

The inexorable connection between colonial history and contemporary society is also powerfully visualized by the filmmaker John Akomfrah. His longtime engagement with Stuart Hall's intellectual legacy informs much of his work. *The Stuart Hall Project* (2013) and the accompanying three-channel video installation *The Unfinished Conversation* (2012) are unparalleled in terms of conveying Stuart Hall's thinking visually and sonically, and provide crucial insight into processes of migration, both historical and contemporary.

The Stuart Hall Project begins with the following statement: "Identities are formed at the unstable point where the unspeakable stories of subjectivity meet the narratives of history—Stuart Hall." The inclusion of Miles Davis's music, featured chronologically, is an effective artistic device that creates a clear sense of temporality that situates Stuart Hall's biography within a relevant historical context. Nothing could be more appropriate, especially considering what Stuart Hall once said, which is also captured in Akomfrah's film:

> I suppose when I was nineteen or twenty, I would say Miles Davis put his finger on my soul. The various moods of Miles Davis have matched the evolution of my own feelings. They continue to be a regret for the loss of a life that I might have lived but didn't live. I could have gone back; I could have been a Caribbean person. I'm not that anymore. I can't ever be English in the full sense, though I know and understand the British like the back of my hand. The uncertainty, the restlessness and some of the nostalgia for what cannot be is in the sound of Miles Davis's trumpet.[83]

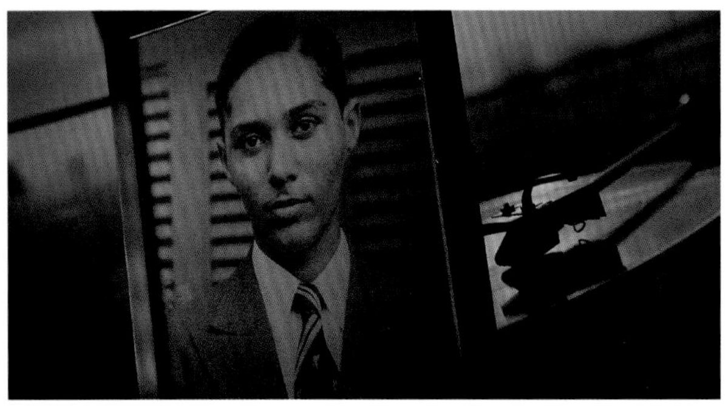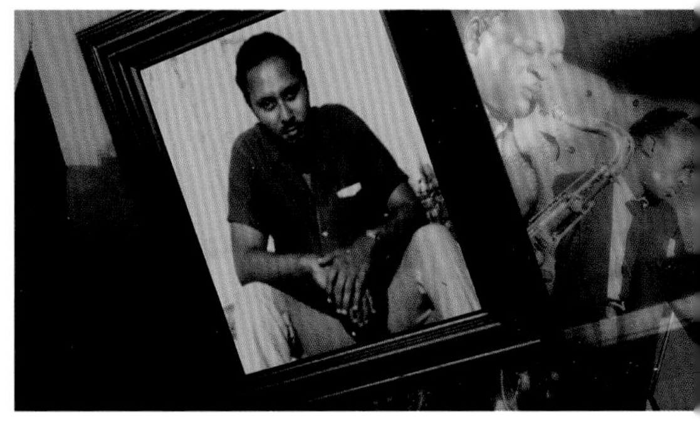

A similar uncertainty, restlessness, and even nostalgia is conveyed in *Auto da Fé* (Act of Faith) (2016), which looks at migration through the lens of religious persecution. This work, which was featured in *The Sea is History*, addresses a series of eight historical migrations over the last four hundred years, starting with the fleeing of Sephardic Jews from Catholic Brazil to Barbados. As the film develops, we are presented with disturbing stories of populations that are displaced in the name of religion, up to and including contemporary migrations from Hombori, Mali and Mosul, Iraq.

Auto da Fé begins with a torrential rainstorm at sea followed by a series of visually captivating scenes and the caption: "We Left Because They Were Burning Jews—Bahia, 1680." We are subsequently guided on an arduous journey through history, across oceans and continents. Along the way we encounter abandonment and ruin, emptiness and despair. A man and woman stroll on a desolate, storm-ridden beach; seawater threatens to destroy a collection of family photos; a desolate cemetery creates a sense of foreboding, while exterior and interior views of a mansion paint a vivid picture of a colonial space. The intense visual narrative is perfectly punctuated by the sound of thunder and rain, while respite is found in the sound of singing.

The journey continues, bringing us continuously back and forth between the West Indies and Africa, as well as France, bringing us to multiple sites of religious persecution. During the course of the film we eventually come to Martinique, Nigeria, Barbados, Côte d'Ivoire, Mali, and Iraq. Historically important dates appear on the screen, alerting us about shifts in the narrative. Spanning hundreds of years of history, from 1680 to 2015, although the costumes and the music change with each new story, the narratives remain hauntingly similar. These overlapping and entangled histories are emphasized by seamless visual transitions that transcend time and geographic location. The visual narrative is further accented by overgrown colonial structures throughout, bringing to mind the strangely poetic justice of Stuart Hall's comment regarding the implications of "the tropics reclaiming colonial buildings."[84]

An equally haunting visual narrative is conveyed in Akomfrah's three-channel video installation *Vertigo Sea* (2015). Typical of Akomfrah's films, here he combines historical documentation with BBC *Natural History Unit* footage, offset by enigmatic scenes that bring to mind the kind of existential angst typical of Henrik Ibsen. Literary references to Herman Melville's *Moby Dick* and Virginia Woolf's *To the Lighthouse* add additional layers of meaning to a mesmerizing visual essay about whaling, polar bear hunting, and environmental issues. However, *Vertigo Sea* is more than a spectacular visual narrative about humanity's conflicted relationship with the ecosystem and the fate of endangered animals in the Arctic Circle; it's a story of epic proportions that is as poetic as it is cautionary. The acted sequences are filmed in a manner that emphasizes a sense of human loss and longing, further accentuated by visual references to the passage of time. The narrative relates as much to human emotions as the damage that humans cause. Documentary footage from the high seas and images of whaling and polar bear hunting in the Arctic are set against overwhelmingly beautiful scenes from nature, resulting in a powerful tale about humanity and its relationship to the sea conveyed in a timeless narrative that balances perfectly between fact, fiction, history, and contemporaneity.

Filmed on the Isle of Skye, the Faroe Islands, and Northern Norway, *Vertigo Sea* combines visual references to colonial history with passages of

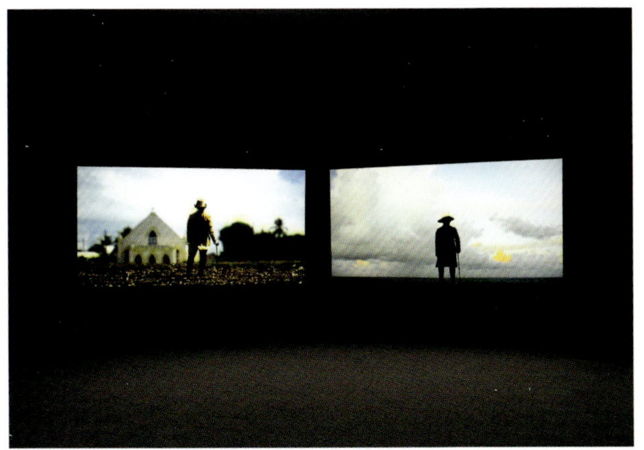
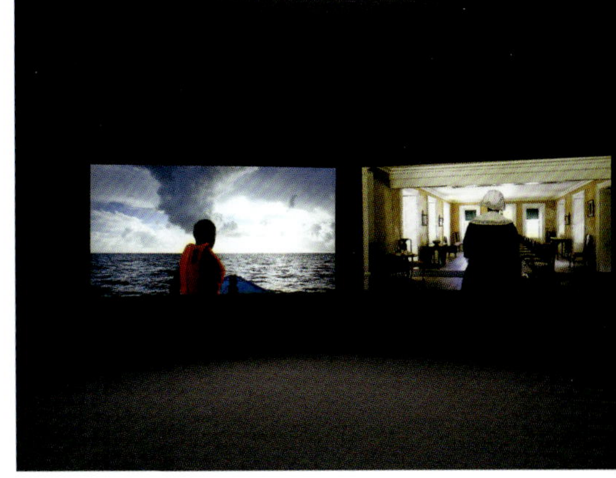

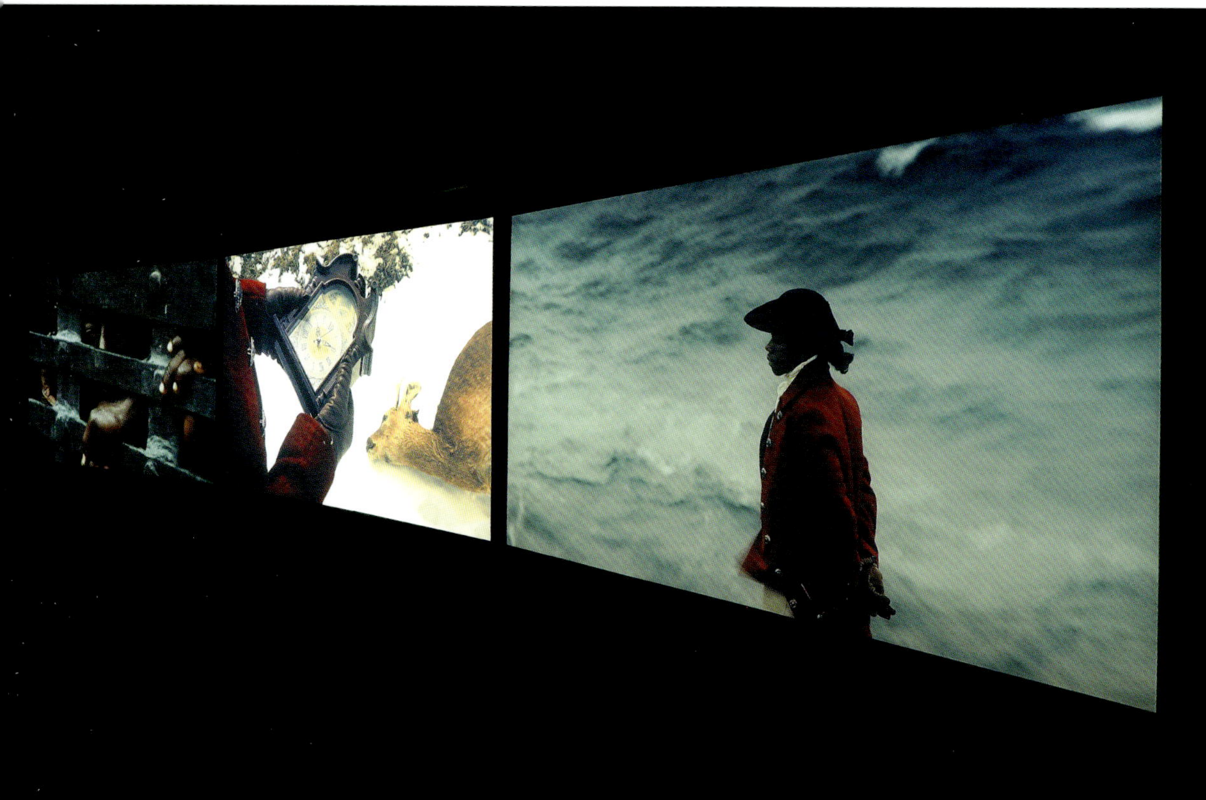

text. Scenes of characters dressed in eighteenth-century European clothing are punctuated by literary quotes, including passages from the first-person narrative of Olaudah Equiano, the West African-born survivor of the transatlantic passage who played a vital role in the British abolitionist movement. Equiano, who also participated in colonial expeditions to the Arctic and Central America, is perhaps most widely recognized for his book *The Interesting Narrative of the Life of Olaudah Equiano, or Gustavus Vassa, the African* (1789).

As a detailed first-hand account of the Middle Passage written by an enslaved African who later managed to purchase his freedom, the significance of Equiano's autobiography cannot be understated. Although some scholars have questioned whether Equiano was actually born in Africa, there is no denying the importance of his book, particularly at the time, in terms of raising awareness about the horrors of the slave trade. Any discussion that raises doubt about the true origins of an enslaved individual who subsequently acquired his freedom, wrote a best-selling book, and went on to fight against slavery comes across as a misguided attempt to discredit and

John Akomfrah
Vertigo Sea, 2015
Three-channel video
installation, HD color,
7.1 surround sound
48 minutes 30 seconds
© Smoking Dogs Films
Courtesy the artist
and Lisson Gallery

thereby silence Equiano's voice. Fittingly, carefully selected passages from Equiano's book are juxtaposed with scenes of an actor playing the role of Equiano. He is impeccably dressed and comes across as brave and powerful standing alone in the rugged arctic landscape.

Throughout John Akomfrah's films the sea is understood as the repository for all the crimes of Empire: ranging from enslaved Africans who were subjected to the Middle Passage to the contemporary version of the Middle Passage—forced migration across treacherous seas to escape dire political, social, and economic circumstances. During an artist talk about *Vertigo Sea* in conjunction with his solo exhibition at Talbot Rice Gallery, University of Edinburgh (2017–18), Akomfrah described the journey across different histories and geographies as an attempt to reboot colonial histories. Prior to making the film, Akomfrah saw a young Nigerian migrant on television who described being capsized at sea. This immediately reminded him of Olaudah Equiano's description of his own experience as a displaced African. With a contagious level of laughter and excitement, Akomfrah exclaims that he believes in ghosts and heeds their call. If his films are haunted by the ghosts of colonialism, he also knows exactly how to exorcise those demons. He describes the challenge of getting these figures (animals and human beings) to talk to one another, and it all makes perfect sense. *Vertigo Sea* is about ghosts talking to each other, sharing a language of love and solidarity. The sea is the history that binds them together. Through the seamless weaving of a narrative that extends through time and across geographies, Akomfrah creates powerful decolonial counter-narratives that rightfully position Black subjects front and center.

Following pages
John Akomfrah
Vertigo Sea, 2015
Film still

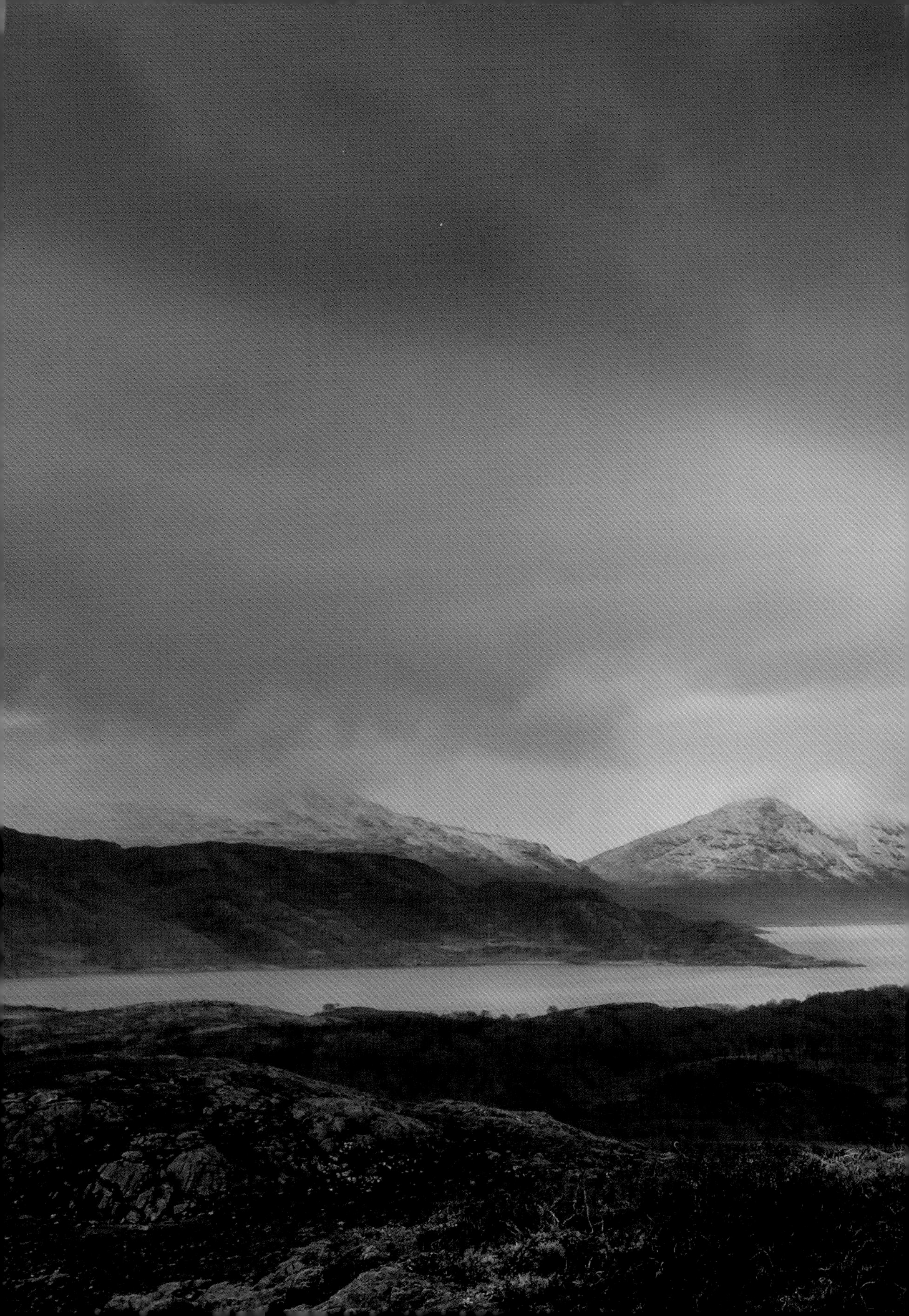

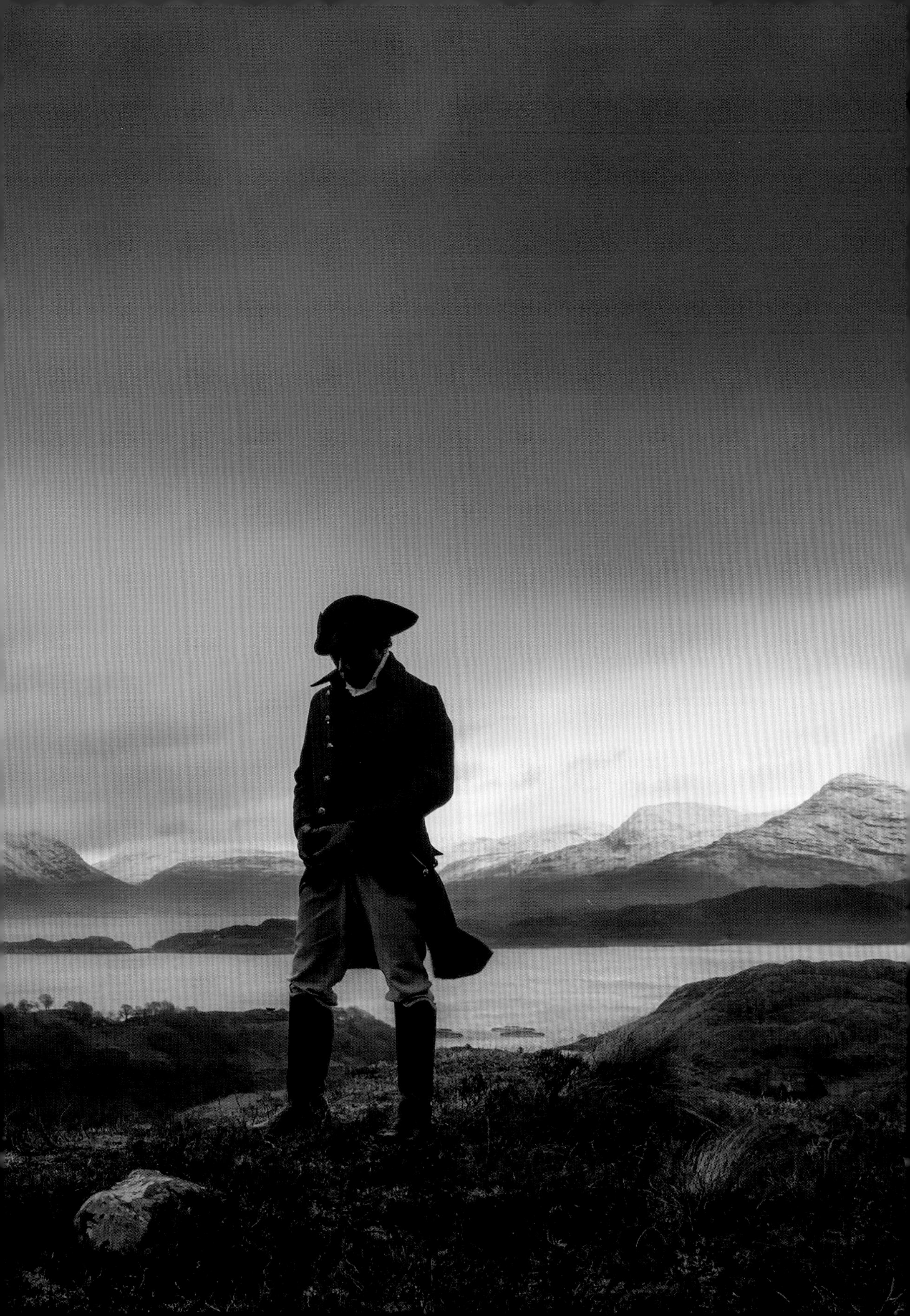

*For all the colonial statues that need
to be removed, there are equally
as many contemporary artists whose
decolonial perspectives could fill
those spaces, and who truly deserve
recognition and visibility.*

Healing from the Past
and Reimagining the Future

At a time when forced migration is affecting the lives of an ever-increasing number of individuals worldwide, the ongoing question is how contemporary artists can address the topic of displacement in ways that can contribute to increased awareness, tolerance, and understanding. As more and more people become aware of the factors which lead to forced migration, as well as the numerous social, cultural, and economic injustices experienced by people of color in terms of systemic and everyday racism, it seems that we are finally on the brink of real change. Although there is still a lot of work to be done, it's a significant step in the right direction that there is increased consciousness about the direct connection between colonial history and the social injustices of our time.

As the artists featured in this book make abundantly clear, the colonial past cannot be ignored, dismissed, or swept aside. This is precisely why we are witnessing historical statues and monuments being toppled down worldwide. As Achille Mbembe describes it in *Critique of Black Reason*, "The role of colonial statues and monuments is to resurrect, in the present, those who during their own lifetimes had threatened Blacks with the sword and with death. The statues function as rituals that conjure dead men in whose eyes Black humanity counted for nothing, which was reason enough for their lack of scruples at spilling Black blood over a trifle."[85] In the United States, the primary focus has been on the dismantling of Confederate statues and monuments, initially witnessed as a sign of protest against the brutal murder of George Floyd. Statues that honor those who were involved in slavery and colonization, such as Robert E. Lee and Christopher Columbus, are finally being taken down once and for all. Clearly, those who supported slavery and who actively fought against the abolition of slavery have no rightful place on a pedestal.

Europe, with its own colonial history, has witnessed the rapid demise of statues honoring colonial monsters such as Edward Colston and Leopold II. On both sides of the Atlantic, the names of streets, neighborhoods, military bases, and institutions are also in the process of being questioned and renamed. Although dismantling statues and renaming sites are mostly symbolic actions, real and lasting change can and will happen through decolonial thinking and actions. In Bristol, Richard Colston's statue wasn't only taken down, it was thrown into the harbor in a powerful act of resistance which makes it abundantly clear that these decolonial interventions won't stop until real change has occurred. In various cities throughout Belgium, statues of King Leopold II have been painted over, tagged, and removed, and there are countless others whose day of reckoning has finally come.

The slightly lesser-known individuals who were involved in the Danish-Norwegian slave trade deserve no exception from the decolonial actions that are currently taking place. And yet, what strikes me about the ongoing debate in Norway about the removal of racist statues is the general lack of interest in achieving a nuanced discussion. Norwegians who are categorically against the toppling of statues have been given noticeably more media coverage, free to voice their opinions in entire newspaper columns with simplistic argumentation that often borders on mockery, while those who attempt to argue against the legitimacy of statues that honor colonialists and racists, are typically silenced and dismissed as having no understanding of history. As a result, the debate has been reduced to an extremely polarized either/or discussion. Nearly everyone involved is thereby reduced to being either antiracist (and presumably a vandal who enjoys tearing down statues for the fun of it) or a law-abiding citizen who is respectful of history (with the argument that taking down statues is an erasure of history). Of course, the real erasure is the one that involves silencing the voices of those who have been left out of Western historical narratives.

In Bergen there is an entire neighborhood, Møhlenpris, named after the slave trader Jørgen Thormøhlen. There is also a painting, hanging on one of the walls of the City Council in Bergen, painted by Mathias Blumenthal entitled *Justitia Majestata* (1762) depicting the goddess of justice standing on the back of a dark-skinned individual. It doesn't help that this individual turns out to be Tisiphone, one of the Furies from Greek mythology. It's quite clear that there will be no peace in relation to these matters until

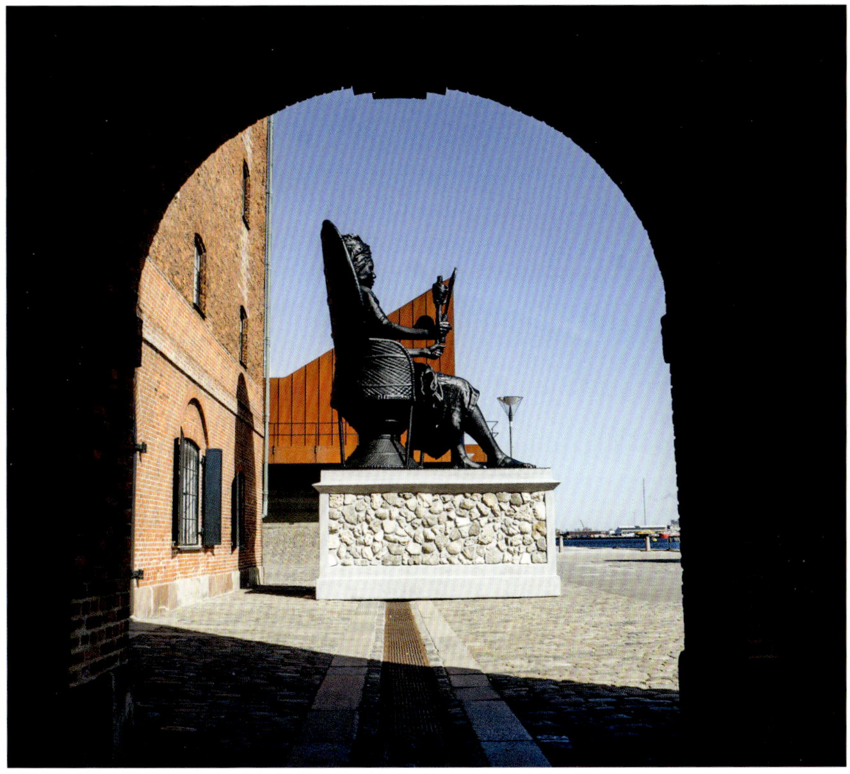

justice has truly been served. While the average Norwegian probably isn't aware of these details, hopefully more people will eventually understand why Møhlenpris must be renamed and why Blumenthal's painting should be transferred to a museum where it can be properly contextualized.

We are at a time in history when decolonial strategies in contemporary art are more important than ever. When it comes to taking down colonial and racist statues, there are plenty of constructive solutions. These range from adding informative plaques to statues, or moving them to museum collections where they can be properly contextualized, to more innovative gestures such as inviting artists to create decolonial interventions in dialog with existing statues or commissioning artists to create completely new works that pay homage to those who fought against slavery and colonial rule. It's as simple as that. For all the colonial statues that need to be removed, there are equally as many contemporary artists whose decolonial perspectives could fill those spaces, and who truly deserve recognition and visibility. Jeannette Ehlers's and La Vaughn Belle's *I Am Queen Mary* is a perfect example. Hew Locke's *Patriots* series, a photo series whereby he intervenes and re-interprets colonial monuments, could also be beautifully executed in real life.

At best, artistic interventions that question the legitimacy of colonial statues and monuments have the potential to raise consciousness while also signaling hope for the future through healing gestures. For instance, Dominican artist Joiri Minaya's interventions involve wrapping colonial statues in tropical print fabrics, as seen in her bold redressing of statues of Juan Ponce de León and Christopher Columbus in Miami (2019). Her most recent intervention *Encubrimiento* (Concealment) (2021) is a thoughtful reimagining of the statue of Christopher Columbus situated in the central square of the colonial historic district of Santo Domingo. These are radical and timely gestures whereby she strips colonizers of their power by playing cleverly with notions of visibility and invisibility. She effectively erases visible traces of colonialism from contemporary space, replacing them with colorful, flamboyant interventions. From a decolonial perspective, these works achieve what Achille Mbembe pinpoints as the primary function of art, which is "to confuse and mimic original forms and appearances."[86] Minaya literally exposes the colonial past by covering it up, while her specific choice of patterned fabric highlights the sociopolitical underpinnings of the work. As she describes it:

> In 2019, I started designing my own version of 'tropical' patterns, highlighting plants that as opposed to being merely decorative, were also culturally meaningful and had a rich history to Native and Black people of the Americas and the Caribbean. I've been particularly drawn to species that relate to (hi)stories of resistance, plants that symbolize the resilience and hope of the Caribbean people in the face of hardship and adversities, flora that speaks of transformation and healing, highlighting stories of survival but also speaking of continuity, nurture, solace and spiritual strength.[87]

As for commissioning completely new monuments, Kehinde Wiley's statue *Rumors of War* is a stellar example. First shown temporarily in Times Square, it now stands permanently in front of the Virginia Museum of Fine Arts, in empowering contrast to the remaining Confederate monuments still on display along Monument Avenue in Richmond, Virginia. These kinds of decolonial monuments have real potential for making a long-lasting sociopolitical impact and there are many, many more simply waiting to be commissioned. By now it should be clear that the only way to ensure that history is not erased, is not by preserving colonial monuments, it's by thinking consciously and constructively about viable alternatives that will open people's minds to decolonial thinking and increase general awareness about the direct link between slavery and the continued prevalence of racism and social injustice throughout the world.

Few have written more poignantly about slavery and the transatlantic slave route than Saidiya Hartman. Her research involves a careful examining of enslaved people and their descendants, an approach which she describes as troubling the line between history and imagination. Hartman tells a very personal account of her journey to Ghana in search of her own ancestral routes in *Lose Your Mother: A Journey Along the Atlantic Slave Route*. She stands alone in terms of how she recounts the horrific details of the slave trade, told with precision and introspection in the captivating language of a true storyteller. Similar to all the artists featured in this book, Hartman makes it abundantly clear why colonialism cannot be dismissed as part of the past:

> The past is neither inert nor given. The stories we tell about *what happened then*, the correspondences we discern between today and times past, and the ethical and political stakes of these stories redound in the present. If slavery feels proximate rather than remote and freedom seems increasingly elusive, this has everything to do with our own dark times. If the ghost of slavery still haunts our present, it is because we are still looking for an exit from the prison.[88]

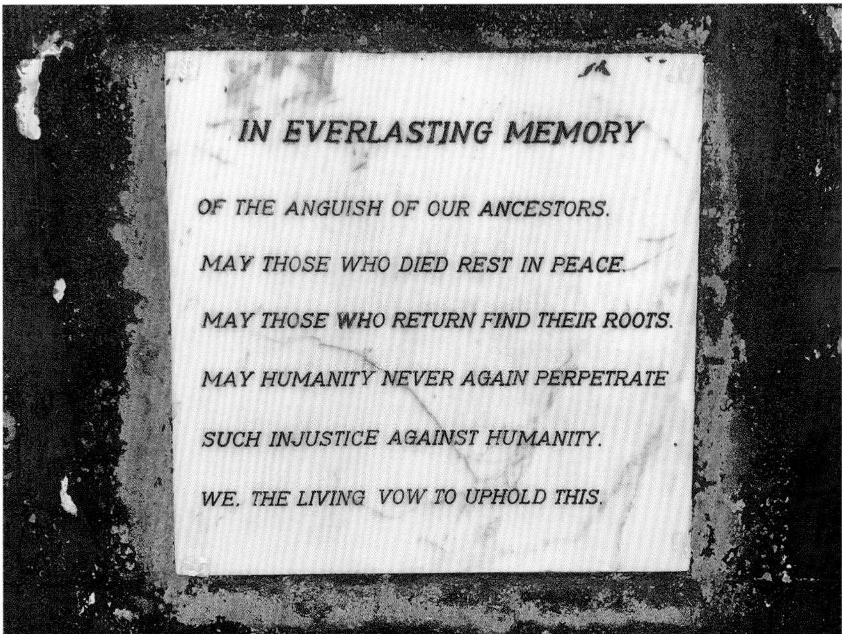

Commemorative plaque
at Elmina Castle, Ghana
Photo: Selene Wendt

Notes

Introduction

[1] Temi Odumosu, Lill-Ann Körber, and Mathias Danbolt are a few of the scholars who are at the forefront of decolonial research in Scandinavia.
[2] Norway was under Danish rule from 1537 and gained independence from Denmark in 1814, coinciding with Norway's union with Sweden.
[3] Stuart Hall, *Through the Prism*, 278–79, cited in David Scott, *Stuart Hall's Voice* (Durham: Duke University Press, 2017), 56.

The Sea is History

[4] Stuart Hall with Bill Schwarz, *Familiar Stranger* (London: Penguin Random House, 2017), 248.
[5] Hall, *Familiar Stranger*, 140–41.
[6] Manthia Diawara, artist statement cited from an email exchange.
[7] Diawara, artist statement.
[8] Manthia Diawara, *An Opera of the World: A Remake of Bintou Wéré, An Opera of the Sahel*, featured in Koulsy Lamko, *Bintou Wéré: African Opera* (Amsterdam: Prince Claus Fund, 2017).
[9] Hall, *Familiar Stranger*, 21.
[10] Hall, 140.

Listening to the Echoes of the South Atlantic

[11] Paul Gilroy, *The Black Atlantic: Modernity and Double Consciousness* (London: Verso, 1993), 14.
[12] Édouard Glissant, *Poetics of Relation*, trans. Betsy Wing (Ann Arbor: The University of Michigan Press, 1997), 73.
[13] Édouard Glissant, *Poétique de la Relation* (Paris: Éditions Gallimard, 1991), 107. Author's translation.
[14] Glissant, *Poetics of Relation*, 159.

From Africa to the West Indies on Danish-Norwegian Slave Ships

[15] Tranquebar was sold to British East India Company in 1845.
[16] Øystein Rian, *Ove Gjedde i Norsk biografisk leksikon* ("Ove Gjedde" in Norwegian Biographical Encyclopedia), published February 13, 2009, https://nbl.snl.no/Ove_Gjedde. Author's translation.
[17] *Ulefos Jernværk i Store norske leksikon* ("Ulefos Jernværk" in Great Norwegian Encyclopedia), last updated September 24, 2019, https://snl.no/Ulefos_Jernværk. Author's translation.
[18] For a general overview of Denmark-Norway's colonial ties to West Africa and the West Indies, the most comprehensive and reliable source for information in English is the Danish National Archives, made accessible online in 2017, https://www.virgin-islands-history.org/en/search-the-records/.
[19] The Christiansborg Archaeological Heritage Project is led by Rachel Ama Asaa Engmann, a descendant of a Danish governor and his wife from the local Ga ethnic group. Relationships between Ga women and European men were quite common, as thoroughly researched and documented in Carina E. Ray's book, *Crossing the Color Line* (Athens: Ohio University Press, 2015).
[20] Rachel Ama Asaa Engmann, "Slavers in the family: what a castle in Accra reveals about Ghana's history," The Conversation, published November 25, 2018, https://theconversation.com/slavers-in-the-family-what-a-castle-in-accra-reveals-about-ghanas-history-104172.
[21] Christiansborg Archaeological Heritage Project, "The History of Christiansborg Castle," accessed August 5, 2019, https://christiansborgarchaeologicalheritageproject.org/history/.
[22] Catherine Roth, "Cape Coast Castle (1652-)," Black Past, published December 2, 2009, https://www.blackpast.org/global-african-history/cape-coast-castle/.
[23] The Danish National Archives, "The Danish West-Indies: Trading Companies in the West Indies," accessed May 5, 2019, https://www.virgin-islands-history.org/en/history/trade-and-shipping/trading-companies-in-the-west-indies/.

24 Niels Brimnes, "Vestindisk-Guineisk Kompagni 1671-1754," Danmarkshistorien ("The Danish West-India and Guinea Company" in Denmark's History), Aarhus University, accessed May 5, 2019, https://danmarks historien.dk/leksikon-og-kilder/vis/materiale/vestindisk-guineisk-kompagni/. Author's translation.

25 The Danish National Archives, "The Danish West-Indies: The voyage to a life as a slave," accessed May 5, 2019, https://www.virgin-islands-history.org/en/history/trade-and-shipping/the-voyage-to-a-life-as-a-slave/.

26 "The Danish West-Indies: The voyages across the Atlantic," in the *Danish National Archives*, accessed May 5, 2019, https://www.virgin-islands-history.org/en/history/trade-and-shipping/the-voyages-across-the-atlantic/.

27 Anders Bjarne Fossen, *Jørgen Thormøhlen* i *Norsk biografisk leksikon* ("Jørgen Thormøhlen" in Norwegian Biographical Encyclopedia), published February 13, 2009, https://nbl.snl.no/Jørgen_Thormøhlen. Author's translation.

28 Ingvild Velure, *Slaveskipet Fredensborg* i *Norges historie* ("The Slave Ship Fredensborg" in Norwegian History), University of Oslo, published January 20, 2020, last updated October 21, 2020, https://www.norgeshistorie.no/enevelde/1251_slaveskipet-fredensborg-.html. Author's translation.

29 Leif Svalesen was one of the three divers who discovered the shipwreck in 1974 and dedicated himself to researching and documenting the history of *Fredensborg* during his lifetime.

I Am Queen Mary
30 Jeannette Ehlers and La Vaughn Belle, artist statement, accessed April 23, 2020, https://www.iamqueenmary.com.

31 In *Whip it Good*, Jeannette Ehlers reenacts one of the brutal punishment methods used during slavery. By using the same method on a white canvas, she creates a personal and simple act of striking back. The performance was first presented for BE.BOP 13 in Berlin and at Ballhaus Naunynstrasse in 2013, and later recreated as a video piece at Vestindisk Pakhus (West Indian Warehouse) in Copenhagen.

Occupying Colonial Space
32 Jeannette Ehlers, artist statement, accessed March 3, 2020, http://www.jeannetteehlers.dk.

33 Fred Moten, *In the Break: The Aesthetics of the Black Radical Tradition* (Minneapolis: University of Minnesota Press, 2003), 223.

34 The Danish National Archives, "The Danish West-Indies: Peter von Scholten and the journey to emancipation," accessed March 22, 2020, https://www.virgin-islands-history.org/en/history/fates/peter-von-scholten-and-the-journey-to-emancipation/.

35 The Danish National Archives, "The Danish West-Indies: The slave rebellion on St. Croix and Emancipation," accessed March 22, 2020, https://www.virgin-islands-history.org/en/timeline/the-slave-rebellion-on-st-croix-and-emancipation/.

36 Martin Luther King Jr., audio recording of speech, accessed March 22, 2020, https://archive.org/details/MLKDream.

The Story of Venus Johannes
37 George F. Tyson, Virgin Islands Social History Associates, *St. Croix African Roots Project*, accessed March 30, 2020, https://www.ft.dk/samling/20091/almdel/KUU/bilag/27/747359.pdf.

38 Moten, *In the Break*, 22.

Fragments of a Shared Colonial History
39 La Vaughn Belle, artist statement, accessed June 30, 2020, http://www.lavaughnbelle.com.

40 Belle, artist statement.

41 Frederik VI (1768–1839) was king of the dual monarchy of Denmark-Norway between 1808 and 1814 and continued as king of Denmark until 1839.

42 Adapted from Belle, artist statement.

Building a Bridge Across the Atlantic
43 Temi Odumosu, "Spiritual Diaspora
in Montage: This Particular Masquerade
Unmasked," in *BAT: Bridging Art + Text*, edited
by Michelle Eistrup and Annemari Brogaard
Clausen (Copenhagen: Hurricane Publishing,
2017), 15–20.
44 Eistrup and Brogaard Clausen, *BAT*, VII.
45 Currently known as The Historical Museum,
which is part of the Museum of Cultural History
at the University of Oslo.
46 Espen Wæhle, "Entrepreneurs in the Congo?,"
University of Bergen, published June 24, 2014,
https://www.uib.no/en/rg/.colonialtimes/
78215/entrepreneurs-congo.

The Past is Present
47 Conversation between Édouard Glissant
and Manthia Diawara featured in Diawara's film
Édouard Glissant: One World in Relation (2009).
48 Glissant, *Poetics of Relation*, 35.
49 Édouard Glissant, *Traité du Tout-Monde* (Paris:
Éditions Gallimard, 1997), 116. Author's
translation.
50 Celeste Hamilton Dennis, *MS Magazine*.
Cited from an interview with Grace Aneiza Ali
about the exhibition *Women's Work*, which
featured work by Sama Alshaibi, María
Magdalena Campos-Pons, Suchitra Mattai,
Miora Rajaonary, and Ming Smith, "The Ms. Q&A:
How Curator Grace Aneiza Ali is Reimagining
'Women's Work'," published July 22, 2019,
https://msmagazine.com/2019/07/22/
the-ms-qa-how-curator-grace-aneiza-ali-is-
reimagining-womens-work-as-art-activism/.
51 Suchitra Mattai, artist statement, accessed
April 20, 2020, http://www.suchitramattaiart.com.

The Sound of the Black Atlantic
52 Alberta Whittle, *You Can Never Touch
the Same Water Twice* (UK/Barbados, 2017).
53 For a more detailed account of Caribbean
immigration to the UK please see Linda
McDowell, *How Caribbean migrants helped to
rebuild Britain*, British Library, published October
4, 2018, https://www.bl.uk/windrush/articles/
how-caribbean-migrants-rebuilt-britain#.
54 For an overview of the 2018 Windrush

Scandal please see BBC, *Windrush generation:
Who are they and why are they facing problems?*,
published July 31, 2020, https://www.bbc.com/
news/uk-43782241.
55 While the reference to rubber production is
very specific, linking rubber manufacture in
Scotland with Caribbean and African regiments
who fought for the UK in World War I and World
War II, it also has wider implications in terms of
what Whittle refers to as "an exploitation of
colonial subjects". North British Rubber
Company profited from the production of rubber
wellington boots in trench warfare. The boots
connect with the people who were fighting the
trenches, which includes Africans and West
Indians.
56 Alberta Whittle, artist statement, accessed
April 20, 2020, https://www.albertawhittle.com.
57 Whittle, artist statement.
58 Whittle.

A Seat at the Table
59 BE.BOP. was established to tackle central
questions on Black European citizenship within
global affairs. BE.BOP. directly confronts colonial
legacies and continuities with artistic strategies
that enable the retelling of such violent histories.
60 Patricia Kaersenhout, artist statement,
accessed May 5, 2020, https://www.
pkaersenhout.com.
61 Teaching American History, "Many Thousand
Gone: Jubilee Singers 1872," accessed June 4,
2020, https://teachingamericanhistory.org/
library/document/many-thousand-gone/.
62 W. E. B. Du Bois, *The Souls of Black Folk*
(New York: Bantam, 1989), 198. First published
1903.
63 Among the thirty-nine seats at Judy Chicago's
table, in addition to Sojourner Truth and Susan
B. Anthony, the only two African-Americans,
there were only six BIPOC participants, including
Hypatia, Hatshepsut, Sacajawea, Ishtar, Kali, and
Aspasia.
64 Sojourner Truth, born Isabella Baumfree,
was recognized as one of the first people
to identify the similarities between the
struggles of black slaves and the struggles
of women.

As an abolitionist and suffragist, she was a powerful force in the fight for justice and equality for both African Americans and women in the U.S. See the Brooklyn Museum website, "Sojourner Truth," accessed May 2, 2020, https://www.brooklynmuseum.org/eascfa/dinner_party/place_settings/sojourner_truth.

[65] Susan B. Anthony's life and work offer a glimpse into the extraordinary events of both the abolitionist movement and the women's suffrage movement in the late nineteenth century. Anthony was the face of the American suffrage movement and one of its primary organizers. Her actions contributed to significant progress in the inclusion of women in the United States political process. Susan B. Anthony's place setting at The Dinner Party represents Judy Chicago's belief in the activist's position as "queen of the table" (Judy Chicago, *The Dinner Party: A Symbol of our Heritage*, 89. Hamburg: Anchor Academic Publishing, 1979). See the Brooklyn Museum website, "Susan B. Anthony," accessed May 2, 2020, https://www.brooklynmuseum.org/eascfa/dinner_party/place_settings/susan_b_anthony.

[66] Kaersenhout, artist statement.

[67] The work is still ongoing. Last year, Kaersenhout added two trans women, Marsha P. Johnson and Sylvia Rivera, to make the table more inclusive and to commemorate the Stonewall riots. The project continues because women from Curaçao still need to be added. Dyonna Bennett who is a cultural heritage professional focusing on forgotten and invisible histories of Curaçao and The Netherlands, has encountered names of three heroines of resistance: Sablika, Diana, and Wela Markita Kanga, but up until now, there is no information about their dates of birth, their lives, or their deaths. Kaersenhout is currently conducting research about these women to eventually add them to the table.

[68] Kaersenhout, artist statement.

[69] Renée Cox, artist statement, accessed June 4, 2020, https://www.reneecox.org.

[70] Kaersenhout, artist statement.

[71] Kaersenhout.

Plantation Memories

[72] Grada Kilomba, artist statement in relation to her participation in the 32nd São Paulo Art Biennial *Incerteza Viva* (Live Uncertainty), curated by Jochen Volz, Gabi Ngcobo, Júlia Rebouças, Lars Bang Larsen, and Sofía Olascoaga, accessed May 26, 2020, http://www.32bienal.org.br/en/event/o/3183/.

[73] Kilomba, artist statement.

[74] Kilomba.

[75] Suely Rolnik in conversation with Grada Kilomba, "When Words are Displaced from the Colonial Subconscious," *Episodes of the South* Magazine, Goethe-Institut. Originally published by the magazine *ARTE!Brasileiros* and reprinted on the Goethe-Institut's website in Brazil, accessed May 26, 2020, https://www.goethe.de/ins/br/lp/prj/eps/sob/en16199210.htm.

[76] Grada Kilomba, *Plantation Memories: Episodes of Everyday Racism* (Münster: Unrast Verlag, 2019), 14. First published 2008.

[77] Kilomba, *Plantation Memories*, 19.

[78] Kilomba, 22.

Shooting as a Radical Decolonial Gesture

[79] Sasha Huber, artist statement, accessed May 12, 2020, http://www.sashahuber.com.

[80] Huber, artist statement.

[81] Huber.

[82] Huber.

The Unfinished Conversation

[83] Cited in John Akomfrah's films *The Stuart Hall Project* (2013) and *The Unfinished Conversation* (2012).

[84] Akomfrah, *The Stuart Hall Project*; *The Unfinished Conversation*.

Healing from the Past and Reimagining the Future

[85] Achille Mbembe, *Critique of Black Reason* (Durham: Duke University Press 2017), 128.

[86] Mbembe, *Critique of Black Reason*, 173.

[87] Joiri Minaya, artist statement, accessed January 19, 2020, http://www.joiriminaya.com.

[88] Saidiya Hartman, *Lose Your Mother: A Journey Along the Atlantic Slave Route* (New York: Farrar, Straus and Giroux, 2007), 133.

About the Author

Selene Wendt is an art historian, independent curator, and writer based in Oslo. Her ongoing curatorial focus is on decoloniality and socially engaged art practices, with emphasis on interdisciplinary projects situated at the intersection between contemporary art, music, and literature.

With an MA in Art History from University of Chicago, she worked six years as Curator at Henie Onstad Art Center and eight years as Director and Chief Curator at The Stenersen Museum before founding The Global Art Project in 2013.

She has curated many international exhibitions through the years. Noteworthy thematic exhibitions include *Art Through the Eye of the Needle* (Henie Onstad, Oslo, 1999); *A Doll's House* (Henie Onstad, Oslo, 2002); *Postcards from Cuba: A Selection from the 8th Havana Biennial* (Henie Onstad, Oslo, 2004); *Equatorial Rhythms* (The Stenersen Museum, Oslo, 2006); *Beauty and Pleasure in South African Contemporary Art* (The Stenersen Museum, Oslo, 2009); *The Storytellers: Narratives in International Contemporary Art* (The Stenersen Museum, Oslo, 2012, and El Museo de Arte del Banco de la República, Bogotá, 2013), and *Mind the Map* (Punkt Ø Galleri F15, Jeløya, 2014).

More recent exhibitions include *Jamaican Routes* (Punkt Ø Galleri F15, Jeløya, 2016); *The Art of Storytelling* (The Museum of Contemporary Art – MAC, Niterói, Rio de Janeiro, 2016), which featured a book project and series of workshops developed in collaboration with the Dulcinéia Catadora collective that actively engaged youth from the local community; *Orhan Pamuk: The Art of Fiction* (The Museum of Cultural History, Oslo, 2017); *A Sheet of Paper Can Become a Knife* (The Prince Claus Fund Gallery, Amsterdam, 2018–19), and *The Sea is History* (The Museum of Cultural History, Oslo, 2019). In 2019 she co-curated *Ríos intermitentes* (Intermittent Rivers), a large-scale exhibition project initiated by María Magdalena Campos-Pons for the 13th Havana Biennial. She was an invited participant in Goethe-Institut São Paulo's three-year interdisciplinary research project *Echoes of the South Atlantic* (2018–20), which also resulted in the exhibition *Listening to the Echoes of the South Atlantic* at Oslo Kunstforening in 2020.

Her ambition is to create meaningful transcultural dialogs that extend beyond the parameters of the art world and to find innovative ways to use art as a unique tool for societal awareness and change. Her expertise as a curator has been greatly influenced by a consistent focus on contemporary art from Africa, Latin America, and the Caribbean, including artists of these diasporas. She places particular emphasis on research-based exhibitions that address contemporary art within the context of cultural studies and is dedicated to exposing the continued impact of colonial history on today's society, most evident in terms of social injustices such as poverty, forced migration, and racism. She writes regularly for publications and art journals such as *NKA Journal of Contemporary African Art* (Duke University Press), has written and edited numerous books and exhibition catalogs, and is a member of the Norwegian Non-Fiction Writers and Translators Association.

For more detailed information about her work please see the website www.theglobalartproject.no

Artist Biographies

John Akomfrah

John Akomfrah is an artist and filmmaker whose works are characterized by their investigations into memory, postcolonialism, temporality, and aesthetics, often exploring the experience of the African diaspora in Europe and the U.S. Akomfrah was a founding member of the Black Audio Film Collective, which started in London in 1982 with the artists David Lawson and Lina Gopaul, who he still collaborates with today.

Recent works include the three-screen video installation *The Unfinished Conversation* (2012), a portrait of the cultural theorist Stuart Hall's life and work. More recent works include his three-channel video installation *Vertigo Sea* (2015), which explores what Ralph Waldo Emerson calls "the sublime seas;" *Purple* (2017), an immersive six-channel video installation addressing climate change and its effects on human communities, biodiversity, and the wilderness, and *Precarity* (2017), which premiered at *Prospect.4: The Lotus in Spite of the Swamp*, New Orleans. Through archival imagery and newly shot footage, *Precarity* follows the life of forgotten New Orleans jazz singer Buddy Bolden.

On the occasion of his participation in the first Ghana Pavilion at the 58th Venice Biennale, John Akomfrah presented *Four Nocturnes* (2019), a three-channel video installation that reflects on the complex intertwined relationship between humanity's destruction of the natural world and our destruction of ourselves.

He has had many solo exhibitions at museums including New Museum, New York; Bildmuseet, Umeå; Nasher Museum of Art at Duke University, Durham, North Carolina; SFMOMA, San Francisco; Museo Thyssen-Bornemisza, Madrid; Barbican, London; Nikolaj Kunsthal, Copenhagen; Edythe Broad Art Museum, Michigan; Tate Britain, London, and a week-long series of screenings at MoMA, New York. He has participated in numerous international group shows, including *All the World's Futures*, the 56th Venice Biennale (2015); Sharjah Biennial 11 (2013), and Liverpool Biennial (2012), to name only a few. He has also participated in many international film festivals.

La Vaughn Belle

La Vaughn Belle is a visual artist who makes visible the unremembered. Borrowing from elements of architecture, history, and archeology, Belle creates narratives that challenge colonial hierarchies and invisibility. Belle explores the material culture of coloniality, and her work presents counter-visualities and narratives. Working in a variety of disciplines, her practice includes painting, installation, photography, writing, video, and public interventions. Her work with colonial era pottery led to a commission with the renowned brand of porcelain products, Royal Copenhagen.

She has exhibited her work in the Caribbean, the U.S., and Europe in institutions such as El Museo del Barrio (New York), Casa de las Americas (Havana), the Museum of the African Diaspora (San Francisco), and a solo exhibition at the National Nordic Museum (Seattle). Her art is in the collections of the National Photography Museum and the Vestsjælland Museum in Denmark. She is the co-creator of *I Am Queen Mary*, the groundbreaking artist-led monument that confronted Danish colonial amnesia while commemorating the legacies of resistance of the African people who were brought to the former Danish West Indies. The project was featured in over 100 media outlets around the world including the *New York Times*, *Politiken*, *VICE*, the BBC, and *Le Monde*. Belle holds an MFA from the Instituto Superior de Arte in Havana and an MA and BA from Columbia University, New York. She was a finalist for the *She Built NYC* project to develop a monument to memorialize the legacy of Shirley Chisholm and for the *Inequality in Bronze* project in

Philadelphia to redesign one of the first monuments to an enslaved woman at the Stenton House Museum. As a 2018–20 fellow at the Social Justice Institute at the Barnard Research Center for Women at Columbia University she worked on a project about the "citizenless" Virgin Islanders in the Harlem Renaissance. Her studio is based in the Virgin Islands.

Manthia Diawara

Manthia Diawara is a writer, filmmaker, cultural theorist, and art historian. He is professor of Comparative Literature and Film and director of Africana Studies at the Institute of African American Affairs, New York University (1992–present). He is the founder of the *Black Renaissance/Renaissance Noire* journal. Among his films are *An Opera of the World* (2017), commissioned by documenta 14; *Negritude: A Dialogue between Soyinka and Senghor* (2016); *Édouard Glissant: One World in Relation* (2009); *Maison Tropicale* (2008), and *Who's Afraid of Ngugi?* (2007). He has received awards from both documenta 14 and the Prince Claus Fund for Culture for *An Opera of the World*. He has also won a prize from the Sundance Institute Documentary Fund for a documentary on Kathleen Cleaver (2012), among many others.

He has published a number of articles and books, including "Malick Sibide: Smell the Perfume… Or When the Youth Was Free in Bamako," in *Malick Sidibe: Mali Twist*, edited by André Magnin and Brigitte Ollier (Fondation Cartier, Paris: Xavier Barral Edition (2017); *Édouard Glissant's Worldmentality: An Introduction to One World in Relation* (documenta 14, 2017); *The Films of Abderrahemane Sissako* (Artforum, 2015); *African Film: New Forms of Aesthetics and Politics* (Prestel, 2011); *We Won't Budge* (Basic Civitas Books, 2003), and *Mali Kow: Un monde fait de tous les mondes*, an exhibition catalog written with Jean Paul Colleyn, photography by Catherine De Clippel (Indigenes Editions – Parc La Villette, 2001). Diawara has been an editorial board member for the publications *Transition*, *October*, *African American Review*, and *Public Culture*, a member of the Scientific Committee for Revue Communications, an advisor for Haus der Kulturen der Welt in Berlin, and a jury member for numerous awards and film festivals, such as the Festival International du Cinéma d'Alger, Algeria (2013). Diawara received a Master of Arts from American University, Washington D.C. (1978) and a PhD in Comparative Literature from Indiana University, Bloomington, Indiana (1985).

Jeannette Ehlers

Jeannette Ehlers is a Caribbean diaspora visual artist born and based in Denmark. She completed her studies at The Royal Danish Academy of Fine Arts in Denmark in 2006. Her practice takes shape experimentally across photography, video, installation, sculpture, and performance, and engages with coloniality, decoloniality, blackness, and black identity, inspired by her own Danish-Caribbean background. She confronts the history of Denmark's involvement in colonialism and slavery, and their afterlife in the present. Until recently, this violent chapter of national history has received only scant attention in Danish public discourses. She recently gained international recognition for her public monument *I Am Queen Mary*, commemorating resistance against Danish colonial rule, co-created by Ehlers and La Vaughn Belle. The sculpture is situated in front of the West Indian Warehouse – The Royal Cast Collection in Copenhagen.

Recent solo exhibitions include *We're Magic. We're real #3*, a live performance at VEGA/ARTS, Copenhagen (2021); *Until the lion*, Nuuk Nordisk Kulturfestival, Nuuk Art Museum, Greenland (2019); *I Am Here*, in collaboration with Base Milano and Careof, Milan (2019); *Into the Dark*, a live performance at Teater Får302, Copenhagen (2017); *Say it Loud!*, Nicolaj Contemporary Art Center, Copenhagen (2014); *Black Bullets*, Videokunst.ch, Bern (2014) and Parisian Laundry, Montreal (2013); *Atlantic*, Århus Art Building (2009).

Select group exhibitions include *Listening to the Echoes of the South Atlantic*, Oslo Kunstforening (2020); *Aftershocks*, Kunsthal Charlottenborg, Copenhagen (2020), The Carl Nielsen and Anne Marie Carl-Nielsen Foundation's Honorary Award, Den Frie Centre of Contemporary Art, Copenhagen (2020), *Face to Face: Thorvaldsen and Portraiture*, Thorvaldsens Museum, Copenhagen (2020); *Relational Undercurrents: Contemporary Art of the Caribbean Archipelago*, Sugar Hill Children's Museum of Art & Storytelling (2018), New York and Museum of Latin American Art, LA (2017); *Blind Spots*, The Black Diamond National Photo Museum, Copenhagen (2017); *Whip it Good*, live performance at the Royal Cast Collection, organized by the Copenhagen Architecture Festival and the National Gallery of Denmark (2017); *Caribbean: Crossroads of the World*, Perez Art Museum, Miami (2014); *BE.BOP 2014 Black Europe Body Politics: Spiritual Revolutions and the Scramble for Africa*, Berlin and Copenhagen, and DakArt 2014, Dakar, to name only a few.

Michelle Eistrup

Michelle Eistrup is a visual artist, arts producer, and initiator of artistic collaborations who lives in Copenhagen. Eistrup's art incorporates themes of identity, corporeality, faith, memory, and postcolonialism, and her transnational background (Danish, Jamaican, American) is sometimes a point of departure.
She traverses varied artistic expressions, including photography, drawing, video, sound, and performance, all integrated in a practice that is led by spirit and a strong belief in the transformative potential of collectivity. Rooted in a vibrant global arts community, she has exhibited internationally, and organized events that facilitate in-depth dialog and research between artists, writers, and curators, for the overall purpose of encouraging a more integrated, sensitive, and equitable creative exchange.
Eistrup has exhibited in Europe, the Caribbean, Asia, and Africa, including institutions such as Aarhus Art Museum; AGWA, Art Gallery of Western Australia (Perth); Arnolfini (Bristol); Kunsthal Charlottenborg (Copenhagen); Galleri Image (Aarhus); Momentum: The Nordic Biennial of Contemporary Art (Moss); The Japanese Palace (Dresden); Haugar Vestfold Kunstmuseum (Tønsberg); Moderna Museet (Stockholm); Sparwasser HQ (Berlin); Pingyao Photography Festival, (Shanxi); The Taitu International Art Center (Addis Ababa), and The National Gallery of Jamaica (Kingston). Between 2012–18 she curated *BAT: Bridging Art and Text* (workshop and seminar) with coordinator Annemari B. Clausen and published the three-volume, 800-page publication *BAT* in 2017. Eistrup also co-curated *NotAboutKarenBlixen* with Brooke Minto, and *Face à Face* with curator and artist Amadou Kane Sy for My World IMAGES Festival 2010.

Sasha Huber

Sasha Huber is a visual artist of Swiss-Haitian heritage, born in Zurich. She lives and works in Helsinki. Huber's work is primarily concerned with the politics of memory and belonging, particularly in relation to colonial residue left in the environment. Sensitive to the subtle threads connecting history and the present, she uses and responds to archival material within a layered creative practice that encompasses performance-based interventions, video, photography, and collaborations. Huber is also claiming the compressed-air staple gun, aware of its symbolic significance as a weapon, while offering the potential to renegotiate unequal power dynamics.
She is known for her artistic research contribution to the *Demounting Louis Agassiz* campaign, aiming at dismantling the glaciologist's lesser-known but contentious racist heritage. This long-term project (since 2008) has been concerned with unearthing and redressing the little-known history and cultural legacies of the Swiss-born naturalist and glaciologist Louis Agassiz (1807–1873), an influential proponent of "scientific" racism who advocated for segregation and "racial hygiene."
Huber has had solo exhibitions at institutions such as the Hasselblad Foundation (Project Room) in Gothenburg, and participated in numerous international exhibitions, including the 56th Venice Biennale in 2015 (collateral exhibition *Frontier Reimagined*), the 19th Sydney Biennial in 2014, and the 29th São Paulo Biennial in 2010. Huber will start her first solo exhibition tour of *You Name It*, commissioned by The Power Plant Contemporary Art Gallery in Toronto and Autograph in London (2021–23). She holds an MA from the University of Art and Design Helsinki and is presently undertaking practice-based PhD studies at the Department of Art and Media at the Zurich University of the Arts. Huber also works in a creative partnership with artist Petri Saarikko. Together they have initiated the long-term project *Remedies Universe* (since 2011), which explores aural family knowledge in different geographical and cultural contexts, and been invited to artist residencies around the world. Alongside her practice, Huber has edited the book *Rentyhorn* (2010) and was co-editor with Maria P. T. Machado of *(T)races of Louis Agassiz: Photography, Body and Science, Yesterday and Today* (2010) on the occasion of the 29th São Paulo Biennial. In 2018, Huber was the recipient of the State Art Award in the category visual arts given by the Arts Promotion Center Finland.

Oceana James

Oceana James is an interdisciplinary artist who was born in St. Croix, USVI. Her work retells and re-imagines her Caribbean roots and American experiences. It comments on the sociopolitical, cultural, and economic realities of people of African descent. Her research is centered on epigenetics, the biology and mythology of trees, the intersection of science and religion, and the use of the body to exorcise traumas of the transatlantic slave trade. Her work revolves around min(d)ing "jumbie spaces"—the (in) between—spaces of resistance and reclamation. James has successfully shown her one-woman experimental piece, *For Gowie: The Deceitful Fellow*, in Germany, Denmark, NYC, and

St. Croix. James recently presented her paper "Weaving Jumbie Time: Translocational Storytelling and Praxis" at the Royal Danish Art Academy of Fine Arts's Archives that Matter conference-residency. She is a core-collaborator in choreographer Paloma McGregor's *Building a Better Fishtrap* and principal member of Sibyl Kempson's 7 Daughters Perf. Co., a theatre company that has just completed a three-year residency (12 Shouts to the Ten Forgotten Heavens) at the Whitney Museum of American Art. Her most recent residencies include EmergeNYC at the Hemispheric Institute of Performance and Politics at New York University; El Residencial 2018 in Carolina, Puerto Rico (where she worked with Las Nietas de Nonó and other Caribbean artists), and *Migrating Histories* (curated by Monica Marin) on the island of St. Croix. James grew up hearing stories and folktales and is proud to continue the long legacy and tradition of storytelling from the Caribbean. James has an MFA in theatre from Sarah Lawrence College (Bronxville, NY) and a Bachelor of Arts (BA, magna cum laude) in English Literature from the University of the Virgin Islands (St. Croix, USVI).

Patricia Kaersenhout
Patricia Kaersenhout is a Dutch visual artist and cultural activist of Surinamese heritage. She studied Social Studies at the Aemstelhorn, Amsterdam, and Fine Arts at the Gerrit Rietveld Academie, Amsterdam. Her work investigates the fact of invisibility as a condition of the African diaspora. She also considers colonialism in relation to her upbringing in Western European culture. The political thread in her work raises questions about movements within the African diaspora and its relation to the history of slavery, racism, feminism, and sexuality. Her first solo publication *Invisible Men*, containing 42 works on paper inspired by Ralph Ellison's book *Invisible Man* (1952), was released in June 2009. Since then, her work has been exhibited internationally. Her solo show *Proud Rebels*, about an important black feminist wave in the eighties in Amsterdam, opened at CBK Zuidoost in 2015. In the same year she also participated in the group exhibition *Embodied Spaces* at Framer Framed, Amsterdam, curated by Christine Eyene, featuring works on the themes of body, gender, and identity. Additionally, she has participated in group exhibitions at Gammel Holtegaard, Copenhagen; *BELL invites: Global Performance* at Stedelijk Museum, Amsterdam; Queens Museum of Art, New York, and the Museum of Contemporary African Diasporan

Arts (MoCADA), New York in 2012; BE.BOP 2014, Volksbühne, Berlin, Framer Framed, Amsterdam, and Van Abbe Museum, Eindhoven; DakArt 2014; *Bloed Suiker* at Cargo in Context, Amsterdam in 2017, as well as *Your Voice Matters* at Museum Arnhem in 2019. She also participated in Manifesta 12, Palermo in 2018 and in 2019 she had a solo exhibition of *Guess Who's Coming to Dinner Too?* at de Appel, Amsterdam.
Kaersenhout is a regular lecturer at the Decolonial Summer School in Middelburg, the Black Europe Summer School in Amsterdam, and for BE.BOP (Black Europe Body Politics). She currently lives and works in Amsterdam.

Grada Kilomba
Grada Kilomba, born in Lisbon, is an interdisciplinary artist, whose work draws on memory, trauma, gender, and postcolonialism, interrogating concepts of knowledge, power, and violence. "What stories are told? How are they told? And told by whom?" are constant questions in Kilomba's body of work, to revise postcolonial narratives.
Kilomba subversively translates text into image, movement, and installation, by giving body, voice, and form to her own critical writing. Performance, staged reading, video, photography, publications, and installation are platforms for Kilomba's unique practice of storytelling, which intentionally disrupts the proverbial "white cube" through a new and urgent decolonial language and imagery.
Her work has been presented in major international events, including La Biennale de Lubumbashi VI; the 10th Berlin Biennale; documenta 14, Kassel; the 32nd São Paulo Biennial, as well as being featured in both solo and group exhibitions at venues such as the Pinacoteca de São Paulo; Bildmuseet, Umeå; Kadist Art Foundation, Paris; The Power Plant, Toronto; Maxim Gorki Theatre, Berlin; MAAT-Museum of Art, Architecture and Technology, Lisbon; Secession Museum, Vienna; Bozar Museum, Brussels; PAC-Pavillion Art Contemporanea, Milan, among others.
Kilomba's work features in public and private collections worldwide.
Strongly influenced by the work of Frantz Fanon, Kilomba studied Freudian Psychoanalysis in Lisbon at ISPA, and there she worked with war survivors from Angola and Mozambique. Early on she started writing and publishing stories, before extending her interests into staging, image, sound, and movement.
Kilomba holds a distinguished Doctorate in Philosophy from the Freie Universität Berlin. She has lectured at several international universities, such as the University of

Ghana and the Vienna University of Arts and was a Guest Professor at the Humboldt Universität Berlin, Department of Gender Studies.

For several years, she was a guest artist at the Maxim Gorki Theatre in Berlin, developing Kosmos 2, a political intervention with refugee artists. She is the author of the acclaimed book *Plantation Memories* (2008) a compilation of episodes of everyday racism written in the form of short psychoanalytical stories. Her book has been translated into several languages and was listed as the most important non-fiction literature in Brazil in 2019. Kilomba lives and works in Berlin.

Suchitra Mattai

Suchitra Mattai is a multi-disciplinary artist who lives and works in Denver, Colorado. Mattai was born in Guyana and has also lived in places as diverse as Halifax, Wolfville, Philadelphia, New York, Montpellier, and Udaipur. Her mixed media work communicates the complexities of living amidst multiple cultural spheres and explores how individual and collective memory allows us to unravel dominant historical narratives. She weaves narratives of the "other," giving voice to people whose voices were once quieted and celebrates the experiences of immigrant diasporas.

Suchitra received an MFA in Painting and Drawing and an MA in South Asian art, both from the University of Pennsylvania, Philadelphia. Recent projects include a commission for Sharjah Biennial 14, inclusion in State of the Art 2020 at Crystal Bridges Museum of American Art/The Momentary, a Denver Art Museum/Biennial of the Americas jointly sponsored installation, a group exhibition at Pen and Brush NYC and solo/two-person exhibitions at K Contemporary Art (Denver), Hollis Taggart (New York), and the Center for Visual Arts, Metropolitan State University of Denver. Upcoming projects include a solo exhibition at Building Bridges Art Exchange (Los Angeles) and group exhibitions at the Art Gallery of Ontario (Toronto) and the San Antonio Museum of Art. Her work has been reviewed and featured in numerous publications and on-line platforms such as *Hyperallergic*, *Document Journal*, *Cultured Magazine*, *The Denver Post*, *The Korea Times*, and *Wallpaper Magazine*, and is in museum and private collections such as Crystal Bridges Museum of American Art, the Denver Art Museum, the TIA Collection, and the Taylor Art Collection. She is represented by K Contemporary Art (Denver), Hollis Taggart (New York), and grayDUCK Gallery (Austin).

Alberta Whittle

Alberta Whittle is an artist, researcher, and curator. She was awarded a Turner Bursary, the Frieze Artist Award and a Henry Moore Foundation Artist Award in 2020. She is a Research Associate at the University of Johannesburg. She was a RAW Académie Fellow at RAW Material in Dakar in 2018 and is the Margaret Tait Award winner for 2018–19.

Her creative practice is motivated by the desire to manifest self-compassion and collective care as key methods in battling anti-blackness. She choreographs interactive installations, using film, sculpture, and performance as site-specific artworks in public and private spaces. Alberta has exhibited and performed in various solo and group shows, including at Grand Union (2020), Eastside Projects (2020), DCA (2019), GoMA, Glasgow (2019), Pig Rock Bothy at the National Galleries of Scotland, Edinburgh (2019), the13th Havana Biennial (2019), The Tyburn Gallery, London (2019), The City Arts Centre, Edinburgh (2019), The Showroom, London (2018), National Art Gallery of the Bahamas (2018), RAW Material, Dakar (2018), FADA Gallery, Johannesburg (2018), the Apartheid Museum, Johannesburg (2017), Framer Framed, Amsterdam (2015), Goethe On Main, Johannesburg (2015), the Johannesburg Pavilion at the 56th Venice Biennale (2015), and BOZAR, Brussels (2014), among others.

Her work has been acquired for the UK National Collections, The Scottish National Gallery Collections, Glasgow Museums Collections, and The Contemporary Art Research Collection at Edinburgh College of Art among other private collections. Over 2021, Alberta will be sharing new work as part of Art Night London, British Art Show 9, Liverpool Biennial, business as usual: hostile environment at Glasgow Sculpture Studios and Right of Admission at the University of Johannesburg.

Alberta's writing has been published in *MAP magazine*, *Visual Culture in Britain*, *Visual Studies*, *Art South Africa*, and *Critical Arts Academic Journal*.

Bibliography

• Baker, Houston A., Jr., Manthia Diawara, and Ruth H. Lindeborg, eds. *Black British Cultural Studies: A Reader*. Chicago: The University of Chicago Press, 1996.

• Baldwin, James. *Go Tell It on the Mountain*. London: Penguin Modern Classics, 2001. First published 1953 by Alfred A. Knopf, New York.

• Césaire, Aimé. *Cahiers d'un retour au pays natal*. Paris: Éditions Présence Africaine, 1953 and 1983.

• Césaire, Aimé. *Discours sur le colonialisme, suivi de Discours sur la Négritude*. Paris: Éditions Présence Africaine, 1955 and 2004.

• Danbolt, Mathias, Mette Kia Krabbe Meyer, and Sarah Giersing. *Blind Spots: Images of the Danish West Indies Colony*. Copenhagen: Det Kongelige Bibliotek, 2017.

• Diawara, Manthia. *In Search of Africa*. Cambridge: Harvard University Press, 1998.

• Diawara, Manthia. *We Won't Budge: An African Exile in the World*. Oxfordshire: Ayebia Clarke Publishing Limited, 2005. First published 2003 by Basic Civitas Books, New York.

• Du Bois, W. E. B. *The Souls of Black Folk*. Mineola: Dover Thrift Editions, 2012. First published 1903 by A. C. McClurg, Chicago.

• Eistrup, Michelle, and Annemari Brogaard Clausen. *BAT: Bridging Art + Text*. Copenhagen: Hurricane Publishing, 2017.

• Ehlers, Jeannette, Mathias Danbolt, Alanna Lockward, and Rolando Vázquez. *Say It Loud!*. Copenhagen: Nikolaj Kunsthal, 2016.

• Equiano, Olaudah. *The Interesting Narrative of the Life of Olaudah Equiano; or, Gustavus Vassa, the African, Written by Himself*. Self-published, London, 1789.

• Fanon, Frantz. *Peau noire, masques blancs*. Paris: Éditions du Seuil, 1952.

• Gilroy, Paul. *Darker than Blue: On the Moral Economies of Black Atlantic Culture* (W. E. B. Du Bois lectures). Cambridge: The Belknap Press of Harvard University Press, 2010.

• Gilroy, Paul. *The Black Atlantic: Modernity and Double Consciousness*. London: Verso, 1993.

• Glissant, Édouard. *Le discours antillais*. Paris: Éditions Gallimard, 1997.

• Glissant, Édouard. *Poétique de la Relation: Poétique III*. Paris: Éditions Gallimard, 1990.

• Glissant, Édouard. *Poetics of Relation*. Ann Arbor: The University of Michigan Press, 1997.

• Glissant, Édouard. *Traité du Tout-Monde: Poétique IV*. Paris: Éditions Gallimard, 1997.

• Glissant, Édouard. *Poèmes complets*. Paris: Éditions Gallimard, 1994.

• Glissant, Édouard, and Manthia Diawara. "One World in Relation: Édouard Glissant in Conversation with Manthia Diawara." *NKA: Journal of Contemporary African Art*, no. 28 (Spring 2011): 4–19.

• Hall, Stuart. *Critical dialogues in cultural studies*. Edited by David Morley and Kuan-Hsing Chen. Oxfordshire: Routledge, 1996.
• Hall, Stuart, and Paul du Gay. *Questions of Cultural Identity*. New York: Sage Publications, 1996.
• Hall, Stuart. *The Fateful Triangle: Race, Ethnicity, Nation*. Edited by Kobena Mercer. Cambridge: Harvard University Press, 2017.
• Hall, Stuart, with Bill Schwarz. *Familiar Stranger: A Life Between Two Islands*. London: Penguin Random House, 2017.
• Hansen, Thorkild. *Slavenes kyst*. Oslo: Gyldendal, 1968.
• Hansen, Thorkild. *Slavenes skip*. Oslo: Gyldendal, 1969.
• Hansen, Thorkild. *Slavenes øyer*. Oslo: Gyldendal, 1970.
• Hartman, Saidiya. *Lose Your Mother: A Journey Along the Atlantic Slave Route*. New York: Farrar, Straus and Giroux, 2007.
• Kilomba, Grada. *Plantation Memories: Episodes of Everyday Racism*. 5th ed. Münster: Unrast Verlag, 2019. First published 2008.
• Lamko, Koulsy. *Bintou Wéré: African Opera*. Edited by Els van der Plas. Amsterdam: Prince Claus Fund and Sahel Opera Foundation, 2017.
• Mbembe, Achille. *Critique of Black Reason*. Durham: Duke University Press, 2017.
• Mercer, Kobena. "Stuart Hall and the Visual Arts." *Small Axe: A Caribbean Journal of Criticism* 19, no. 1 (46) (March 2015): 78–87.
• Mercer, Kobena. *Travel & See: Black Diaspora Art Practices since the 1980s*. Durham: Duke University Press, 2016.
• Mignolo, Walter D., and Catherine E. Walsh. *On Decoloniality: Concepts, Analytics, Praxis*. Durham: Duke University Press, 2018.
• Miller, Kei. *Augustown*. London: Weidenfeld & Nicolson, 2016.
• Moten, Fred. *In the Break: The Aesthetics of the Black Radical Tradition*. Minneapolis: University of Minnesota Press, 2003.
• Moten, Fred. *Black and Blur: Consent not to be a single being*. Durham: Duke University Press, 2017.
• Noudelmann, François. *Édouard Glissant: L'identité généreuse*. Paris: Éditions Flammarion, 2018.
• Ray, Carina E. *Crossing the Color Line: Race, Sex, and the Contested Politics of Colonialism in Ghana*. Athens: Ohio University Press, 2015.
• Scott, David. *Stuart Hall's Voice: Intimations of an Ethics of Receptive Generosity*. Durham: Duke University Press, 2017.
• Svalesen, Leif. *Slaveskipet Fredensborg og den dansk-norske slavehandel på 1700-tallet*. Oslo: Grøndahl og Dreyer, 1996.
• Wendt, Selene. *The Sea is History*. Milan: Skira, 2019.

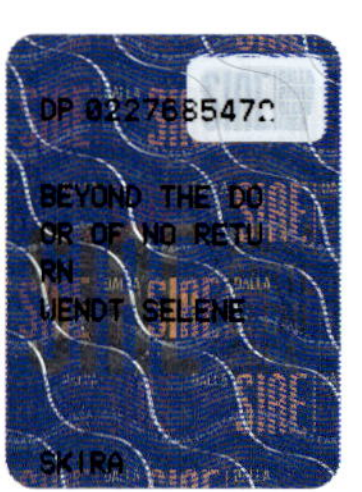
DP 0227685472
BEYOND THE DO
OR OF NO RETU
RN
WENDT SELENE
SKIRA